PRAISE FOR *GIRL POSITIVE*

"This book is about the real, sometimes awkward, essential conversation that can be a life-altering opportunity if we as parents, youth, mentors, teachers and citizens take an honest look at ourselves. . . . This is a call to action. Words matter. Actions speak louder. Let's get moving."

—SOPHIE GRÉGOIRE TRUDEAU

"You need to read this new Trudeau-approved book about mentoring girls. Sophie Grégoire Trudeau says this new book is a 'call to action' and it totally is. Consider it your handbook on how to encourage girls to be strong and independent."

—*TODAY'S PARENT*

"[A] hopeful exploration of what it means to be a girl [today]."

—*TORONTO STAR*

"Girls are one of the most powerful demographics on social media, but they face a lot of challenges with that power. *Girl Positive* . . . looks at stories from young women who are making a difference and more; what an important book."

—CBC RADIO, "All in a Weekend" (Montreal)

"Timely. Generous. Accessible. Provocative. I hope every teacher, health-care professional, social worker, policy-maker and parent will read."

—MICHAEL KAUFMAN, co-founder of the White Ribbon Campaign and author of *The Possibility of Dreaming on a Night Without Stars*

"Equal parts smart, sassy and savage, *Girl Positive* will inspire girls around the world."
—SAM MAGGS, author of *The Fangirl's Guide to the Galaxy*

"Tatiana Fraser and Caia Hagel are out to change girl culture. . . . *Girl Positive* . . . spotlights real-life struggles, like the crushing pressure to meet beauty standards."

—*CHATELAINE*

"I was moved to tears first at the possibility of a world where girls can grow up individual, different, free, safe and proud. A world where a female president is not an aberration, a world where little girls can be little girls and dream out loud. A world where girls have a voice and can become women without guilt or fear to shape the lives that become them best. Fraser and Hagel make a strong case for such a world. But *Girl Positive* is all about the girls, their voices, their particular visions and stories. It's in their words, all together, in one voice coming in loud and clear. It's that voice that we can no longer ignore. It's that voice that will win in the end and when it does, we will all win."

—**AGATHE SNOW,** artist and performer

"As exciting and candid as a late-night dorm room discussion, *Girl Positive* knows the issues young women face today are similar to previous generations, but on a much more complex level—like a video game's highest difficulty setting. Anyone reading this book, no matter how alone they might feel in real life, will become totally enveloped by the community of funny, smart and inspiring young people who populate it. Best of all, *Girl Positive*, which treats young women with respect for their intellect and choices that is all too rare these days, proves the kids are all right—and will be, as long as they can benefit from the celebration of strength, intelligence and positivity that Tatiana Fraser and Caia Hagel know is at the core of every teenage girl navigating the world today."

—**DUANA TAHA,** author of *The Name Therapist*
and contributor on *LaineyGossip.com*

GIRL
POSITIVE

HOW GIRLS ARE
SHAPING A
NEW WORLD

TATIANA FRASER
AND CAIA HAGEL

VINTAGE CANADA

305.2308
Fraser

Published by Vintage Canada, a division of Penguin Random House Canada Limited, in 2018. Originally published in hardcover by Random House Canada, a division of Penguin Random House Canada Limited, in 2016. Distributed in Canada by Penguin Random House Canada Limited, Toronto.

Vintage Canada with colophon is a registered trademark.

Pages 323 to 324 constitute a continuation of the copyright page.

www.penguinrandomhouse.ca

LIBRARY AND ARCHIVES CANADA CATALOGUING IN PUBLICATION

Fraser, Tatiana, author
    Girl positive / Tatiana Fraser, Caia Hagel.

Includes bibliographical references and index.

ISBN 978-0-345-80840-0
eBook ISBN 978-0-345-80841-7

    1. Girls—Attitudes. 2. Girls—Psychology. 3. Self-esteem in women.
4. Women—Identity. I. Hagel, Caia, author II. Title.

HQ777.F724 2018   305.23082   C2016-902564-0

Cover design by Leah Springate
Cover image © gpointstudio/Shutterstock.com

Printed and bound in the United States of America

2 4 6 8 9 7 5 3 1

Penguin
Random
House

VINTAGE CANADA

To all girls everywhere, with love

CONTENTS

HELLO FROM US TO YOU

GIRLS ARE CHANGEMAKERS. They are at the frontiers of the digital world and they leverage digital platforms better than anyone else. They are co-creating media. They are forming communities that speak out and take action for and against the issues they feel strongly about. They are the greatest force behind the powerfully rising female dollar and are the fire at the heart of movements like the Arab Spring, Occupy Wall Street, Black Lives Matter, girls' education and community building in emerging economies, and dress-code reform and ending campus rape culture in Western society. Girls are busy in all kinds of ways, transforming the world we live in, on the front lines and behind the scenes.

We are honoured to introduce the girls and young women in this book to you. They'll be speaking from across North America in their own voices about their lives and the many things they're passionate about. We—Tatiana Fraser and Caia Hagel—will be narrating their stories, while also weaving together commentary from girl-issue experts and loving mentors, cutting-edge research, alternative opinions and our own expertise and analysis.

Tatiana brings to the discussion twenty years of leadership on gender issues, social innovation and systems-change. She is the co-founder and past executive director of Girls Action Foundation, a not-for-profit that seeds and supports trailblazing and transformative girl programmes nationally. Born of her vision that girls and young women are powerful change agents, she spearheaded the creation of an unprecedented network of organizations dedicated to advancing girls' equality, leadership and empowerment. Her own experiences and struggles growing up as a girl were a catalyst to building a movement for social justice that was inclusive of *all* girls. Throughout her career, Tatiana has recognized the problematic disconnect between girls' realities and the popular discourse about girls, and the need to shine light on *real* stories about girls, about their vision and resilience. This is what inspired her to write this book.

Caia comes to this book with many years of writing and speaking on pioneering movements in culture, on activism in art and design, and on groundbreakers in youth culture. She is the co-founder and director of GuerrillaPop+MediaLab, an international communications lab that creates message-driven media like #YouthTalks, the United Nations Girls' Education Initiative blog, and ethical advertising that uses "moral offsetting" to involve lucrative brands in funding emerging and grass roots causes. As co-founder and co-director of HungryForFortune, she brings together creative girl collectives and provides opportunities for them to produce and impact culture. Her work opens bridges between the old and new economies, intellectual and pop culture, and established and emerging generations. The opportunity to identify the power, insight and energy that girls bring to our changing world—and offer advice on how to nurture that and connect it to mainstream thinking—inspired her to write this book.

Because we share a vision of a world in which all girls grow up with the resources and support they need to realize their greatest potential, we wanted to write a book that would capture and amplify the powerful stories we know girls live, dream for themselves and imagine for our collective future. Rather than reporting secondhand on what girls think and say, we wanted to hear from the girls. We interviewed girls and young women between the ages of nine and 29 (by "girls" we generally mean girls between the ages of nine and 15 and by "young women," we mean young women between the ages of 16 and 29), in communities across North America. We asked them to tell us about their lives, to share what they believe in, care and worry about and struggle with. In doing so, they reveal how they see themselves—and offer insights into what stands in their way, what they want to change and the solutions they have discovered along their paths. The experiential reflection offered by the older participants adds richness, depth and a retrospective understanding to the contemporary issues and realities girls are living. We believe that girls and young women are the experts on their own lives and are wise in ways that are often overlooked; we have a lot to learn from, and with, girls.

As two white, educated, heterosexual and able-bodied women, we are aware that our identities interact with and shape this narrative, and we recognize the limitations this brings. To engage with diverse girl experiences, we invited others to take part in our journey—girl mentors who act as portals into communities across North America. Many of these women have worked with Girls Action Foundation for years; through their added perspectives, we have woven insight and context into the issues the girls themselves raised. We are so grateful to them, and to the many others who have helped us tell these stories in the strongest possible way.

What does a world shaped by girls' visions look like? What will it look like when girls and women are leaders and co-creators at all levels of power? We know how this potential can positively impact culture and ecology, build community and transform the economy and politics. By sharing the stories of girls' and young women's victories and their smart approaches to solving the many challenges the world faces, we are presenting potent images of a future where girls are engaged as powerful citizens forming new foundations for tomorrow.

Girl Positive is an invitation to participate in this new, dynamic culture that girls are shaping. It is a guidebook for anyone who wants to hear from girls, and understand and support them. It is also an activist manual, to arm *all* girls and to celebrate and support them as they realize their destinies and take up their pivotal roles at the most promising horizons of the twenty-first century.

INTRODUCTION

WHY GIRLS?

IT WAS A BALMY SUMMER weekend in Montreal when we found ourselves standing in line on the steps of a church, rubbing latex shoulder pads with a retro–glam punk crowd. Twilight fell as the colourful ensemble slowly milled into the venue, and it wasn't long before we heard the familiar caterwauling of excited fans, eager for the opening notes of this concert featuring five teenage girl bands. The inner doors opened and the audience hustled for their seats, or prime spots in standing-room zones. Deep inside—under hairspray vapours, flashes of glitter and paparazzi cameras—a boy, already under the spell of this scene, asked his mother, "How come rock camp for *girls*, Mom? Isn't there any rock camp for *boys*?" The mother tousled her son's hair and smiled down at him before answering: "*Life* is a rock camp for boys, darling."

What's an eight-year-old boy to make of that wry comment? It might very well seem confusing and unfair, especially if he has an older sister. To him, it might appear as if the world is populated with plenty of ferocious, bodacious girls—and why do these girls get to rock so hard on a lit-up stage, primped by a hair and makeup team and fawned over by press, camera crews and hundreds of adoring fans? Why a rock camp for girls only?

What this boy didn't know—and what his mother only cryptically articulated—is that, in this second decade of the twenty-first century, we are just beginning to carve out a stage for girls; that in the wake of a very long legacy of erasure, much longer than even a *10*-year-old boy could imagine, we are finally allowing girls to step into the spotlight.

Historically, Western societies have produced girls who were their father's property, groomed for marriage by learning to be helpful, sweet and obedient, and hard-working without complaint. But as women's roles expanded beyond the domestic sphere in the mid-twentieth century, people began asking questions about the "girl experience." Politically, girls landed on the map in 1995, during the United Nations Fourth World Conference on women, in Beijing, where the "girl child" was identified as a priority. Gains that had been made by the women's movement were extended to girls, and policies began to identify and respond to girls' needs. Inequities in education, employment, health, sports, leadership, science and technology were suddenly on the agenda, with the goal of effecting change and bringing girls into the sphere of advancing women's equality.

And so, in this day and age—when it would seem that girls have the same freedom and access to resources as boys, not to mention equal standing in society—the easy answer to "Why girls?" is: because we love them and want what is best for them. They are our daughters and sisters. We are their friends, their aunts and uncles, their grandmas and grandpas, teachers and mentors. We want to provide them with everything they need to navigate the transition from childhood into adulthood with a strong sense of self, and with full opportunity, confidence and liberty to act.

But that's the easy answer. The real answer is much more complex.

+++

Today's girls live in an intricate, sped-up reality where technological advancements play out very personally in their social-media-centric lives by making their every move visible and open to public scrutiny and criticism. Within this fast-paced lifestyle, girls are both acting and being acted upon, absorbing vast amounts of information daily and responding to it with information of their own. Whether following Selena Gomez on Instagram and then posting inspired selfies[1] on their own feeds, reading #YesAllWomen[2] and tweeting support, or watching a Taylor Swift video and forwarding it to a hundred friends, girls are immersed in, and *participating in*, the creation of culture.

Little wonder, then, that we experience so much public debate about girls in Anglo-American societies—about the clothes they wear, about how they conduct themselves in social media (provocative selfies and sexting are high on the list of topics), about the fear of potential predators and the pressure to negotiate sexual activity and its ever-morphing boundaries. High school teachers bemoan the girl-on-girl aggression that plays out in classrooms and the schoolyard. Voices from various media outlets chime in with warnings about "bad girls" and "mean girls" who are disrupting the classroom and sending ripples of fear through communities at large. Parents tell us that their adolescent girls are upsetting the social dynamics of the family, that they are texting until 3 a.m. and ruining the cohesion of the home. More broadly, we hear discussions of how bullying is taking on insidious virtual forms and how, from within their bedrooms, on computers and smart phones, girls are up to no good. And yet, amid all of this, girls themselves are asking for a little freedom. "Please give us some room to experiment in our lives," they seem to be saying. "Let us test our boundaries and new technologies. Give us support, but trust us to know what is best for us and to develop our sense of what is right."

What are we to make of this? How can we better understand the reality of girls' lives, and help them to navigate the often choppy waters of adolescence? Unfortunately, those of us looking to do just that may not have the best information or tools at our disposal, and we've made missteps along the way. During the last two decades, media discussions have focused on girls largely through a psychological lens. Research and policy experts tend to frame girls as suffering from low self-esteem, no doubt the result of a constant barrage of media that objectifies and devalues women. One popular reaction has been to try to save girls from losing themselves, to inject them with the confidence they need to become capable and ambitious adults. Look around and you'll see a whole market based on this approach—in pop psychology, in self-help books, and in advertising campaigns for everything from Dove soap to Always hygiene products to Kellogg's cereal. Somehow, girls' self-esteem has become a commodity—a brand—to buy and sell.

Ironically, despite this overwhelming fascination with girls, we don't often hear what girls themselves have to say about who they are or where they feel they are situated within the buzz around their social, economic and political presence. We don't ask girls what they think they need, or about how they see their world. The conversation is certainly *about* girls, but has not really *included* girls—until now.

With this book, we set out to try something new. We wanted to hear directly from girls about their lives. Popular narratives tend not to reflect the realities that so many girls are living. At the same time, they also tend to obscure the innovative and inspiring ways in which girls navigate their intellectual, social and emotional development during the critical years of adolescence. Aside from robbing us of these interesting *true* stories, these popular narratives also do a much greater disservice: they prevent us from seeing what we might do to usefully respond to girls' needs, and to serve and support them better through this pivotal time in their lives.

Girl Positive seeks to share these true stories—told by girls in their own voices and on their own terms—and in doing so, to reframe the ideal image of a girl put forth by the media. In the making of this book we embarked on a North American Girl Tour. We travelled to a small reserve on James Bay in northern Quebec. We flew along the West Coast from the Yukon, stopping in Vancouver and then heading south to San Francisco and Los Angeles. We drove ten hours to New Haven, Connecticut, and flew back and forth to Detroit. We spoke to girls in Texas, Ottawa, Montreal and Toronto. We hung out in coffee shops, dance studios, classrooms, gyms, skate parks, beaches and bedrooms. We interviewed girls as young as nine and as mature as their late 20s. We talked to middle-school girls, high-school students, college girls and young women in the early stages of their careers. We met artists and athletes, computer coders, gamers, journalists, activists and businesswomen. We did one-on-one interviews and met with small focus groups, and we gathered more than a hundred compelling stories through an online survey.

We spent many hours talking with girls and really listening to what they had to say. We wanted to find out how they see themselves, how they make sense of their worlds and how they are living—if they are thriving, coping or struggling (hint: it's often all of the above). We wanted to understand their relationship to pop culture; we wanted to know what they think of social media, sexuality, the Internet and the changing world; we were curious to hear from them on social and environmental issues such as emerging technologies, poverty and climate change. We wanted to discover how these forces are shaping their experiences and concerns, and how they, in turn, are shaping these realms. We also wanted to talk about the difficult stuff, like their experiences of sexual harassment and racism.

Along the way, we also spoke to experts in media, health, race and gender politics, sexuality, education, leadership and girl-led social change. Their advice and input allowed us to bring context to the issues we explored, and to better equip ourselves as parents, friends, educators, mentors and activists.

The stories we share here were gathered from hundreds of conversations. Our talks were conducted with the understanding that we would include the girls' voices in this book, but that we would do so anonymously. The names of the girls you will meet on these pages are pseudonyms, but the patterns and themes are as real as can be.

When we were planning our travels, we knew we wanted to talk to girls from various locations. But we weren't thinking only about geography. How a girl experiences her world is influenced by many intersecting spheres, such as race, class and sexual identity. Much of the mainstream focus on girls revolves around the white middle-class experience, as if this is somehow representative of all girls. Clearly it is not, and yet many assumptions about a girl's reality are built on these generalizations. How we understand girls' needs and how we choose to care for and value girls are informed by what is, in essence, incomplete knowledge. Unfortunately, this leaves a lot of girls out of a discussion that is supposed to be about them. When we don't see *all* girls—and when we assume that all girls experience girlhood in the same way—we are in danger of missing some of the most dynamic and inspiring stories girls have to tell. With this in mind, we gathered stories from many contexts and perspectives, and worked hard to survey the true complexity of girls' lives.

Many of the girls in this book, whether from Indigenous communities or skate culture, showed us that girls who are unseen and overlooked in the mainstream due to racism and class bias are sometimes the most powerful and pivotal forces for change—locally, nationally and internationally. We owe it to them, and to ourselves, to listen to their stories.

1

UNFINISHED BUSINESS

IT SEEMS HARD TO BELIEVE, in these early years of the twenty-first century, that we are still discussing girls in terms of equity and still attempting to gain a better understanding of their experiences. How is it that we still find ourselves here, when so many gains have been made? Because our work is not finished.

Girls' lives unfold in such a complex environment: in Anglo-American contexts, girls inhabit a world defined by historic achievements of women's rights, the privilege of developed wealth, the many waves of feminism and their backlash waves. Within this, girls live their own messy challenges spanning hormones, peer politics, self-image, autonomy, smart-phone politik and sexuality, along with the dramas, expectations and baggage the world has projected onto them.

Girls have traditionally been a symbol of innocence and of the ripening of a new generation. Girls embody the hope and new life—quite literally, in their maturing bodies—of the evolution of our species. They fascinate and intrigue with their youth, innocence, intelligence and beauty, and they offer a new promise of power and vitality. They also embody the social anxieties of the day; where idealization and morality is placed on our cultural imagination of a girl's experience.

Before we hear from girls themselves, it's worth taking a moment to explore the current landscape that girls are living in, in historical context.

CHALLENGES NEW AND OLD

This is a unique time for girls. Girls and young women between the ages of 12 and 25 get a lot of attention in the media, certainly more than ever before. In 2012, the World Bank's *World Development Report on Gender Equality and Development*[1] declared that investing in girls is smart economics. Corporate culture has identified girls as among our greatest consumers, and lobbies them relentlessly through slick advertising and social-media campaigns. Pop culture cherishes girls as its greatest aficionados, celebrating the vision of a girl in her innocence and emerging sexuality with high-octane entertainment (fashion spreads, music videos, television shows and video games) while the non-girls among us look on in fascination and discomfort.

Research indicates promising news for girls. We are told that girls are outperforming boys in educational settings, have access to the equities won by their foremothers: essentially, that girls have it all. But it's not easy being a girl. It never has been, and today's girls face entirely different challenges from the ones their mothers and grandmothers and great-grandmothers faced. These days, the benchmark for being a successful girl is set high—very high. Girls feel pressure to achieve in school, sports, and extracurricular activities. Many are also expected to take part-time jobs and help out at home with siblings and domestic chores. On top of this, tween and teenage girls feel the need to navigate pop culture pressures that demand they be beauty queens, shape their bodies to fit the latest ideal, showcase an enviable life in pictures over social media and secure an ever-elusive win in an ongoing and pervasive popularity contest.

Despite the fact that all eyes seem to be on girls, gauging their success, girls themselves can feel quite alone. So much of the way the rest of us talk about girls' issues is framed by the individualistic spirit of our times. Academics discuss the neo-liberal era, which, when applied to girls, leaves them individually responsible for their successes and their failures, regardless of the social and economic conditions in which they are living.[2] And yet, these conditions have always had—and continue to have—a real and sometimes debilitating impact.

Consider, for example, that one in three American women lives in poverty,[3] and that many women are still working in traditionally pink-collar jobs and bearing a disproportionate responsibility for unpaid care work. In the US, women make, on average, 77 percent of men's wages;[4] in Canada, 81 percent.[5] Women hold only 18 percent of leadership positions in the US including 17 percent in politics, 16 percent in business,[6] 23 percent in academia, and 16 percent in film and television.[7]

In addition to these unyielding realities, beliefs and cultural attitudes set up competing and contradictory expectations for girls. They continue to be told to be pretty, but not too pretty; to be smart, but not too smart; to be sexy, but not too sexy; and to save the world, but not to die trying. The girls we spoke to on our tour talked a lot about the double standards that play out in their daily lives, from the seemingly banal to the more consequential. "Boys can say what they want, be supersmart, be mean, be angry, and act it out," said 14-year-old Melanie from LA. Sari, a 16-year-old Torontonian, said, "Girls are expected to have better manners. Girls are expected to do better in everything. Boys can sleep with lots of people and not get judged, but if girls hook up with guys then you're a slut. You are screwed if you do and screwed if you don't. You just can't win."

The task of trying to achieve "supergirl" status can be perilous.[8] When girls fall and we don't stop to consider their social conditions and economic realities, *we* fail *them*. Girls' success is not a measure of their personal capacity; it is the measure of a society willing to provide the opportunities, supports and safety nets needed for all girls to experience success.

OUR MOTHERS, OURSELVES

Life may be a tightrope walk for girls, but being a parent isn't easy either. As mothers ourselves, we know that much of what we hope to do when it comes to accompanying girls through life starts with our relationships with our daughters. But what have we inherited from our own relationships with our moms? When our generation was growing up in the 1970s and '80s, women's roles were actively changing. As The Bionic Woman and Wonder Woman took on the world from our television sets, our moms were beginning to do the same—and we had a front-row seat for the action.

Many of our mothers challenged traditional gender roles; they lived on the front lines of a society in transformation. Newly won economic and social freedoms provided more choice around education, career, marriage and child-bearing—and some women tried to "have it all." Major changes on the political and economic fronts made room for mostly white middle- and upper-class women to enter these arenas. Women who worked multiple jobs to pay bills and who faced structural inequality like racism, homophobia and poverty, were often left behind by the new-found power of "women's liberation." Nevertheless, we were told we could do anything—and be anything we wanted. And we believed it.

We inherited some unfinished business from our trailblazing mothers and grandmothers, who hadn't quite solved the gender-inequity puzzle. While our mothers modelled strength and courage, they also passed on some unspoken cues. They wanted us to be confident but were often insecure themselves; they wanted us to be proud of our bodies but they dieted relentlessly; they wanted us to be free but they had hang-ups about sexuality. Whether our moms went to work or not, they did the majority of the housework, the child-rearing and the family nurturing. Some of our moms got divorced, and paid the price by enduring economic instability. Some continued to struggle with the persistence of inequity.

We daughters responded in a variety of ways. Some of us rebelled, some inherited degrees of self-loathing, some conformed and some became hyperachievers. Whichever path we chose, we found voices to echo our own. Naomi Wolf and the Riot Grrrls helped to push the boundaries of girl and woman power. Feminist writers Audre Lorde and bell hooks wrote passionately about the intersections of gender, race and sexual identity. Musicians Liz Phair, Tracy Chapman, Courtney Love and Sinead O'Connor gave us anthems and fuel for rebellion. Madonna showed us we could be sexually powerful, and Cyndi Lauper set us free to have fun. But our generation was also on the receiving end of a backlash against feminism, and a new story was written, declaring the feminist project over. In privileged enclaves across the Western world, a new mantra could be heard: the women's movement was a *fait accompli*. Elsewhere, marginalized voices continued to work tirelessly to speak out against discrimination and violence.

Many feminists and women's groups kept working and organizing action despite funding cuts, "postfeminism" and backlash politics—to address everything from migrant and domestic workers' rights to violence against women; from economic human rights to food insecurity; from environmental justice to Indigenous sovereignty.

Like our moms before us, we did our best in the 2000s to find our own ways of being women. We stayed in school longer, sought non-traditional relationships and careers. Many of us delayed or opted out of starting families and expected male partners and friends to meet us on equal ground. *Sex and the City* inspired a fresh sense of independence built around female friendships, cosmopolitans, casual sex and career ambition. Thanks to Carrie Bradshaw and her entourage, it's now socially acceptable for women to drink and talk about sex in public. The adult beverage industry seized the brand-new day, and alcohol is now a lucrative female-dollar market. It's also a sanctioned escape from our work as mothers, corporate players, activists, economic agents and romantic partners, to name just a few of our many roles.

So, some things have certainly changed, but many others haven't. Our mothers didn't solve everything, and nor have we. And yet, we are repeating history in some important ways. Just as our mothers thought they were setting us up for success, and telling us that we could have it all (without really stopping to think about what that meant, or whether it was even desirable), we, too, are projecting some hazy ideas onto today's girls—ideas that have us believing, or at least wanting to believe, that *they* have it all figured out. Girls are now on top, we tell ourselves (and them); *it's a girls' world*, and they should assume their entitlement because they have it all.

A nice thought, certainly, but that's all it is. Girls and young women tell us that it's not so easy, and there's plenty of evidence to support their claim. Statistics on the state of girls' lives reveal a clear need to separate our projections from their lived experience. Recent studies in North America show that girls are dealing regularly with sexual harassment, sexism, racism and discrimination. They are facing growing rates of HIV infection, and sexually transmitted infections and diseases. The psychological issues that most affect girls—such as depression, negative body image, anxiety and stress—are on the rise. We're also seeing an increase in acts of self-harm, such as cutting and binge drinking.[9]

Despite the progress that has been made, there is much to do before we will have created a truly equal place in the world for and amongst women and girls. The cultural shift we've experienced over the last few decades is still a very new phenomenon in a long legacy of living in a man's world, and we are carrying that baggage. As parents, we must be mindful of passing on outdated beliefs and attitudes and be thoughtful about how we contextualize the world for girls.

How, for example, do we feel about our bodies? Are we comfortable in our own skin? Do we (like our mothers) expect girls to love their bodies, yet at the same time obsess over the five pounds we can't lose, or our aging flesh? Do we expect girls to find power in "sisterhood" although they see us pick apart other women for their imperfections or their successes, or tear down those who haven't made the same choices we have? Do we walk around with guilt or shame? Are we high-performance supermoms, inadvertently raising the bar for our daughters to impossible heights? Are we perpetuating deep cultural legacies through internalized sexism? How do we participate in maintaining or transforming racist structures that ignore the realities many girls are living with?

Taking stock of our own lives with this type of questioning can be an eye-opening experience. Being aware of who we are as women—and as role models—allows us to serve our daughters and our nieces, students and friends better. And continuing our own evolution toward freedom and acceptance, of ourselves and others, will make it easier for girls to do the same. Looking back to our mothers and grandmothers, and the many generations before now, gives recognition not only to where we have come from, but also to the many cultural and diverse stories "we" as women hold in this project of healing and transformation.

SECRETS, SHADOWS AND VIOLENCE

We also need to be willing to cast light into the dark spaces, to ask tough questions that may encourage new ways of thinking. Today's girls have secrets just like their mothers and grandmothers did, and these secrets can be isolating. Many girls are taught to take on the problems of our world personally. Emotional and sexual taboos can be projected onto them, and discrimination through racism and classism can become internalized. Girls are often on their own trying to make sense of this.

Among many other topics pulled from their daily lives, we talked with the girls we met about sex, cutting, eating disorders, homelessness, racism and slut-shaming. Through this sharing, they discovered that they are not alone. When girls can take internalized struggles and locate them within a larger social context, they are able to see that they themselves are not the problem. They begin to understand, often for the first time, that they are experiencing the effects of larger social and systemic problems. And perhaps even more important, they get to share coping strategies, and generate ideas about how to make change happen.

The need for change becomes urgent when we start to unveil how normal and pervasive violence is in the lives of girls today. In the US, one in five girls experiences teen dating violence.[10] In Canada, one in four girls in grade ten does not feel safe in her school, and almost half of girls report being the target of unwanted sexual comments or gestures.[11] In hearing from girls directly, we learned that violence is a regular fact of their lives, and is often erased by friends, adults, authorities and even legal representatives who invalidate their experience by blaming them, making them feel ashamed or further victimizing them. It happens often that girls are blamed for sexual violence. "Don't dress like a slut," they might be told. "It means you're asking for it." "What did you expect, if you were drinking so heavily," they might be asked when reporting a rape. Girls should not be made to feel responsible for a culture that perpetuates sexual violence and then fails to believe them when they try to get help after suffering an attack.

Thankfully, social-media platforms are beginning to effect change on this front. Tired of waiting for someone official to do the right thing—

or anything at all—girls are taking to Twitter, Tumblr, Facebook and Instagram to shout out their experiences. They're fighting back against revenge porn and date-rape photos gone viral, and they're enlisting digital crowds to bring about justice when justice is needed. *All* girls have valuable insights to share on these issues. It would serve us well to hear them.

And let's not forget to include boys in this conversation. They are implicated in girls' stories, but they need help to understand those stories and find positive positions within them. Boys are going through their own changes as the balance of power shifts, and they, too, receive mixed messages about what it means to succeed or, in their case, to "be a man." Little wonder, then, that when boys are told that "life is a rock camp" for them, it can set up expectations that are not fulfilled. Learning about historical social and gender inequities can help boys find a role to play in the politics of transformation.

ROCK ON!

If the girls we have met are any indication, this generation of young women is *strong*. They have their own ideas about how best to pick up the unfinished business of achieving equity and moving forward with change. Girls are the experts in their own lives. They have a lot to say, and they can offer parents, educators, politicians and culture at large new ideas not just about how to be a girl today, but also about how to tackle our wider social, environmental and economic challenges.

Here's what you will learn in the pages that follow: girls aren't just lighting up rock 'n' roll stages, they are lighting new trails through life. By stretching beyond the stereotypes, contradictions and double standards that have been imposed on them for far too long, and by using the potentially radical new media that is the hallmark of their generation, girls are reinventing what it is to be a girl.

While hanging out with them, we learned that despite the visibility that many girls enjoy in this brave new world, so many others are still not seen. The conditions that girls grow up in are diverse and complex, but the systems we have traditionally put faith in—like the health care and education systems—all too often employ a "one size fits all" approach. At the most basic levels, they often don't understand how to care for girls.

But girls are learning how to take care of themselves and each other, and, in doing so, they are gaining the ability to teach us what we can do to help them thrive. Despite claims that today's youth are apathetic and individualistic, we've seen how engaged and passionate girls can be about changing the world. Whether they are taking on classroom issues, tackling inequities in their own communities, or building projects on a global level, girls are on the move with great ingenuity.

If girls are leading the way toward true and lasting change, overturning the media and storming unexplored territory in everything from sexual self-expression to global politics, what more are they capable of doing? We have the ability to find out. By shifting the axis and supporting their visions, we can help ensure that life is a rock camp for boys *and* girls.

ABOUT THE SURVIVAL KIT

At the end of each chapter in this book, you'll find a section titled "Survival Kit," full of practical tips on how to be better informed and better equipped to support girls. By including this information—which will sometimes feature direct input from girls themselves, and from the many experts we spoke to in the course of our research—we hope to inspire new conversations with girls and new actions by girls for girls. We also hope to encourage you to open yourselves up to new ideas or to discuss any issues that may feel challenging. Tips range from personal advice to ways to get involved in activism and advocacy. We will also connect you to organizations, websites and books that offer further information and resources on the topics covered. Knowledge, after all, is power.

DISEMPOWERED AND DUPED?
CALIFORNIA GIRLS

WE LANDED AT LAX on a balmy autumn afternoon. Sunlight streamed in from beyond the exit doors. People plugged into iPods mobbed in and out of lineups and raced to departure gates. Teenagers posed with their phones to send digital postcards into the digital world. Here, we thought, is social-media central: the land of the selfie with the Hollywood backdrop.

We were in Los Angeles to meet Sarah Banet-Weiser, an author, media studies professor at the University of Southern California and "girl culture" scholar who has documented phenomena from Nickelodeon television heroines to beauty pageants to self-branding. We came to talk with her about the proliferation of girl stories and growing girl awareness in the media, and about whether this increased visibility is empowering girls.

A quick glance through a magazine or website, or a flip through the hundreds of channels available online or on your television, reveals an interesting dichotomy. On the one hand, we have trends that continue to promote hyperfeminine idealized "norms": YouTube beauty tutorials, and the rise of the Kardashian clan (with their endless cosmetic surgeries and beauty tips that conform to Barbie's original standards). On the other, we see progressive messages that are redefining beauty norms coming from and inscribed in pop culture. There are a growing number of efforts to diversify our ideas of beauty: Dove's Campaign for Real Beauty; HBO's popular hit series *Girls*; Ellen DeGeneres's Gap fashion line for girls; and Disney sensations such as 14-year-old Rowan Blanchard (who actively shouts out to support racial diversity) and 19-year-old Zendaya (now the model for a black, dreadlocked Zendaya Barbie doll). At the time of writing, Blanchard and Zendaya have 3.7 and 23.5 million Instagram followers, respectively, while Kim Kardashian [was until recently] the most followed person on earth with more than 65.9 million followers (Taylor Swift and Selena Gomez took over at more than 70 million each). Is it any wonder that girls might be feeling an overt tension between upholding and transgressing stereotypical gender norms?

On the tranquil and leafy USC campus, students were huddled together or roving in packs, discussing their classes, political passions and sorority and fraternity associations. There were groups sitting outside in the sun eating lunch and drinking iced smoothies. We found Sarah in her office, a cozy book-lined room with a window overlooking a courtyard. She was running to teach her next class on communication, gender and culture. The topic of the day was Beyoncé, and guest lecturer and "Beyoncé expert" Dayna Chatman was set to lead the conversation. *A Beyoncé expert?* What a glamorous job title! The students obviously thought so, too, since the lecture hall was expected to be full. Sarah disappeared out the door, promising to send along some students who had volunteered to speak with us.

A few minutes later, a group of young women aged 17 to 21 sat with us in a circle on Sarah's office floor, our backpacks, notepads and iPhones spread out all around. On our minds was the fact that in mainstream culture, feminists have been talking for a long time about the impact of the objectification of women and girls. At the end of the 1970s, Jean Kilbourne introduced her critique of advertising with her groundbreaking documentary *Killing Us Softly*, and Naomi Wolf continued this awareness in the 1990s with her bestselling book *The Beauty Myth*. Today, it is well documented that girls are bombarded by negative sexualized images that come at them across media platforms. This, combined with sexual objectification, can lead to diminishing self-esteem. Recent studies suggest this goes even further: objectification leads to body monitoring and body shame, which leads in turn to variations of self-objectification, self-exploitation, cognitive dysfunction, depression

and damaging competition among girls and women.[1] In this toxic domino effect, girls are often positioned by pop culture and media as passive
recipients of the damaging messages.

We wanted to find out how Sarah's students—media-literate young
women who hail from all corners of the US from diverse cultural and
ethnic backgrounds—negotiate beauty standards, gender codes, relationships and pop culture influences. We asked them whether girls are really
disempowered and duped by media, or whether they are actually tran-
scending these expectations. They answered with tales about how they
play with self-expression, clothes, makeup and identity in an effort to
renegotiate feminine stereotypes. They discussed the tension between
performing and at the same time pushing against idealizations of beauty
and body in order to achieve what they want, to assert their voices and
take their place in today's world. They also talked about how this tension
plays out in their relationships.

Cara, a white 19-year-old, told us, "I've always struggled with the
superficial weird society I'm a part of. It's an inner conflict. I never dress
in a way that appeals to men during the school week. I wear bizarre
things; it's part of my self-expression. When I go out, though, I totally
fit the mainstream mould. I look like every single other girl wearing her
crop top; I lose my sense of individuality. Essentially I'm conforming to
fit that male gaze, so that I look like I'm desirable. This class has been
interesting. Now, I've kind of reverted back to dressing like I would normally dress, to dress for myself instead; to try and fight that expectation
to please a man."

"I struggle with that, too," said Terese, a 20-year-old Latina. "I don't
know if it's wrong though. If I'm dressing to appease the male gaze, is it
wrong? Is it wrong to dress in a slutty outfit if I have a goal in mind to
meet guys? Am I now taking advantage of a situation that benefits me?
It's really complicated. I don't know what's right or wrong."

"I can dress to feel confident and to feel comfortable," reflected Joah,
an 18-year-old bi-racial young woman of colour. "But we are still practising the disciplinary power of femininity." Joah explained that for her this
meant conforming to "feminine" expectations—like wearing makeup,

working to make sure her body is shaped a certain way, looking "presentable," being pretty but not overly sexual. "It's like, 'Be a lady and sit with your legs crossed, not sprawled open,'" she told us. Sarah's class had made her aware of the contradictions inherent in these expectations, and how those contradictions influence girls' lives—even when they are choosing to resist this cultural norm. Joah gave us an example. "I work hard and I'm tired and sometimes I look like crap. College isn't easy. I put on makeup; it's my battle outfit, but, at the same time, I try to fight for myself and be authentic in my expression."

"We always feel like we have to be presentable, happy and peppy all the time," added Elise, who is 19 years old and from Mexico.

"I used to feel confident in my feminism, and in my behaviours," Yasmine, a white 19-year-old, reflected. "I considered myself [as] subverting expectations and gender codes in some ways. I'm feminist. I've been like, 'If I don't feel like shaving my legs, then screw you, I won't.'"

"There is a norm—a feminine code—that girls are expected to follow," added Cynthia, a white 17-year-old. "If you follow it, you perpetuate it. I used to think that if I rebelled, then I was subverting. But there is no subverting. If you rebel, you re-enforce it. It 'others'[2] you. It's weird. Before, I felt more powerful in my individual actions and choices. Now I feel like trying to be different by breaking those rules doesn't really do anything at all."

"You are screwed if you do, screwed if you don't," Amalia, white and 21, threw in, referring to the struggle between conformity and push back, both of which are policed by peer pressure and pop culture's definition of "cool."

"There is nothing I can do to change all this. It has to come from somewhere else," said Mela, an Asian 18-year-old, expressing a desire for social change. The entire group agreed.

+++

We moved from Sarah's office to an outdoor patio, taking advantage of the beautiful day. Over iced tea, Elizabeth, 19, told us how she wanted to feel attractive and desired but also struggled with those feelings. "The truth is, it's pretty hard to escape the adolescent-girl battlefield. There are a lot of contradictions. I've always considered myself outspoken, feminist and confident. Now I've become a little more self-critical. The way I dress, for example. I used to wear short skirts and crop tops to look good for guys. I realized I was doing it for attention, which can be seen as bad. But at the same time, isn't that human? I'm realizing that there is a way that reality is set up."

Cara agreed. "Everybody's version of what they think needs to change [in order to achieve social equity] is so different, and everyone's version about how to go about changing it is so different. I don't think being a feminist is about 'don't wear makeup, never shave your armpits.' There is no right or wrong; people can make different choices and still be a feminist. But there are so many layers. This class helps make us aware of all these small things I never would have noticed before. A lot of what I aim to do by subverting expectations makes me a feminist."

"What we're learning is being able to think critically about what we do," added Elise. "I always thought I embodied girl power. I went out, hooked up with a guy and was on to the next. I thought I had a sense of power. When I reflected on this, I realized my nights out depended on the guy and on external validation to determine my self-esteem and self-worth."

"If a guy comes up to you, it's hard to not feel like the guy has all the power," said Amalia. "If we take the power, or say no, we are seen as a bitch. Guys do the approaching and girls are the receiver."

"I say we should think of girl power in terms of just going out and having fun," concluded Yasmine. "It should be, 'Did I have fun? Did I get to scream along to that song with my friends?'"

By the time we finished our iced tea, it was clear that these girls, like so many others, are caught in a tricky dance involving identity, media and pop culture. And yet, they are far from being disempowered dupes, or "victims" of media objectification. They are smart and aware, constantly on the lookout for ways to play with and to tackle confusing and contradictory messaging. As they left the patio to make their last classes, they told us how happy they were to have found a platform for critical reflection and a place to grapple with and navigate cultural currents. Their media studies class had given them a new way of seeing themselves amid the norms of femininity and masculinity, and an informed way of talking back to the world around them.

This self-awareness and critical reflection isn't limited to life on campus. It can be seen in the myriad ways that girls choose to express themselves: dresses and makeup one day, and sports uniforms and bare faces the next; short haircuts and high heels; BMX bike races won by gripping the handlebars with long, elaborately manicured nails. Girls reimagine and get creative with traditionally defined gender roles by blurring the masculine and the feminine. While the second wave of feminism rejected high fashion and traditional feminine markers like makeup and heels, this generation of girls is bringing back some of these "outlaws"—and enjoying the sense of fun and empowerment that comes from embracing their femininity on the one hand and actively dissolving traditional gender roles on the other. And all the while they are creating a new space, one in which outdated social constructs can be redefined.

GIRL POWER AND THE ECONOMY OF VISIBILITY

After our meeting with her students, we followed Sarah Banet-Weiser to her home in the suburbs, weaving through LA's heavy traffic (and our GPS directives!) to get there. Sarah greeted us at her door as serene as if she hadn't just braved the same traffic after a long day at work. Tall and vivacious, with an infectious laugh, Sarah eagerly told us how visibility has become an end in itself for girls.

We reminisced about the Riot Grrrl punk movement that peaked in the 1990s, and recalled how girl power momentum took on issues around racism, sexual expression and sexual abuse that challenged the feminine codes of conduct and pushed a new vision of what was possible for girls into the Western collective imagination. Armed with electric guitars, activist blogs, zines and mauve mohawks, these punk avatars were outspoken and dynamic; they took over a bright corner of pop culture with their punchy messages backed by an earnest desire for reform. It didn't take long, though, for girl power's anti-consumer DIY roots to be hollowed out. When consumer culture took on the imagery and symbols of this political movement for use in mass production, its political force was reduced to a brand with a slogan. The idea of girl power became mainstream. Commercial productions like pop music's Spice Girls used "girl power" as one of their catchphrases, and through their accessible personas, songs, movies, apparel and merchandise, turned the idea into a safe, sexy and sellable feminist project.[3] Since then, girl power's message has been gutted even further.

"We live in a world of commodified imagery," Sarah explained. "We are constantly being told to look at girls—they are everywhere, on the cover of magazines, on billboards, on TV shows and all over social media—but this proliferation of visibility is not tied to any political project. It's an economy of visibility as a destination."

The "economy of visibility": it's a term Sarah coined to describe the contemporary trend of visibility for the sake of being visible. But how did we get from the original counterculture girl power—complete with political agenda—to this, where being seen and admired is the only goal? Sarah points out that there's nothing new about girls wanting to be liked, and experiencing varying degrees of peer pressure around this desire. What's changed, she says, is the means to the end. Today's economy of visibility manifests like a classic popularity contest, but one held in the Wild West of the Internet. "It used to be what they *did* that made them visible. [But] kids now want to be famous more than they want any specific job or career. Visibility is the goal; 'likes'[4] take on meaning. Being visible and visibly liked is an end in itself that has commercial rewards. If you put a video up on YouTube and you get enough views, you can become a YouTube partner. If you're 'Facebook famous,' or have huge Instagram or Twitter followings, you are seen to have peer and therefore market influence, and then you can be approached by brands to be a brand ambassador. So you have these girls doing makeup and shopping tutorials, that are earning money and becoming remarkable material successes just by being visible."

Because microcelebrity status and great earning power are now so tangible online, the promise of celebrity and profit has swept the digital generation into a narcissistic scramble. Have girls become embroiled in a capitalist sellout with no political message except "Mirror, mirror, on the wall, who is the fairest of them all"? Is this the Cult of True Womanhood, which in the nineteenth century sought to assert that womanly virtue resided in piety, purity, submissiveness and domesticity, making its foray into the twenty-first century? If so, is social media the vehicle that most invisibly recycles and revamps this ideal? Where does that leave us?

ARMY-STYLE SURVEILLANCE AND FITTING IN

If some of the most visible girls are rewarded for propelling the capitalist machine, how does this impact girl culture generally? Even if the so-called democratic digital world offers the most followed girls fame and fortune for online popularity, in this economy of visibility, the rules of play are very narrow. "Like culture" is the electronic version of peer pressure; it mirrors the same policing we have always seen in social power dynamics. On this public forum, girls are being constantly evaluated on the basis of their bodies and what they do with them. This value system reinforces that a girl's worth is predominantly in her body, and rewards girls for conforming to and achieving an accepted and modest version of beauty, desirability and femininity.

And what is that accepted version of beauty? In the vast majority of cases, the aesthetic being promoted is white and Western. YouTube tutorials posted by women of colour demonstrate how to make their eyes look bigger, or how to use contouring and shading to accentuate cheekbones and make the nose look thinner and longer.

Likes and mainstream beauty tutorials reject girls who fail to meet these white Western standards. They also either praise or punish them—and no one knows if it will be one or the other—for posting things like bikini or underwear shots, for being "slutty" or overtly sexual. In this way, girls are recruited by the machinations of social media to monitor each other. "There are two well-pronounced moral messages at play," Sarah explained. "One which says, 'Use your body to be confident and go rule the world but only if you stay within the established rules,' and the other which says, 'We don't trust your body, it's too sexy and unpredictable, you need to be protected.'"

The negative feedback loop that this army-style surveillance and public appraisal generates can set girls up for competition, comparison and judgment—dynamics that seep into their social lives, where they jockey for acceptance, approval and validation.

We told Sarah about some of the girls we'd met in Whitehorse, Yukon, in the northwest of Canada, who were very articulate about how they're dealing with this form of surveillance and media pressure. They told us about extreme cases of policing on Ask.fm, a social networking website where users can ask other users questions, and responses are anonymous. Users hope that they will be complimented, and very often they are. But the TBH trend ("to be honest," a parlour-style phrase that dares kids to tell the truth about what they think of each other) can also bring out harsh criticism. Ask.fm has more than 150 million unique users each month, from all around the world, and has been heavily criticized for its lack of regulation.[5] Fourteen-year-old Sophie told us, "On Ask.fm you get posts on your wall like, 'You are a fat stupid slut.' People go crazy saying what they wouldn't ever want to say to your face. It's incredibly hurtful. I haven't been victimized on social media but I see some of my friends getting hurt by it. It's the evil side of TBH."

Zadie, 14, told us about her experience. "Someone wrote in the boys' washroom that I have a big ass. I'm getting a lot of that; it makes me feel like I'm fat. I don't like it when people say stuff about me, like on Ask.fm, where they say the same kind of stuff. You don't say that to a girl. It's not a compliment when I'm being objectified because of what I'm wearing and what kind of ass I have. It's horrible; you judge yourself all day. You want to be that person who doesn't judge your body, who doesn't say, 'I don't like how big my butt is, I don't like my thighs,' but there is always something holding you back, there is always something that makes you want to lose weight. It sucks, I hate it."

So many of the girls we met talked about the pressure to conform to beauty norms, to be popular, and how they feel this has to happen on every platform. Tara, 16, told us, "Now you have to be popular online and in real life. You can be popular online and not popular in real life. It's, 'Oh, I have more likes on my pic. Oh, I'm texting more people than you. Oh, I have more Snapchats than you.' It's a competition."

Tara's friend Candace, 15, offered a personal glimpse into how the economy of visibility and the culture of policing can breed internalized sexism and self-hatred. "Jealousy is the root of all the problems. I get jealous sometimes. I don't want be jealous. I'm jealous of other girls' friends, their looks, how many people like them, what boys like them, how many friends they have. [Instead] I could just learn that I'm good enough. I think people get jealous because people are comparing themselves. You can't always be comparing yourself; you make yourself feel so bad. You are always going to be jealous, but you can turn it down. If a popular girl is really pretty, and she has perfect eyebrows, you know you can't have the same thing. It's so pointless and such a waste of time to get emotional about it. There is a good jealousy that helps you improve yourself, and then a jealousy that just makes you mad at yourself for things you can't change."

Sarah agreed that today there is an even greater surveillance of and pressure on girls because of their digital presence. Girls are required to create and build an enviable existence both online and in what they refer to as IRL ("in real life"). Juggling the digital representation of herself with the self she presents every day at school can be like a full-time job. This competitive marathon to win likes and gain visibility also makes girls turn on each other, and this perpetuates the contradiction they feel around how to be both validated and authentic.

"Digital culture is varied, but much of it functions like a rating system," said Sarah. "It's a beauty pageant. I worry about girls policing other girls and this happening in public with the focus on their bodies all the time. The judgment and fear around 'fat' polices girls' bodies to such an extreme, and starts so early. Having a sexy body is the most desirable currency, and it's a visible, public currency, constantly negotiated and evaluated. It's a losing battle for self-esteem. Why make advertising campaigns with slogans like, 'You're beautiful the way you are'? It makes feeling good about yourself all about physicality. Everything we do to bolster self-esteem is focused on the body.

"If we don't get the focus off their bodies," she continued, "girls are always going to be found wanting; their bodies are always going to be something that is a deficit in their minds. This solidifies the thin, hypersexualized body as the desired norm."

Sarah's 12-year-old daughter, Lillian, walked in then with a group of her water polo teammates. They said hello, grabbed some snacks and retreated to her bedroom. "What would it look like if my daughter wouldn't worry about whether or not her legs are fat?" Sarah asked. "Or if she wouldn't be competing for beauty, popularity and visibility everyday? I wish she didn't have to check herself all the time. My oldest is 21; he wrote his college essay on how ruthless conformity made him not want to be like anyone else. He is entitled to say that. Lillian, she wouldn't say that. She is subject to ruthless conformity in a totally different way."[6]

Sarah tries to mitigate this by setting rules around Lillian's online presence. Lillian has an Instagram account; she's allowed to show pictures of food and her dogs and some of her hobbies but she's not allowed to show her body. "Having an upsurge in tween girl culture [to tap into] is also really important," said Sarah. "Things like the Divergent and Hunger Games book series. There's some good music too. Becky G raps about positive Latina girl images, and Lorde writes lyrics that are critiquing a lot of the stuff girls are living. If my kids are singing the lyrics of Lorde, then good. Part of the way gender norms work is that you just hear the stereotypes. [You] read them and see them so much that you repeat the stereotypes and they just become who you are. So if we know what's out there and we channel popular culture in particular ways to our children, we do help them to focus on the more empowering messages."

Later on, we visited Lillian and her girlfriends in her bedroom. They were eagerly anticipating a win in their upcoming water polo game, and told us how much they love participating in sports. Winning is more fun than losing, they all agreed, and simply playing helps them deal with the social pressures they feel. It's clear that they take pride in their achievements and are less worried about aspects of a beauty regime. Abby, 12, explained how she "lost a toenail just by putting a goal in!"

"Yeah, it's a tough sport," Jolie, also 12, added. "People won't mess with you because it makes you stronger. It takes your mind off of stuff, and if you've had a bad day it's a great way to vent your anger."

It wasn't the last time we'd hear about the empowering benefits of sports on a girl's psyche.

AT VENICE BEACH

The next morning was a Saturday. We went to the beach early and hung out around the skate park, hoping to meet a few skater girls. The first girl we met was Joya, a tall, 15-year-old black girl wearing a loose dress with the iconic Rolling Stones lips emblazoned on the front. She was there with her mother and her brother, who was the skater.

After hearing about the visibility rat race, we were thrilled to meet Joya, who turned out to be a breath of fresh air. Her interests were reading and theatre and she was really happy within herself. She offered proof that not all girls participate in a school popularity contest every day only to go home and pine over how many people "like" her—or don't. "I like my school," she told us. "I really like drama class. I want to be an actress. When you become a character you get to be other people. You're not you, but their stories might be similar to yours. It's an escape and a way to experience life that you can learn from, and that's really fun."

Joya has a social-media presence, but she doesn't let it rule her life. "I have Facebook, I have Twitter," she said. "But Facebook can be annoying. Some of the things that people post can be weird and negative. I like Instagram. Twitter is just drama but I like reading some of the feeds; it's entertaining."

She told us about a friend who was receiving death threats on social media from fellow students. This friend had been popular, but because of rumours about sex with a boy (which hadn't happened), she was under attack. Joya did her best to help, but she couldn't really understand her friend's relentless drive to be popular—a drive that was so strong it put her in harm's way. She thinks being too visible is damaging, and that social media is mostly a pointless acting out of a lot of drama that she'd rather play with productively in theatre class.

Where she does feel pressure, however, is around her body image. "I've never been a small girl," she told us. "I've always been the tallest in my class. I felt judged by those pressures to be a certain size and shape. My classmates would be like, 'Oh, she's not little, she's not normal size.' It's hard, but acting helps, reading helps. I can escape in a good way."

Joya's story was echoed by many of the girls we spoke to. Media influences and social-media pressures are certainly real, but lots of girls have other interests, social networks and values that keep them engaged in life. At the skate park we also met Beth, an 18-year-old white skater girl. Her cropped hair, cut-off jean shorts, grunge top, and faded blue Converse gave her a streetwise look. She did a few rounds in the bowl on her short-board and showed off some of her tricks. After we had admired her skills she sat down with us to chat. When we asked if it was hard to be one of the few girls on the skating scene, a story emerged.

"When I started riding at 14," she told us, "it would be like, 'So, do you ride that?' The guys thought I was being a poseur. I would sarcastically say, 'No, I just carry it around,' but then I'd jump on it and show them and they'd see, 'Oh, she's not just doing this to be cool.'

"I go out by myself. It's intimidating being a girl at a skate park. At first I would wear my sweatshirt so the boy skaters wouldn't see my boobs, so from a distance they wouldn't know I was a girl. It was important that they didn't think I was a girl with an accessory—like my board was a purse—to pick up guys. I'm actually really into skating; I do it for me.

"Testosterone fills this space. The boy skaters flood it with their bullshit. They aren't bad people; they're just enjoying a privilege they don't even realize they have. The [skate park] provides a stage for boys to feel good about themselves. It's normal for them to show off and build their self-esteem. [For me], it sucks. I've been sitting here for a bit and no one's like, 'Hey, Beth, come take a turn.' I have to wait till the guys all get their turns. I have to . . . push my way in. The way I work it is I talk a lot of shit, too. I talk about gross shit, like this guy landed on his nuts the other day and I was like, 'Man, it must suck to have a nut sack.' I'm pretty blatant, but once you start talking shit with them and you [say] that you [already] have a boyfriend, then it's cool."

We asked Beth how she came to be "one of the guys" at the skate park and what advice she has for other girls who want to push back against gender conformity. Before answering, Beth seized an opening between the guys and got a round of her own skate tricks done, and then came back to us with her reflections. "There were cliques of girls that I grew up with; we had sleepovers and did manicures. I remember being made fun of by them. I was brown-haired and they could see the hair on my legs. They cared so much about image, even in second grade.

"I didn't fit in with other girls that much, so I always tried to keep up with my brother, who is three years older than I was. I didn't see a difference because he was a boy. I was just like, 'That looks like fun!' and I would join in on everything he was doing. I remember one time, he and his friends were building the curb at the bottom of the street, making it a huge pile of dirt. I would see them riding [their bikes] up into it and down the field to the creek. I loved that but I wanted to do the highest hill, the one that none of them had even tried. I ripped the tassels off my purple bike and was like, 'I can do this,' and I did it. I did the most sensational run over the highest hill. It was really exciting. It was awesome. It was me as a person, not as a girl."

Beth told us about the way she understands society and sees it trying to coerce girls into an age-old script. "The first years of life are preparing you for, 'Are you pretty?' I also grew up with a tomboy sister, who is five years older than me. She is driven and she worked really hard at everything. She didn't care about what she looked like. She was awesome. We have girls making a strong presence in snowboarding and BMXing. It would be really nice to see more girl skateboarders getting out there. Girls are told, 'You're so pretty, I love your dress,' and they're always asked, 'Do you have lots of friends?' We don't ask girls hard intellectual questions. I would like to see girls caring about their minds, what they do, how they have changed things," Beth said.

Asked how her IRL experiences help her navigate dominant cultural messages, Beth responded by telling us a bit about how she spends the rest of her downtime. She plays (and really loves) video games. If they give you confidence and you have a good time, she says, they can be great. She had other ideas about social media, though. "Social media sucks. People always ask me, 'Are you on Twitter, are you on Instagram, are you on Facebook?' and I'm like, 'No—I'm right here.'" While Beth sees the benefits of connectivity, she also sees how media streaming through hand-held devices breeds conformity and causes stress. Her advice for girls? "We need to break away from the whole 'being liked' culture. Just breathe. Take a week off, take a vacation with yourself. Don't worry so much about pressure, about what you are going to be when you grow up, about wanting to be older, about clothes. It doesn't matter if you're 'pretty.' Someone is going to find you pretty, someone is going to like you, and you don't have to like everyone who likes you. Don't sell yourself short. Don't worry about what people are saying about you on the Internet, because honestly, they aren't going to remember."

And with that, Beth spotted another opening in the flow of boys and ran off to take another turn in the bowl.

RE-IMAGINING BEAUTY IN SAN FRANCISCO

On our way to LA, we'd stopped in San Francisco to meet with Christine Grumm, a well-known leader in philanthropy. During her time as CEO of the Women's Funding Network, she co-chaired Women Moving Millions, an international group of extraordinary individuals who pledged gifts of a million dollars or more to organizations for the advancement of women and girls. In Christine's hilltop living room, with its panoramic view over the city and the harbour, we sat and talked about the corporate glass ceiling, Geena Davis's Institute on Gender in Media, the contemporary feminist project and why there are still challenges for girls. Miley Cyrus's "girl gone wild" antics were all over the news at the time, and we talked about that, too. "Miley has gone from Hannah Montana to this sexual coming out," Christine said. "We too often bifurcate the conversations about girls between the 'good girls' and the 'bad girls.' On the one hand they are supposed to be prim and proper girls, and on the other hand the media often makes them into young temptresses. In the US, it is difficult to grow up and express one's sexuality with these competing messages. Watching Miley Cyrus go through these changes in front of us is an interesting case study of those confusing messages. If you look at what she is wearing and how she is dancing . . . compare that to how Rihanna or Jennifer Lopez or Madonna dress and perform when they are entertaining: What is the difference? Is the shock because it is a young white woman moving from the innocence of Hannah Montana to an expression of her sexuality? As a society we have a difficult time with women's sexuality in general, but more specifically for young women who we want to put in either the 'virgin' or 'slut' category. Add to that mix class issues and racism, and the sexuality question of young girls becomes even more bifurcated."

We discussed the problematic nature of the moral fears that surface when Disney's It Girl turns out to be sexually alive, and how this evokes ideas of a fragile, white middle class, heterosexual femininity that needs to be protected while at the same time "othering" black girls or Latina girls as oversexualized, marginalized and unexploitable. These are the implicit and explicit messages that girls are dealing with in their cultural landscape. Christine feels we are ready as a society to have honest and frank discussions about the many ways we perpetuate and accept these messages. She asks questions like, "When will we, in a public space, begin to analyze what advertising, the media and society are telling us?"

We talked a lot about the prescribed roles that get projected onto girls via the media machine, and how important it is to arm girls with the tools to recognize and label these roles, societal attitudes and expectations, and to be able to decide how to make independent choices through life. When we discussed some of the media analysis that could be taught to girls, Christine gave us a radical example: "I believe that violence against women on the Internet and often in video games is gratuitous.

Pornography as well as video games often portrays girls and women in bondage being overpowered. It is within this media context that there needs to be a discussion about healthy sexuality. Sexual fantasy and reality are very different, but when they become merged, violence against women and girls increases. We need to be careful about suppressing sexual expression, but at the same time we need to talk to young people about what they are seeing and feeling. Let them speak freely about their own sexuality and be heard. It would be interesting to ask the question: 'If you were going to produce a film on sexuality, what would it be? If you were going to make a video game, what would it be?'"

With these provocative thoughts[7] in mind, we walked from Christine's place down the steep alleys and staircases to Mission Street, where we stopped for coffee. Twenty-three-year-old Safia, of Jamaican heritage, was our waitress. We noticed her confidence and complimented her on her retro eyeglasses and the red scarf she had tied into her hair. When we told her we were in town specifically to talk to girls, she said she would love to chat before she left for her other job as a photographer at Shameless Photography—a boutique studio that takes photographs of clients dressed up, dressed in lingerie or undressed, as their fantasy-fulfilling selves.

Safia told us about her trajectory from teenage timidity through film school and the male-dominated field of professional photography to where she is now, in what she calls her dream job. She echoed some of the ideas we had explored in our conversation with Christine when she told us, "Being a feminist doesn't mean you don't get to be sexy, too." At Shameless, she helps women to own their beauty, and redefine it on their terms. "A woman comes in," she told us, "and then we do her hair and makeup and fit her for clothing. We tell her, 'You can be anyone you want to be today.'" Using vintage clothing, customized hair and makeup, and props that recall anything from 1950s Hollywood to a contemporary circus, clients create whatever story they want to inhabit to experience their beauty.

After working for a fashion photo agency where her male colleagues earned more and got most of the work, and where her boss wasn't supportive, Safia feels valued in this new job. "I felt much better about photography when I started interning [here]," she said. "All these women came in with their amazing stories, stories you could never even imagine. It showed me for the first time in my life that it didn't matter what size a woman was, what colour her skin was and how physically able she was. She could be sexy if she just believed it. Pin-up is interesting, it is sexy, it's suggestive, it's about real beauty and valuing that. It's been an empowering experience for me to give that to other women, to be able to say, 'You can do anything you want to do. It's your day to be naked or to dress up and to be gorgeous the way you define it.'"

Like Beth from the skate park, Safia has found both a way to challenge traditional notions of beauty, and the confidence to reimagine and appropriate age-old scripts. Through her work, she is creating media that goes against corporate packaged beauty norms and porn trends. How did she get here? She talked to us about how she turned the pressures she felt growing up into a will to fight for her place in the media and against the corporate status quo. "In high school, I compared myself to other girls. I put myself down and had a lot of anxiety," she said, explaining that there was a great deal of pressure to be thin and a lot of girls were anorexic. But Safia told us she couldn't have starved herself even if she'd wanted to. "That's not a part of our culture. My mom would notice and the family would be on me so quickly about food, it wouldn't work. Jamaicans love food." She laughed and then said, "I wasn't comfortable in my body. I wore big sweatshirts to cover myself. I remember always chasing this level of beauty that was crazy, and not attainable, always on the inside feeling never good enough, looking at other girls and feeling, 'I don't have that, I will never have that.'"

For Safia, things changed when she left high school. She met new friends and had experiences that taught her new things. Safia said that hanging out with the smart, worldly women she met while working helped her see how hard she'd been on herself and how much the desire to please boys drives girls to police and compete with each other, and to stay quiet. "I finally realized no one could attain that impossible standard of beauty, that it's crazy for everyone. Maybe that's how you get smart enough to know who is playing you, when the media is playing you against each other as women."

Safia now knows that this tactic keeps women isolated and prevents them from being a powerful group that sticks together, fights for each other and creates a force for solidarity. She told us her film programme was highly competitive and that she was one of the few girls enrolled. She had to take her place among male peers who underestimated her. "They really think we are less because we are girls, that's what shocked me. So I was just like, 'I'm going to be a woman and do it in a skirt and you can't tell me what to do.'"

But when Safia started in her career, she hit a wall. She found out she was being severely underpaid compared to her male colleagues in similar positions. She had to assert herself and try to combat the "boys' club" attitude that was advancing men in their careers and curtailing hers. She learned to ask her employers for what she wanted, even though she realized that this was frowned upon. "It doesn't make sense. A guy can be a douche and get away with it," she told us. "It doesn't work the same way with women. Girls often lack the tools to be assertive and outspoken in the world—and when we do we are labelled bitchy." Safia also explained how black women have to face the fear of being labelled as the "angry black bitch" for asserting themselves in even the most subtle ways.

Christine Grumm shared similar views about how we are preparing girls for the workplace. "We are telling girls a lie," she said. "We lead them to believe, 'You can do anything, be anything.' We need to be honest with girls about what they are facing. You can't have it all at once, or ever have it all. Women go into corporations and then, on the third or fourth rung up, they hit the glass ceiling. Why do women leave the corporate structure? They don't have training to deal with the barriers. Girls need to understand their rights and to demand their rights. We need to arm them to battle, to analyze a situation and understand the underlying causes. If you don't have an analysis, you blame it on yourself and it becomes your fault. The fear is, what if they speak up and lose their job?

Which is an echo of the fear of losing the boy—that they will not be accepted by the guy/the [male] boss/the male colleague. The peer pressure to be with the guy, and to please the guy, is high."

Safia said she was learning how to be assertive in the right situation and freeing herself from the need for male approval. She's into helping others do this, too, through her photography and by being a mentor in a photography club for high school kids. "As I've gotten older [she's in her early twenties] I've learned to celebrate my peers, celebrate the women around me and see that as long as I'm lifting them up I'm lifting myself up, too. Caring is important to me," she said.

Safia's insights into "being played" by the media are interesting. Is this insight a skill that could serve girls at a younger age? Analyzing media messages develops girls' critical thinking and their creative abilities to broaden their experience of media, to free themselves from the constraints of the messages and to develop their own media messages. Being supported to produce media and their own visions of beauty—by making videos, practising photography and writing their own scripts—could help girls shift the outdated beauty and behavioural codes that currently bombard them.

Some of the girls we spoke to learned media literacy with mentors, or in girls' programmes or media classes like Sarah Banet-Weiser's at USC. Some found information through Internet activism—feminist memes and funny, savvy youth-driven medias that reach girls in new, simple ways (such as exploring #feminism or #girlactivism). Alternative influences help girls transcend the mainstream code of conduct and begin to see what is possible beyond these constraints and limits.

With Safia, we reflected on what the impacts might be if all girls were taught to deconstruct masculine and feminine stereotypes and the perceived rewards for conformity. Could girls learn to celebrate their girlfriends instead of constantly trying to win a ruthless beauty pageant? If girls were explicitly told that they were being manipulated by an industry that makes billions of dollars every year by keeping them insecure, would that change the negative dynamics of competition that seem to be accepted as normal? If girls were better armed with tools and the early practice of self-assertion, self-care and honest conversations about the "real world," would they feel less coerced into playing the narrow roles that culture assigns to girls?

Safia acknowledged that diversity is under-represented among the mainstream role models available for girls today, but pointed to a few women who stand out for pushing boundaries. "I like Christina Hendricks because she owns her fuller physique. I love women who are outspoken, too, like Zadie Smith; she owns her culture. I love Beyoncé, but I don't look up to her in that way because she is so commercial. I like Beyoncé's sister, Solange. She is funky and I love her hair!"

Like Lillian and her water polo–playing girlfriends, and skateboarder Beth, Safia, too, finds strength in being athletic. Her sport is boxing. "I've always been into fighting sports," she told us. "I have brothers. I could always throw a punch. This makes me feel powerful but I'm also realistic. Some dudes are just bigger, right? I think it's really important for girls to take a course in self-defense, at least to know what's possible. It's like warrior class. If you know that you're a warrior and can take someone on, it's just a stronger way to face the world."

And perhaps, also, a secret ingredient in combatting the pressures of media and conformity.

MISSION GIRLS

When Safia left for her shift at Shameless Photography, we continued our walk through the Mission neighbourhood. It took us past a community centre called Mission Girls—a bright space where girls gathered around a table with art supplies, pop music playing in the background. The energy was high and the girls, in their preteens and early teens, were excited and engaged. Executive director Susana Rojas welcomed us and agreed to an impromptu interview.

Mission Girls has been operating for twenty-five years. It is a local organization that empowers girls to achieve academically, express

themselves creatively and become agents of change in the community. Susana showed us the artwork the girls had been creating—huge
painted and graffitied murals, and rooms full of crafts. Over tea in her
office, we listened to a demo CD produced by the Young Queens, working with Future Youth Records—one of the Mission Girls' music groups
for those in their mid-to-late teens.

Susana explained that a lot of the neighbourhood girls who come
regularly to the after-school and weekend programmes are being dis-
placed by gentrification. Many of the local families have been forced to
move to the Tenderloin district (where there is no similar programme),
an area on the other side of town where girls and all youth have to contend with the risk of violence from drugs, alcohol and unsafe situations.
This is negatively impacting the girls in Susana's programme, many of
whose parents are working two to three jobs to get by and can't be home
after school and into the evening. Mission Girls provides an environment where these girls can let their guard down, have fun together and
talk about what's happening in their lives. So many of them who have
moved away still come back because they feel safe and at home.

When we asked Susana what systemic changes she would like to see
for her girls, she named three things: more funding for better education; media literacy programmes in schools; and the teaching of critical-
thinking skills through media arts like music and videography. "Our
little girls are growing up with songs that call them bitches and hos"[8]
she told us. "They grow up with images that tell them their worth comes
from shaking their booties and how many people want to sleep with
them. A few years ago, people were concerned that girls were anorexic,
that they want to be skinny like in the movies. Now the big-booty
women are really popular. Our Latina and black girls don't feel pressure
to be skinny. Now, you have to be a ho to be cool and girls want small
waists, big thighs, big butts and big boobs. There is a lot of pressure to
be sexual at a very young age. These days there is no dating and first
kiss. Now boys expect that having a girlfriend means you are having sex.
If they're not dating they are dancing, watching the videos, twerking on

the wall. It's in the little girls that we are really seeing the shift. This is a really dangerous shift because they think they need to be a rap video ho in order to be loved. They aren't learning to love themselves first."

This, of course, has always been a hard lesson in growing up, for both genders. But today's world seems to pose many more challenges in this area because of how social media and pop culture have coalesced into a mythical reality, which young people aspire to reproduce. A lot of Mission Girls' work is rooted in letting girls know that they don't have to have sex to be loved. During workshops and while hanging out, they ask girls questions like, "When you hear that kind of talk, how does it make you feel? If you don't like it, why don't you like it? What does 'love' mean and what are the many ways to be loved?" They listen carefully to songs and discuss the content. Susana told us that before they really heard the lyrics and were asked to think about them, the girls all loved the popular songs because the music had a great beat and made them want to dance. When they listened to what these songs were saying, though, Susana noticed a change. "They were starting to think, 'Wait a minute, I might not want to be called that.' Some girls were really into learning this."

When we, in turn, listened to their demo CD and the lyrics of the songs these girls were writing, we were very moved. The songs were reflections on their life experiences. They were wise songs about loneliness and self-harm, and about transformation, empowerment, self-love and activism—with beats catchy enough for twerking!

When we left Mission Girls, we went for a long walk through the back streets where some of these girls lived. We saw how the neighbourhood was changing. New shops were opening, old apartments were being refurbished and marketed to upscale buyers and hipsters were filling the South American eateries. But we could also feel the grassroots energy dedicated to keeping the community alive in the midst of this gentrification. With the Mission Girls' lyrics still floating through our brains, we walked on, inspired by their strength and creativity. Girls find power, it seems, when they question media influence and become cultural producers themselves.

A DIALOGUE WITH THE BEYONCÉ EXPERT

Our final interview in California was with Dayna Chatman, the woman whose lecture we missed when we met with our group of USC students in Sarah Banet-Weiser's office. Dayna is a black feminist media scholar who explores images of black women in popular culture and black women's responses to those images online. We sat with Dayna in the late-afternoon sun to get her take on today's reigning pop queens.

While the popular culture has in the past idealized white, thin beauty standards, these norms have shifted over the past decade. Today, Rihanna and Beyoncé dominate North American pop stardom, and they, in turn, are following JLo and Mariah Carey's rule-changing leads. These women, and others like them, have been instrumental in redefining what we consider the norm. "White and skinny" may once have ruled the world, but today, big bums and curves are all the rage. In fact, current beauty standards are even more diverse than this, depending on where you live. K-pop, the Korean musical craze, and Bollywood, the Indian film, fashion and singing craze, show how a globalized pop culture community can break down the dominant Western white gaze and democratize beauty ideals and their influence.

Despite this advancement in mainstream pop culture, Dayna told us that the realities for girls are still challenging. While we are seeing an increase in diverse representation in the media—from poets like Diamond J. Sharp and Morgan Parker to the online web series The Misadventures of Awkward Black Girl, in which black women create complex black characters and spark discussions about the issues that women of colour are living with—girls of colour are still severely under-represented, and there are many layers to the stereotypes that continue to be projected onto these girls. "For example," Dayna explained, "Rihanna is a figure that is said to be looked up to—and therefore to function as a role model for young girls. However, she is a young woman who expresses her sexual agency unapologetically, in a provocative manner. On the one hand, this expression is read within the broader context of hip-hop culture, where women's bodies are sexually objectified. On the other hand, Rihanna is called to task by some because she is a prominent figure in the entertainment world and her perceived sexual self-objectification is viewed not only as potentially harmful to young girls, but is also perceived as making her complicit in perpetuating long-standing stereotypes about black women's sexuality. I wouldn't say that her expression of sexuality is deviant; she strives for shock value and an expression of her self-identity that is tied to the display and celebration of her body."

Jaclyn Friedman, author of *What You Really Really Want*, explains how "girls of colour are often viewed as always sexually available, simply because of their race. Just look at the specific stereotypes: Latina women are 'spicy,' Middle Eastern and South Asian women are simultaneously 'exotic' and 'repressed,' Asian women are 'submissive,' black women are 'wild' or 'animalistic.'"[9] Touching on a deeper layer of what Christine Grumm described as the hypersexualization of black girls, Dayna explained that, "There is an extra-thin line when it comes to sexual agency as black women, whether sex is for her pleasure or for a man's. Black female sexuality is always framed inside a larger reality of racism and sexism, so even if you are expressing your own sexual agency, even if you are saying, 'This is my body, I'm going to do what I want with it,' it is still discussed in terms of objectifying black women's bodies and deeming them deviant." So Rihanna may be sexually unapologetic, but her attitude confirms a pre-existing understanding of black women's behaviour and is therefore seen as just a normal part of what and who black women are.

Dayna said, "Some people are more disturbed by Beyoncé, who is a married mom and is read as classy within the 'politics of respectability.'[10] Yet, at the same time, Beyoncé is sexually provocative in a way that makes mainstream society uncomfortable." Beyoncé sails dangerously close to mixing the "ho" and "mother" roles, which, combined with her fondness for white femininity codes (long, straight, light hair; pale skin), puts too many ingrained and cherished ideals into conflict. "Where is the space for black women to be visible and express sexuality without it being perceived this way?" Dayna asked. Pop culture bloggers like Sesali B. and Maya Dusenbery at Feministing.com are re-centering this conversation by celebrating Rihanna as an artist, a survivor, a fashion icon *and* a woman with a beautiful, unapologetic sexual expression.[11] At the same time, these forward-thinking bloggers are celebrating Beyoncé as a successful pop star who is "navigating how to assert her own agency while subverting the world's expectations of her as a mother and a businesswoman."[12]

Dayna told us there is an emerging group of black girls, like Arielle Loren and Mia McKenzie, blogging about what it means to be sensual and to express their sexuality. Black Girl Nerds and For Harriett are curated websites where girls can access stories that offer a world that challenges long-standing stereotypes. These sites encourage black girls to develop self-love and, from that powerful centre, to exercise and explore their self-expression. "That is progress," said Dayna, "but it's not hugely visible in the mainstream yet."

We talked over the conversations we had had with the USC students and commented on how much they had shown us about the ongoing and complex struggle girls face when it comes to navigating prescribed gender roles and the expectations and consequences around those. Dayna told us that she sees many girls accepting limitations on their self-expression because they're afraid to rock the boat. She said how lucky she feels to have been raised by a mother who encouraged her to follow her path, to be herself and to be critical, to ask questions and not give in to the status quo. We wondered together about how these kinds of conversations could become more common. Wouldn't girls have greater freedom if they had the means to critically analyze stereotypes and contradictions so they could transcend them? We recalled something Christine Grumm had said to us as we were leaving her house: "Education isn't enough. We need to train girls to have the language, the analysis, and a strategy."

GIRLS ONLINE: FROM CITIZENS TO POLITICAL DOYENNES

We'd seen plenty of evidence to suggest that not all girls are being duped by media's influence. Young women like Safia and Beth and the Young

Queens are playing with and troubling social codes. They're using their creativity to raise awareness and influence pop culture. But the forces of conformity are still powerful in girl culture, as they have always been.

These days, the Internet produces self-made branding machines like Acacia Brinley, a 18-year-old Instagram star with over two million followers. She's a microcelebrity making today's version of a big business with brand endorsements and social cachet for the mere fact of being liked; she may be the best illustration of what Sarah Banet-Weiser means when she talks about the economy of visibility. A quick glance at Acacia's Instagram feed reveals a DIY production of idealized beauty and makeup advertising, selfie flirts and hip fashion brands. Acacia dresses up or dresses down, does her makeup, occasionally poses with her dog or her mom, or some food or one of her friends, and routinely receives 150,000 likes for these posts. How do girls consume these peer-produced media messages, and what impact are they having?

"The media doesn't affect me," said Emily, a 13-year-old we met in Vancouver. "I know that people get Botox and stuff, and edit the pictures to make them look a certain way. We know the media is not real. [Instead of following Internet stars,] I judge myself based on girls I know at my school. I'm not tall and skinny, I'm just myself."

Girls aren't duped. They are in a constant dance of shaping and being shaped by their world. Girls told us how they can separate reality from media projections, and suggested that the underlying messages, stereotypes and gender norms are enforced through other means, too, such as peers judging and punishing each other, and deeply rooted cultural beliefs. In fact, much more than being passive recipients of media, girls are influencing opinion by becoming cultural producers and media makers themselves. Even Acacia Brinley fits this mould, in her own way. The ability to project their voices through social-media platforms puts girls in a more powerful position than ever before to resist mass culture's commercialized femininity and sexuality and fight back against being identified solely as prized consumers. Many girls are testing their voices online and, without adult intervention, discussing topics that break through the stereotypes—things like politics, religion and spirituality.

This creates a public self, which is the important first step girls must take in order to see themselves as citizens.[13]

Tasha is a 15-year-old aspiring singer who writes and performs her own songs and posts them on YouTube.[14] Anna is an 18-year-old who posts stories on online forums about her experiences in overcoming the challenges of growing up with violence, sexual abuse and addiction— stories that offer inspiration for many isolated young people who can connect with each other and share advice, regardless of where they live.[15] These young women offer examples of ways in which girls communicate, on a day-to-day basis, with the world.

Both online and offline, a crop of young female artists are playing with messages and meaning around selfies and some of the other outlets for experimenting with identity spawned by the Internet, such as chat room hang outs and webcam sex diaries. Emerging Internet artists and performers such as Mary Bond, RAFia Santana, Hannah Black, Jennifer Chan, Petra Collins, Kate Durbin, Ann Hirsch and Jillian Mayer inspire discussions about the objectifying male gaze and the effects of pornography on culture by asserting sexual self-representation and personal agency. The work they make uses pop culture, and feeds back into pop culture, in ways that pose questions and challenge assumptions around who girls really are—in public, influential spaces.

Amalia Ulman became a phenomenon in 2014 when she documented a self-beautifying programme via selfies on her Instagram account. For four gruelling months, her 73,500 followers, their networks and the media watched like soap opera devotees as she went through treatments ranging from eyebrow plucking to skin treatments to breast-augmentation surgery. Her audience didn't know that her project was performance art, and when they found out, many of them refused to believe it or to let go of their attachment to her violent striving to be beautiful. Ulman has spoken about this work as a rebellious piece of social commentary. For her, it is a statement on the pressure girls and women feel to be sex objects, and how this pits what is real against what is fake. If the purpose of art is to provoke discussion, Ulman's work can be counted as a roaring success.

Without a doubt, it raises important questions about who we are and what we are attracted to, and why.

Sex and beauty are some of the topics with the most visible controversy that girls are taking on with transformational fervour. Young women are also using technology's platforms to raise global awareness about a number of other political causes. Angy Rivera, who was 19 years old when she first came out as an undocumented immigrant to the US in 2010, opened public debate about the reality of immigration and the plight of undocumented people when she ran a unique youth advice column for refugees and immigrants in 2015 called "Ask Angy." Her film, *Don't Tell Anyone (No Le Digas a Nadie)*, about her courageous journey from poverty in rural Colombia to the front page of the *New York Times*, has been a timely beacon in a crucial movement for social justice and immigration policy reform in the US.

Mars, the 15-year-old co-founder of The Art Hoe Collective, is taking to the web to ignite a movement for girl and women artists who are often underrepresented and exploited in the art world. This movement features performance art, photography, written word and dance, by and for women of colour artists to portray themselves on their own terms, free from stereotypes and mediated preconceptions of their identities. Kimberly Drew, a 25-year-old African-American curator at the Metropolitan Museum of Art in New York, is making it a mission to include black girl art in the American culture agenda. Amendla Stenberg, 18, known for her role as Rue in the *Hunger Games*, is a social activist using her visibility in Hollywood to stimulate conversations about cultural appropriation and racism.

Other more established artists such as illustrator-activist Molly Crabapple, who has reported from the front lines of Occupy Wall Street, Guantánamo Bay and various Middle Eastern conflict zones to politicize the digital generations with her accessible, illustrated news stories[16] and artist-activists Angela Washko, who compassionately combats sexism in video gaming and macho pickup-artist culture, as well as Moreshin Allahyari, who's illuminating the Iranian girl experience, and restoring

Islamic cultural artifacts lost under Islamic State rule (by using 3-D digital printing)—are all building awareness about lesser known or understood areas of potential girl influence into the cultural establishment.

Girl-generated media platforms like *Rookie*, Tavi Gevinson's fashion and opinion magazine and VICE's new channel Broadly, invite the wider world into the girl universe. LennyLetter.com, a website and newsletter created by *Girls* sitcom creators Lena Dunham and Jenni Konner, offers an umbrella of health, lifestyle and politics reading for young women across a mosaic of feminist perspectives.

These creative ways that girls and young women generate culture and develop followings around important ideas, new ways of seeing themselves and new angles from which to mobilize for causes represent a very exciting emerging movement where girl citizens are self-made, influential political doyennes.

GAMER GIRLS CREATING CULTURE

Rebecca, a 29-year-old working in tech, met with us in Montreal to fill us in on how girl coders and gamers are playing a powerful role in cultural production and social change. Rebecca's an ex–web designer turned game developer for AAA Studio, and co-founder of Pixelles, a hub for girl and women gamers that helps create space for them in a world that is sometimes considered one of the last frontiers of the boys-only club. According to Girls Who Code, an organization whose mission is to close the gender gap on technology, in middle school, 74 percent of girls express interest in science, technology, engineering and math (STEM), but when choosing a college major, just 0.4 percent of high school girls select computer science and just 12 percent of computer science degrees are awarded to women.[17]

When she began her career in the tech start-up world, Rebecca said, "It was pretty much unchecked guy culture. So I took the opportunity to get a mentor and I switched to video games."

Like Code Liberation Foundation in New York City and Dames Making Games in Toronto, Pixelles works to get more girls and women involved in games—playing games, creating games and expressing themselves in games—to introduce culture to the gaming business. "Having girls in games is an opportunity to turn things around," said Rebecca. Girls now make up 48 percent of the gaming population and as good customers in a thriving industry, deserve access to games that they relate to.

The female presence in the gaming world has been shifting its axis. There's a new Lara Croft who has had a breast reduction and been developed into a more realistic female character. *Assassin's Creed* has good female characters, created by the revolutionary gaming scriptwriter Jill Murray.

Rebecca cites Twine[18] as one of the resources that's helping to give power to girls in the gaming industry. As a new open-source tool for telling interactive, non-linear stories, and that doesn't require writing any code to create a simple story, Twine is accessible to anyone. "This is where a lot of girls are creating visibility for their visions of games," said Rebecca. "There are a lot of Twine games that are changing the larger game—new stories about positive sex experiences, being a strong female who's a master of her sexuality, being gay or bisexual, being emotional; it's garnering a mass audience and transforming the landscape." A great example is *Tampon Run*, created by Sophie Houser and Andrea Gonzales, two 17-year-old high-school students from New York City, to destigmatize menstruation. Players collect tampons, shoot tampons to escape villains, shoot tampons before the villains do and race to finish without running out of tampons. In an interview in *TODAY Health & Wellness* online magazine,[19] Gonzales explained, "The idea of making it funny and quirky kind of makes menstruation a lot more approachable and more comfortable."

Rebecca sees that people are getting tired of first-person shooter games. "People are starting to be more interested in stories, life experiences and social issues. These games help raise awareness and teach us about issues that matter. It's really exciting not to have corporate culture driving everything anymore. There's now a Reddit forum for girl gamers, diversity-focused game blogs and bloggers, and cultural critics. The power is shifting and this is good for everyone." (See more about gaming in chapter 10, where we speak with boys.)

If marketing forms cultural attitudes, consumers have a lot of power. "If you disagree about sexist violence in video games, don't give that game money and support," Rebecca concluded. "Take to Twitter and tweet out, 'I'm not buying this game because I disagree with it,' and say why!"

The growing number of girls who are harnessing tech and coding savvy to carve out new spaces for their intelligence in these traditionally male dominated arenas is a beacon to their emerging leadership. It's also an area of cultural production and skill that gives girls, and their ideas, a powerful stake in co-creating what the world is becoming as it moves more and more deeply into the digital.

SURVIVAL KIT

RECOGNIZE GIRLS AS SMART AGENTS, the experts in their own lives. Support girls to be cultural producers, disrupters and rebels. Encourage and celebrate their efforts, and listen to what they have to say. Tell them not to be afraid!

FIND CREATIVE WAYS to compliment girls. The author of *Redefining Girly*[20] encourages adults to be conscious of what we re-enforce for girls. Condition yourself out of, "You're so cute" or, "You're adorable." Rather, compliment a girl on something she was doing *with* her body: "You are so strong," or, "That was a good hit," or, "You run fast."

PRACTISE CRITICAL THINKING. Critical thinking means asking why, breaking down our ideas and checking up on our values and assumptions. For example, why do magazines airbrush women's bodies? Why do advertisers lighten Beyoncé's skin? Why is there a pink girl aisle and a blue boy aisle in toy stores?[21] Who benefits from this layout and marketing? What do I think about this?

QUESTION STEREOTYPES. By teaching girls and boys about gender stereotypes, we can expand social and cultural norms. As parents, we can start early—when our kids are very young. Introduce the deconstruction of a stereotype by looking at the message it sends and the limits it imposes. We can engage our young children by asking: Why do we assume boys like blue and girls like pink? What other colours can they like? Why do girls play with dolls and boys play with trucks? Why do girls compare themselves to other girls? Are girls expected to please boys? Are boys expected to be tough, go-getters and strong?

CALL OUT SEXIST AND RACIST objectification of or discrimination against women and girls. Challenge yourself, your partner, your kids and your community to become aware of discriminatory talk and action. Notice when media stories, conversations among communities or friends, or incidents that happen in your environment objectify and/or perpetuate racist, homophobic or sexist stereotypes. Point this out to kids and explain why it is wrong to discriminate against others.

GIVE GIRLS DIVERSITY IN THEIR TOYS, clothes and play. There is more than pink, princesses and Disney. Ask friends, search the Internet and question girls about where to find the latest and greatest girl-positive toys, books, clothes, music and movies, and take a look at the boys' toy section, too. Spread the word and make a change. Include variety. Support girls to "try on" different identities and encourage them in a non-judgmental way.

PRACTISE MEDIA SMARTS. Encourage kids to think critically about the messages they receive from music, magazines, films, television and the Internet. Challenge them to think about why the media and the fashion and beauty industries do what they do, and have conversations about this. Be a guardian of the media that comes into your home and other environments. You have the right to say no and also to recognize that what's okay in one place may not be appropriate in others.

SUPPORT AND ADVOCATE FOR critical media literacy programmes in schools for both boys and girls. Critical media literacy includes a gender, race and class lens that unpacks power, systems and social structures. Ask teachers, principals, team coaches, music teachers, babysitters and older friends to support the effort.

BE A SAVVY CONSUMER. Industries make money by making girls and women insecure. Look at the messages behind products and make educated decisions about which ones to buy. Be a conscious consumer. If we expect girls not to be duped by corporate schemes and marketers, modelling conscious consumerism as a parent or other adult role model is a great way to teach them.

BE BRAVE and start conversations. Your kids will love these discussions.

PICTURE BOOKS That Break Out of the Pink, Princess and "Be Pretty" Stereotypes[22]

Fairytale Hairdresser series, by Abie Longstaff
I'm a Girl!, by Yasmeen Ismail
Interstellar Cinderella, by Deborah Underwood

Princess Daisy and the Dragon and the Nincompoop Knights,
   by Steven Lenton
Princess Grace, by Mary Hoffman
The Princess and the Pony, by Kate Beaton
The Worst Princess, by Anna Kemp

MEDIA LITERACY RESOURCES: Feminist Frequency is a video web series that explores the representations of women in pop culture narratives. The series was created by Anita Sarkeesian in 2009 and largely serves as an educational resource to encourage critical media literacy and provide resources for media makers to improve their works of fiction.

GIRLS AND POP CULTURE SITES THAT MAY INITIATE INTERESTING AND EDUCATIONAL CONVERSATIONS:

Racialicious: racialicious.tumblr.com
Feministing: feministing.com
Crunk Feminist Collective: www.crunkfeministcollective.com
Madame Noire: madamenoire.com
Black Girl Nerds: blackgirlnerds.com
For Harriett: forharriet.com
Jezebel: jezebel.com
Art Hoe Collective: @arthoecollective
Rookie: rookiemag.com
Clutch: clutchmagonline.com
VICE Broadly: broadly.vice.com
LennyLetter: www.lennyletter.com
Girls of the Internet Museum: gim-museum.tumblr.com

SUPPORT GIRLS IN TECH: Check out and connect with these inspiring organizations that are working to get girls into technology.

- Girls Who Code, a US non-profit organization working to close the gender gap in the technology and engineering sectors.

- Pixelles, based in Montreal, is a non-profit initiative committed to helping more women make and change games.
- Actua's National Girls Program (Canada) inspires young women to fulfill their role as leaders in STEM and encourages their engagement in STEM fields like engineering and computer science where women continue to be vastly under-represented.
- Black Girls Code promotes and empowers girls of colour to be innovators in the STEM field.
- She's Coding provides education, resources, and actionable guidelines for anyone who wants to help bridge the gender gap in the field of computer science.
- Deep Lab is a collaborative group of cyberfeminist researchers, artists, writers, engineers, and cultural producers advancing women in the digital space.
- Read more about girls disrupting 'bro tech culture' in Dazed Digital's article here: http://www.dazeddigital.com/artsandculture/article/30199/1/the-feminist-groups-disrupting-bro-tech-culture-in-2016

+++

SEXTING
WORKSHOP

PERIOD 2
10:10 –11:25

ROOM 210
Lecture Hall

PROJECT SLUT

I'M SEXY AND I KNOW IT:
MARAUDING THROUGH MONTREAL, PART 1

A FEW MONTHS AGO, we attended "Consenting Sexualities: Teens, Social Media and Anti-Violence Activism," a conference at McGill University that brought to life provocative themes in girl culture and politics. As the early-spring light washed over the second-floor lecture hall, Dr. Lara Karaian, a criminologist at Ottawa's Carleton University, spoke passionately about ineffective legal responses to sexting.[1] Dr. Amy Adele Hasinoff, in the communication department at the University of Colorado–Denver, read excerpts from her book, *Sexting Panic*, and discussed the reactions to sexting in mass media, law and education. And Sarah Banet-Weiser gave a seminar on the economy of visibility.

As the conference and our many conversations with girls across North America make clear, sexuality in the digital age is a challenge. As girls move mercurially from their real lives to their smart phones and back, online sexuality has become a controversial frontier. Girls may be applauded for using social media to talk about music, or to promote a new vision of ecology, or even to incite large-scale political change. But using it to express sexual desires, sexual conquests, sexual confidence and sexual struggles is something mainstream doesn't yet understand.

Inspired by what we'd heard, we decided to see for ourselves how this theme is playing out in the online world. We surfed sites from *Jezebel* to *Teen Vogue*, and conducted searches with keywords like "girls Internet headlines." We saw how popular girls' behaviour is as a topic, and how much the media both warns us about the dangers of the Internet and relentlessly discusses how "sexually depraved" girls have become.

Headlines across North America criticize a perceived pornification of society and the negative roles, as both victims and perpetrators, that girls play in this so-called downward spiral. Magazine covers and articles paint girls as hedonistic tramps, while the Internet stands accused of producing female sexual marauders. We read how authority figures are trying to manage this new realm in which girls are sexting and sending sexy selfies to each other, to eager boys and sometimes, involuntarily, to the larger online world. Thanks to the conference we'd just attended, we knew that, legally, this development is being handled with pornography laws that punish the production and distribution of nude and sexually suggestive images in a one-size-fits-all way (more on this below).

The minefield that girls struggle with here came into sharp focus. While mainstream culture induces fear of girls' impending cyber victimization, it also lobbies for their attention and spending power by using sex to sell. This cultural ecosystem (which is teeming with free porn) sends perplexing messages to girls—about being sexually available and desirable on the one hand, and "bad" and to blame on the other. All of this while they're in the already complex process of discovering and exercising their own sexuality!

Taking it all in, we asked ourselves if society is really degenerating—as the tabloids love to tell us—or is it just that the private lives of girls have been made transparent by technology? If pop culture is a hall of mirrors, what are the competing ideals and ideologies projected onto girls, and what do girls have to say about them?

DESIRE

Montreal is a red-light city. Tourists from all over the world come to enjoy the exotic cuisine, see the historic buildings and contemplate the art on display at the Musée d'art contemporain. Up the street, meanwhile, are the glittery sex shops, peep shows and lap-dancing bars where *danseuses nues* light up the night. The non-Puritan French influence in this city makes it a little more open about sex than any other in North America. It was in Montreal that we met Maude, a white 16-year old francophone. Over café au lait, and in a mix of French and English, she told us her story.

"When I was 14, some of my friends showed me a website with webcams where you could talk with people," Maude told us. "You see a person, if you don't want to talk, you switch off or switch to another person. After a while I met boys, mostly older, but not so old. And that's it. It was a conversation, then it became sexual conversations. I loved it. When you're 14, you don't know that guys think you are cute. I met guys from around the world. I got to see different faces, cute guys, and speak with them. At 14 you don't speak with cute guys at school.

"First it was conversation, then with the webcam, it was more showing. Some boys were long-term, they became friends. It's weird, but it gave me self-esteem, really a lot of self-esteem. I would even say my self-esteem was born from this. I wasn't sexually active at the time and this helped me to understand desire and pleasure. I feel very connected to desire and pleasure. It was great because I started speaking with boys and learning how to drive the conversation, how to lead it, and I liked it. It gave me confidence that I could speak to guys and, when they looked at me, they saw the beauty in me. I learned about my personality, what makes me special. After you know your power, because a few guys tell you often, you believe it. A lot of my friends, they don't know themselves sexually. I've learned what kind of guy I like, what I find physically attractive. I've learned to tell him what I like, what pleases me, what I desire. I express that. Validation is not looking for attention. My personality doesn't change with a guy's approval. It might sound a bit alarming when doing this on the Internet, but in general I don't agree that it's bad. It's a bit scary for parents but it can be really special for girls."

When we asked Maude if her parents knew about her online webcam activities, and the extent of her sexual interaction with others online, she told us, "For me, it was great, but I knew that if my mother knew, she would be angry. She eventually found out, and it wasn't fun. She thought I was not normal. This made me rebel. I wanted to do it even more just because she didn't want me to, because she was telling me I didn't have the right to do it. I was angry at my mom, who made me feel like a difficult child, like I was a teenager who is not good. I was a perfect teenager; I was good at school. She made me see a sexologist, though only once because I told her it was humiliating and she understood. I knew it was not bad, what I had done. I even did it more, in secret. To prove to myself that I was not weird, but it was hard."

All on her own, before and after her mother found out, Maude became street-smart on this platform. She told us how gut instinct and risk strategies were central to her approach to online safety. She said that because this experience was so important to her she always kept herself safe, and told us about some of the practices she developed. "I protect myself online. At first, I never show my face. I'm not naked. But when there is a cute guy and I show my face, it is nicer. To feel safe, I talk with the guy before. I get to know where he lives. After you check the environment, you check how the guy looks—clean or not, his clothes, how he speaks. What does he do? Does he study or work? I have a radar. But you can also research people online. You can check his Facebook page, what kinds of friends he has, if he lives a normal life. If I don't like the person, I just leave. I don't feel bad. If I start to be more sexual, the guy knows it's okay. I take the lead."

While not all girls are experimenting to the extent that Maude has with her webcam, many girls are having online experiences that may give them first-hand knowledge and a sense of self-possession that can serve them well when they do become sexually active in a physical way. Maude told us that when she began having sex in real life, her webcam wisdom made her feel in charge of not only what she wanted to experience but also of saying no to what she didn't want. The assertiveness she developed also gave her a confidence she carries into other aspects of her life.

Maude articulated the importance of listening to her gut instinct and knowing how to ask for what she needs and wants. She said she's not "popular" at school, but she isn't shy. She doesn't like to engage in stereotypical girl drama, and she has perspective and a strong sense of independence when it comes to social, peer and media pressure. She wants to be thinner, but she doesn't believe in using fad diets or pills to get there. Her friends party and do drugs but she keeps her focus on preparing for college. Maude knows what she wants from her life, how to balance her desires with her practical goals and how to hold her boundaries.

In the face of so much adult panic around girls becoming victims online, Maude's story provided an interesting counterpoint. She is happy and doing well at school, in her friendships and with her self-esteem and sexual relationships. Her webcam experiences were clearly positive for her, and were pivotal in the development of her evident self-confidence. Is it possible that the fear we feel over our girls' online activities is unwittingly undermining the progress we have made in the arena of women's rights and freedoms?

As it turns out, Maude's story was corroborated by many of the girls to whom we spoke. While not all were into using technology as a tool for sexual expression, others told us they do use it to explore their sexuality. We discovered that these girls are smarter than many adults and parents give them credit for, and thoughtful when it comes to risk management. Girls told us that they mitigate risk by not giving personal information and by not showing identity markers like their face, bedroom or any particular features such as a mole (see more about risk mitigation in the Survival Kit at the end of this chapter). Several felt secure in knowing their limits and deciding what, and when, they were ready to explore. Self-respect, identity development and social relationships, they told us, are deeply tied up in how girls relate to and grow into their sexuality.

These days, selfies are one of the most common ways girls like to explore their identity and experiment with both expressing their desire and being desired. In some ways, selfies are becoming the mirrors of the twenty-first century, a means of experimenting with your sense of self and a way to project the private self into the public eye. Aidan, a white 19-year-old art student we met in Montreal who is majoring in photography, told us that she takes a lot of nude self-portraits, for herself and as artworks. She likes to capture the moments when she feels really beautiful, and she likes to play with the conventions of beauty and desire in her images of herself. "TV shows and all media, actually, have really precise ways of telling you how to be. They teach you how to play games— other people's games. You have to look a certain way or you're not attractive.

I'm tall and kind of fat and I've got cellulite on my ass, but I'm hot! If you say it first and take great pictures of your cellulite ass and plaster them across the Internet, then no one can say shit about you. I show my bruises and my flaws. I love it that Lena Dunham does that, too—shoving her big, naked body and her badly fitting, floppy bikini and stuff in our faces. It's the best form of subversion. I want to see butt zits on TV, and clothes that don't fit well. I want to identify with real girls. I want girls to be okay with who they are, and all of us being okay with the 'not beautiful.' It's so easy to try to be perfect. It's not so easy to try to be just what you are."

Simona, a white 16-year-old Montrealer, said that she, too, is experimenting with what is possible in her expressions of beauty. "I remind myself by taking pictures of myself in cute outfits, or even semi-nude, that I'm beautiful, sexy and have a great body—even if it's not a mirror image of a body from a music video."

We also talked to girls who told us that the "bygone" sexual double standards are not bygone at all, but are pervasive and a strong force girls mitigate in relation to their own sexual expression. When we were in Detroit, the girls we met[2] told us about how those who post sexy images are seen to be attention-seeking, insecure and slutty, but that they're also pressured into posting them, and into sending private photos to guys. Among Millennials and Generation Z'ers—the kids born from the 1980s to the early 2000s who have grown up immersed in technology—sharing intimate pictures is a common form of communication often laced with gender inequities. Didia, an African-American 14 year-old, explained what often happens after a boy asks a girl to send him a sexy picture: "If a girl shares an image with a boy, the boy thinks she is easy and then he won't respect her. Girls want to be talking to boys but are also afraid to give in to pressure to do more." They are called prudish for not sending naked pictures, Didia said, but when they do send one, they are called a slut. Either way, the boy won't respect the girl and he will move on. "I lose lots of guy friends. It makes me sad. It makes me scared that all guys are dicks. I try to tell myself I don't care, that I'm okay saying no and I don't care if they don't like me anymore, but it makes me shut down my feelings." Being judged and rejected for sexual expression happens much less frequently to boys in a social landscape where they are socialized to be, or appear to be, studs. And what about the girls who take a conscious stand against this by searching beyond judgment for empowerment? Unfortunately, as the entire topic is still taboo, they are often left unsupported and on their own.

Like Maude, 20-year-old Alice told us that she came of age on the webcam, also with very positive results—and also in private. "I was like the 16-year-old quiet girl with good grades version of the Jewish Princess, so when I got horny and started on new technology, it was insane. I had such a great time and I learned so much but I never told anybody because I felt guilty. We are told that it's wrong."

Lou, 18, said she believes that the secrecy and judgments surrounding girls' sexuality are harmful. "The sexual double standard basically means that guys are allowed to mess around and girls can't without getting judged for it. Because of this, I do find that many female friends I have, or girls I have met, still feel that they cannot be assertive."

Fifteen-year-old bi-racial Em believes that "girls should have the ability to express themselves sexually." Sally, a white 14-year-old we connected with in Whitehorse asked, "Why is sex looked at so negatively? We like sex." Her friend Naomi, also 14, added, "If girls didn't care and could just be themselves, they would be 'sluts,' but in a good way." Tandi, a black 17-year-old, whom we had spoken to in San Francisco, took this thinking a step further by linking her sexuality to her sense of confidence and strength. She told us that she is unwilling to hide her sexuality because "what is attractive about me is not a lie, it gives me power."

+++

Michelle Fine, PhD in social psychology at the City University of New York, has been a trailblazer working to reframe the way we think about girls' sexuality—to flip the script from girls being passive recipients to being empowered. She does this by acknowledging the existence of a girl's sexual desire, which works to undo the double standard where a guy is applauded for his lust and a girl is shamed and called a slut for hers. Similarly other theorists point out, "the double standard paints hetero-sexual teen boys as agents, choosers, actors, ready to go, unconfused about their wants and needs, out for pleasure, demanding, and entitled. While teen girls' sexuality has been pictured as more hesitant and fragile, full of chaste longing but not sexual."[3] In an article titled "The Missing Discourse of Desire,"[4] Fine explains how sex for girls is always presented in a negative light. From an early age, girls are taught that sex is danger-ous and they are seen as potential victims of male sexual aggression.

How is it that these outdated ideas persist, in light of the experiences of Maude and Aidan? It's clear that Maude's sexuality is far from fragile, and her assertiveness about it has served her well. Why, then, after the sexual revolution of the '60s and the efforts of the generations since to liberate sex from taboo, is it shocking to so many people that girls are sexual beings with desire? When is the last time we've heard anything *positive* about girls' sexuality and expression?

What we learned from Maude and others is that desire is an impor-tant frontier for girls, a drive they're learning to talk about more openly, and to embrace and explore more freely. Is this the root of the "sexual depravity" we read about? Is it simply the result of girls playing with this area of their self-expression and challenging the expectations that society projects onto them—through the digital communication chan-nels that are their generations' platform? Far from being depraved, what these girls are really doing is questioning the double standards, appropriating and redefining traditional femininity, and recasting ideas about love and relationships in their real-life sexual experiences. Some are doing this assertively and with an unapologetic display of who they are and what they want. Others are doing it more quietly. Rather than interpret their sexual confidence as an indication that they are victims of culture, or as evidence that they are provocateurs without a cause, we can instead see girls as activists in their generation's quest for sexual freedom. The continued reactions of fear, condemnation and censorship when confronted with the new visibility of girl sexuality are in fact more of the same old issues of power and control, just repackaged for our era.

They reveal, more than anything else, how we still don't understand and still fear girls' desire.

REACTIONS, CONVOLUTIONS AND CONTRADICTIONS

For those who are not "digital natives," the power of online experiences may be difficult to understand. It's not surprising, then, that older generations and institutional reactions to girls' sexuality cover a wide territory—all the way from neo-conservative attempts to push abstinence-only sex education to sexy sex-positive campaigns originating from young activists and progressive community organizations. In the first camp, we have kids being told, "Sex is bad! Sex is scary! Sex is dangerous and it can ruin your life!" Sexting is treated with the panicked reactions normally reserved for teens who are actually having sex. In fact, the panic may be even more severe, thanks to the added fear some adults feel when faced with Generation Z's unfamiliar digital lifestyle. And when sexting becomes abusive—in the form, say, of revenge porn (sexually explicit media that is distributed maliciously without the consent of those involved) or non-consensual "forwards" (personal messages that are passed on to others without consent)—legal responses are quick to criminalize girls for sexual expression, and much slower to address the many other issues that may be at hand. Right now, the law is labouring to catch up with the online world, and grappling both with how to determine what constitutes crime in this new realm, and how that crime should be policed. And there are deeper problems, too, like social attitudes rooted in sexism.

Combined, all of these factors contribute to a grey zone in which girls are too often seen as "the problem." Awareness campaigns warn teens of the dangers and risks associated with sexting—all the while painting girls as victims, consensual sexting as self-exploitative and boys as uncontrollable.[5] These initiatives induce moral fear and set up surveillance tactics that undermine girls' ability to exert their own power in this realm, and simultaneously justify an outdated system of control over girls' sexuality.

Following the conference at McGill, we caught up with Dr. Lara Karaian and Dr. Amy Adele Hasinoff, both of whom are contributing substantive and innovative research into this new area of girl sociology.[6] Dr. Hasinoff lamented that the sensational media coverage of sexting puts the moral onus—not to mention the responsibility for sexting and its spin-off problems—on girls. Dr. Karaian agreed, and pointed out that the mainstream media coverage paints sexting as overwhelmingly harmful for teenage girls and tries to prevent it by emphasizing protection, surveillance and control over children. "People feel that there is an inherent harm in sexual images," she told us in her energetic style. "There is no inherent harm in the image. As long as the image is not produced in an exploitative and abusive way, or is a product of sexual abuse, there is nothing inherently harmful in the sexual image. What's harmful is how we respond to the image."

Dr. Karaian's studies of sexting have revealed some compelling statistics:

Among teens who have sent sexually suggestive content, 66% of teen girls and 60% of teen boys say they did so to be "fun or flirtatious"— their most common reason for sending sexy content. 52% of teen girls did so as a "sexy present" for their boyfriend; 44% of both teen girls and teen boys say they sent sexually suggestive messages or images in response to such content they received; 40% of teen girls said they sent sexually suggestive messages or images as "a joke"; 34% of teen girls say they sent or posted sexually suggestive content to "feel sexy"; 12% of teen girls felt "pressured" to send sexually suggestive messages or images.[7]

Clearly, most teen girls are comfortable exploring their sexuality in this new digital realm. But with all of this online flirting, should we be worried about what's happening in the real world? "Cybersex is a way that girls can play in sex without the physical," Dr. Karaian told us. "Teens are using it as a different form of 'cyber petting,' like we used to talk about 'heavy petting'—who even uses the term 'heavy petting' anymore?" she asked, laughing. "Everyone wants to frame sexuality as penetrative sex, sometimes seen as a replacement for broader expressions of sexuality. A lot of the concern around this is about the stepping stone, the idea that those who sext will move on to other things—that is, starting with sexting, ending with sex. But it's not as causal a relationship, or as slippery a slope as it often gets framed to be." In other words, experimenting with sex like many girls do over phones and webcams, and on everything from Skype to iChat, can be a healthy and even normal exploration for digital-generation teens. Plus, it often helps them navigate this tricky learning curve.

Today's teens actually have their first sex later than their parents did. They have fewer sexual partners and lower incidents of teen pregnancies than previous generations. The only marked change in this generation is that the rate of sexually transmitted infections (STIs) is much higher— a statistic that could, in fact, highlight the lack of comprehensive sex education.[8] In a society in which the response to girls' sexuality is still so often conservative, girls are then left on their own to figure out how to have positive, safe and empowered sexual experiences, both online and, when the time comes, in their real lives.

SEXTING AND SELFIES: THE LEGAL FALL

If you think you can bury your head in the sand and wait for this fad to pass, think again. Sexting, it seems, is not going anywhere. Statistics show that 98 percent of kids are online daily, and kids aged 12 to 18 send an average of one to two hundred texts per day, with 84 percent reporting no parental rules limiting their time, or who and what they text. Forty-six percent of teens report sending nude photos of themselves, and 44 percent report sending explicit sexual messages.[9] And despite Dr. Karaian's reassuring research into the implications of all of this sexting, the prevalence of online sexual activity can still be a minefield for today's young people, especially when it comes to issues around consent.

Legally, there is no difference at all between the flirty, fun and consensual sexting that has become so common, and the harmful, non-consensual forwarding, abusive sexting or harassment that does creep into this realm. Instead, the issues blend, and all sexting is treated as illegal activity (a situation that, in essence, reinforces the media-hyped concerns about safety and danger). Responsive policies and practices from law enforcement and schools blur the issue even further by painting girls as self-victimized citizens—or worse, as criminals themselves.

"Criminalized responses in the US have included the prosecution and conviction of teens for possession and peddling of child pornography in cases of consensual and non-consensual sexting alike," Dr. Hasinoff told us in our post-conference chat, "making no distinction between sending sexy photos within a relationship and forwarding sexy photos that are being maliciously redistributed. In Canada, the prosecution of non-consensual teenage sexting has also occurred, but only where an individual sent a picture without the subject of the picture's consent."

Our friend Mona, a social worker who lives on the outskirts of Kingston, Ontario, had us over for dinner to talk about her experiences with sexy selfies. Mona has two boys, one of whom is 16 and plays on the local hockey team. Recently, he had a personal encounter with the legal backlash that can result when a sexy selfie goes viral.

"When boys chat with girls [with the aim of romance], boys are 'wheeling' them," Mona told us. "So kids wheel each other to see if they want to go into a relationship. They have a 'friend zone' when they are chumming or wheeling, and if it gets deeper, they start to ask for more. Things like pictures."

"The girl in this case was in grade eight," Mona continued. "She took a picture of herself in the mirror with her bra and panties on because the boy that she liked had asked her to. She sent it to that boy and he passed it around to his friends and the hockey team." A similar thing had happened the year before, Mona said, and the kid who distributed the photo was investigated by the police.

Mona told us about her approach to the situation—one that Dr. Karaian would undoubtedly have supported. "My son talks to a lot of girls, so we warned him about how quickly it gets to that level, where a girl is being violated," she said, stressing that she's always communicated openly with her boys. "We discussed how he needed to be responsible and to respect girls. It's okay to share photos privately but it is not okay to receive photos from girls and to share them without their consent. We had a good talk about sharing love and caring for partners and friends. He understood the long-term effects. We scared him. We told him anything digital is forever."

Like most parents, Mona had been unaware of the intricacies of the law on this subject. Her son's recent experience, however, brought the realities home in an uncomfortable way. "So this year," she went on, "it was his best friend who received the picture, and he sent it to his friends. A parent reported it to the school and the school in turn reported it to the police. It was serious. The boy in question was called to the police station, he was interviewed and investigated. It really scared him, and us. The initial investigation turned into an investigation of hockey culture. All the boys on the team were implicated even if, like my son, they weren't involved and the issue was really that the one boy kept asking the girl to send pictures and he forwarded these to friends without her consent. In the end, the boy and the hockey team received warnings from the police."

Mona's story offers a glimpse into the boys' side of this thorny issue. Her open communication with her son was admirable, but how many parents have the wherewithal or the knowledge to address these topics with their boys? With a culture that encourages sexual bravado and sexual conquest in boys and men, and a lack of education about how disrespectful attitudes can be harmful—or how forwarding private photos without consent is wrong and actually a form of sexual violence—boys are left in the dark. The recourse for both girls sending photos and boys forwarding photos is a possession-of-child-pornography charge. But criminal punishment without explanation or understanding doesn't get at the root of these issues.

"The simple logic of advising 'sexting is dangerous; don't do it,' may be appealing to parents," Dr. Karaian told us when we talked, "but if the discussion ends there then it does not consider or address the harm produced by abusive sexting." Or, it seems, the legal implications of taking part in this "dark" side of online sexual experimentation.

We heard many echoes of Mona's experience on our tour. At every stop, whether in small towns or inner-city schools, there was a story about a girl sexting and a boy who sent the photos out to friends without her consent. We heard about the many potential types of fallout for the girl—bullying, suspension, a move to a new school or even a new town, police involvement and sometimes criminal charges—and the associated emotional reactions to each.

The lack of knowledge about consent and non-consensual behaviour exacerbates the problem, especially when almost all the attention focused on the issue is aimed at the girls sending the photos. As we've seen, education campaigns warn girls not to create or send sexual content via electronic devices or the Internet; this behaviour is defined as self-exploitation.[10] Girls are framed as both the victim and the perpetrator of self-exploitation, rather than seen as empowered for choosing to share photos (nude or not) for their own reasons. Boys send sexy selfies to girls, too, but the social reaction is the complete opposite. Boys are high-fived and their popularity increases when sexual pictures of them are circulated; girls are slut-shamed and at risk of social ruin (and all its negative spinoffs).

And Dr. Karaian pointed out an added wrinkle. "We see extra crime control and prevention campaigns targeting white middle-class girls, where they've been told that abstinence, self-censorship and self-control are the solution. This approach locates the problem of teenage sexting as originating with girls. The idea that 'without her there would be no crime' is the message. We hear often that without her taking the picture, we have no issue. She is the source of the problem and the target of the crime-control response. In other words, girls are ultimately to blame for all forms of sexual misconduct and are responsible for solving its problems."

But if sexting truly has become a new form of flirting—and if more and more girls are using it to explore and express their sexual power—shouldn't we be supporting kids with accurate information rather than panicking and judging or, worse, panicking and hiding? Shouldn't we be teaching the difference between healthy and defamatory sexting, rather than slapping an inappropriate and ineffectual punishment on every instance, regardless of the circumstances? These are important questions to consider as we raise children, educate youth and support our nieces, sisters and friends in this often-confusing and ever-changing new world.

SEX-POSITIVE PARENTING

In some important ways—and with important repercussions—it seems as if the fears and recriminations around girls and sex have more to do with the adults surrounding the girls than with the girls themselves. We ourselves are raising daughters, and we often reflect together on their brilliance, and on the tests we face as their parents. We have sat over many cups of coffee, asking each other what girls could gain if they were allowed by society to express their desires, and test them, without being judged, ridiculed or shamed. We've even laughed—more than once!— over the ways that parents are sometimes confronted by questions about sex and sexuality.

Before I was educated on LMFAO, a former American electro-rap band, my six-year-old daughter, Morganne, came home and strutted down the hallway singing, "I'm sexy and I know it!" I chuckled, sharing the moment with her, asking myself quietly, "Wow, where did she get that idea?" A few weeks later, a friend shared how she overheard her daughter in the bathtub squealing, "I love my vagina!"—and how she revelled in her daughter's unabashed joy with her body. Historically, reactions to these situations would have been along the lines of alarm, or to squash our daughters' self-expression with punishment or shame but instead, in these cases, we chose to embellish our daughters' confident sense of themselves. My girlfriend continued to share her story as we reflected together on how we attempt to parent our young daughters toward a positive and confident sense of themselves. She shared how, after her daughter's bath, when she was all tucked in and ready for bed, she continued a conversation about her daughter's exciting self-discovery. She told her it's normal to touch herself and that it can be a lot of fun and feel really good. She took this opportunity to talk to her daughter about healthy boundaries and reminded her that her body belongs to her, and that she decides who gets to ever be in her bubble—re-enforcing the idea of her personal space and boundaries. I added another teaching moment I had with Morganne to our discussion. I shared how, recently, Morganne asked me about what her vagina looked like, and how many holes did she have, one or two? I proceeded to google "female anatomy" on my iPad and we spent over half an hour studying the vulva, clitoris, minor and major labia. She was thrilled.

-Tatiana

Empowering our daughters to love themselves without the inheritance of a negative body image and a legacy of sexual shame is one way to encourage self-knowledge, confidence and authority. Sex-positive parenting teaches about consent at an early age and tells the truth about sex. Books like *Where Did I Come From?* and *What Makes a Baby* engage kids in a healthy conversation that can start young, allowing "sex talk" to become an ongoing conversation rather than something to dread as the teen years approach. The truth is that kids are sexual beings from the moment they are born. We can begin to support their development by teaching them about healthy boundaries and by not making them feel ashamed for their curiosity. Sex-positive parenting teaches kids that sex is pleasurable, in an age-appropriate way, and it equips kids with the knowledge and tools to avoid harm while empowering them to know that they can make decisions regarding their own bodies for themselves. According to Airial Clark, MA, author of the website the Sex-Positive Parent, "A sex-positive child is safe, protected, and knows about consent and boundaries. They have access to accurate and age-appropriate information about reproductive biology, as well as the emotional and social realities of sexuality. A sex-positive child is not a sexualized child."[11] We can be sex-positive parents by being open, honest and responding to kids' questions in a non-judgmental, non-fearful way.

Being able to ask questions is part of a girl's empowerment around her body and her sexuality. If girls don't feel free to ask these questions, they won't ever ask them. Sexual curiosity starts early, and it is important to be as open with our answers as young girls are with their questions to us about their bodies, boundaries and, eventually, about sex. If we can do this, the foundation for sexual health and confidence will be laid by the time they get older. These times are also our chances as parents to speak first and early, to frame sex and sexuality in the way we want our children to see and experience it, as opposed to the world outside the home describing it to our kids.

We've also talked together a lot about how strongly our own experiences growing up influence our approach. Dealing with our daughters' emerging sexuality requires us to explore our own, because what we feel about ourselves is passed on to our children, and it can have a powerful influence on their attitudes and values. The way we react to their sexuality can sometimes be more about our projections onto them of our personal fears and feelings than the truth about who they are, or what they are asking or participating in. At the same time, it is important to remember how we, as teens ourselves, came up against outdated attitudes around sexuality, too, and did our part to break through those when it was our turn. It's our daughters' and younger sisters' turn now. They are taking up this multi-generational project, continuing the trek toward empowered and healthy sexuality.

Our memories of the struggles in our own pasts give us the capacity to feel compassion for the plight of girls today, and to understand the lonely places to which adolescence sometimes leads. Reflecting a positive message in terms of beauty, desirability and sexuality is known to give girls access to the strength and wisdom that they innately possess, including their inner sense of what feels good and not good for them in the sexual sphere.

The digital age may be revealing the enormity of this struggle in an unprecedented way. The fact that digital media both exposes and blurs the lines between private and public means that, by its very nature, it gives society a public view of what was once the most private and personal sphere. Sex used to be conducted behind closed doors. Today it is a cabaret show with free front-row tickets for anyone who cares to attend.

THE PORNIFICATION OF CULTURE: THE NEW SEX ED

Pornography is the highest grossing, most easily accessible entertainment in the world, and with free content available for download, it is now being consumed in the greatest quantities we've ever seen. Most kids watch porn and take cues from it; its accessibility makes it a source of information for teens. There are many forms—everything from superplastic macho porn to awkward amateur reality porn—all of which reflect the tastes, aesthetics and changing views of social norms.

Today, many kids experience porn—in all its infinite variety—before they engage in intimate relationships. Mona's son and his friends watch porn, and so do the girls who send them pictures. Nine out of ten boys and six out of ten girls are exposed to pornography before the age of 18, with 51 percent of boys and 32 percent of girls having viewed porn before the age of 12.[12]

Kids today are quick to find their porn preferences and share them with friends. Porn is downloaded and played at parties and on dates. Some young people direct their own amateur versions, or star in their own porn. None of this is terribly shocking. It is normal, after all, to be curious about sex and to try to figure out how sex works and feels, especially in those years when hormones are wreaking havoc.

Beyond the teenage bedroom, a glance through the Internet shows that sex.com and porn.com sit in the top five profit-making domains in the world. PornHub and YouPorn, the top free download sites, have daily visitors in the billions and advertising that grosses millions.[13] Consider this within a cultural atmosphere where mainstream media, advertising, merchandising and pop culture idols are all vying for girls' attention and adulation—luring girls with erotically suggestive imagery and slogans into purchasing push-up bras, G-strings, makeup, heels, and all the music, films and social-media gadgets that go along with these—and it could be argued that a large part of North American culture is in the grip of pornification.

Maude told us that she watches porn. "It gives me ideas and inspiration for experimenting," she said, but added that it made sex with her first boyfriend difficult. "He watched porn, too, and was into girls with small genitals[14] and I was different. At first it gave me a hard time. He wasn't mean, but just to see his reaction was difficult."

Aidan, the girl from Montreal who spoke with us about her selfies, said that she watches porn, too, and enjoys it, but does feel it has a not-always-positive influence on herself and others. "It's the trashy glossy mainstream porn that gives us the unrealistic and misinformed vision of the female body, and the wild ideas about how to approach it, and how to satisfy it. I feel like this damages sexual relationships, because who is actually like that? It's totally fake. Those girls are being paid. They're not actually getting off, and yet we're believing it's true and even modelling ourselves after them. Their bodies are also fake. Why do we all want to be fake and get with fake people?"

Aidan's friend Lou, 18, told us, "I like porn. The argument with porn is usually that it gives young people who are growing up with Internet access unrealistic expectations of what sex is and how it should be. But there has been quite an increase [in availability online] in amateur porn. Porn's female images have definitely evolved from massive silicone breasts and the artificial Barbie type, which don't seem to be that desired anymore. It's more about the natural body/face type. Even if it may give young people, initially, false expectations of what sex is, can or should be, I think we all learn from doing anyways in the end. What I do think is beneficial about porn, especially with its easy access, is that people can find out earlier in life what their desires might be and might not feel so ashamed about them. Watching porn can show them that there are others out there like them who are into the same things."

To get a wider gauge of girl thought on porn, we asked young women between the ages of 15 and 25 to reply anonymously to an online survey question: Do you feel pressured by pornography?

In their answers we heard that porn can send high-pressure messages to teens to perform the porn-star role, which can create fun, but can also lead to insecurity and unpleasant experiences. The pressure girls feel is around expectations for body parts to look a certain way or sexual performance to be acted out in a certain way, both from their side and their partner's.

We also heard that girls are adept at separating porn fantasy from reality. They recognize objectification and can hold their own when it comes to boys' expectations. Many of the girls we talked to said that they watch many varieties of online porn—from the mainstream productions to the amateur—and they enjoy it. They were curious about it, and said they learned new things from it. We also heard from girls who find porn a negative experience, and others who don't watch it at all. Here is a sample of what they said:

- I do feel a bit of pressure. I try to ignore it but I see girls looking and acting a certain way in those sex acts and I wonder if I'm up to par.
- I feel that it creates unrealistic expectations of the woman's body, which makes me somewhat insecure, and I feel that it makes people judge me based on my boobs rather than who I am. I try not to let myself be judged like that.
- I don't feel pressure—it's just entertainment. Besides, boys feel the pressure more, LOL, if you get what I'm trying to say (performance anxiety ☺).
- I don't watch porn. I think I just hang around the right kind of people.
- Ha ha, nope. Porn doesn't get to dictate who I am.
- Porn is unrealistic and is considered acting; not everybody realizes that. Porn is often completely [directed] toward the male's satisfaction and enjoyment of the experience.
- Everyone seems to expect you to be open to trying anything sexual because all the other girls they see online do it. I am not comfortable with certain things, therefore I will not let my partner try them. They usually become whiny when they can't get their way.
- I have seen porn that depicts uncomfortable situations (for me) where the balance of power is shifted [from the female to the male], and the couple seems to be doing the video because it is work for them. I don't like those videos.

- I always think about the women's bodies and wanting their bodies as a replacement for mine. But I think guys know that this isn't realistic and are less into the picture-perfect lady now.
- I don't engage sexually with people who allow porn culture to form their conception of what sex should be.
- I feel like porn should give me pressure, but I don't feel any. I'm not interested in being sexually active anytime soon.
- My partner and I have discussed the unrealistic portrayals of women in porn culture and we just do what we find pleasurable.
- My boyfriend, who is a fitness instructor, knows porn is not realistic and does not pressure me to do anything I'm not comfortable with. I work out and eat healthy and take care of myself so I also don't feel the need to put on that act since I know I look amazing as it is.
- I do feel expected to do crazy things or be really good at it or shave the hair off certain parts of my body.
- I don't feel pressure or expectation. The only thing I sometimes think about is to try intimacy with another girl. I don't know if it comes from pornography or my own inner desire, but it feels exciting . . .
- When I watch porn it is purely private and for my own pleasure. I definitely do not feel degraded by it (I usually watch lesbian porn) and I find it stimulating for my own imagination. Although pornography as an institution and a market *can* be degrading, it is also a very *human* thing to want to participate in or watch.
- A lot of it turns me on and I use it in empowering ways for my own sexuality.

As with sexting and selfies, there is a moral panic around pornography. And just as open communication about those two issues is paramount, so, too, is it necessary to speak candidly with kids about pornography. Arming our preteen and teen children with porn literacy tools—so they can unravel fantasy from reality, misinformation from truth, and performance from pleasure—will give them the skills they need to decode the often violent, male-centred "porn performance" they are seeing onscreen. What lessons about gender are re-enforced when women in pornography are predominantly objectified and depicted as passive, grateful and emotionally void?

Dr. Lara Karaian believes that we also "need better porn." With her, we imagined how great it would be if porn were centred around a woman's pleasure. "If teenagers are performing like porn stars on each other's phones and in each other's bedrooms," she told us, "we need better porn almost as much as good parenting and more social support for the healthy sexuality of girls." She believes that, in general, we stigmatize porn too much. We don't talk about it enough, and yet we all come across it and sometimes use it in our lives. "When I was performing my 'porn star role' [as a young woman exploring how she 'performed' her own sexuality], it wasn't a great teaching tool," she remembered out loud. "I tried things and then I unlearned the porn performances that weren't working for me. But if porn is our default part-time teacher, and kids are modelling themselves and their sexual performances on those films, then we need better porn."

Parental guidance around porn is a new imperative. Without guidance and dialogue, this behind-the-scenes "teacher" remains a taboo subject that educates by default. However, in today's youth culture, with its many pornographic influences, sexting and sex do come together at a certain age—a situation many adults fear and for which they are often wrongly prepared or wholly unprepared. According to Dr. Amy Adele Hasinoff, a lot of advice given to parents for navigating their children's jungle of online temptations and real desires stresses monitoring their activity by setting limits on time and content, locking specific domains and using spying apps. "This is an appealing solution to parents but it's not a good one," she said. "It's not the type of relationship you want to have with your kid. You want to teach them to respect others, not that spying on people is okay. There is no substitute for talking with kids about how they deal with their peers, technology and sex. I don't think spying apps will achieve what conversations about respecting someone's privacy—what's okay with technology, how you recognize what the acts of shaming and insulting are and call out your friends when they do it—will achieve."

Dr. Hasinoff told us that abstinence-only sex education, which advocates no sex until marriage, is proven to be ineffective in preventing teens from having sex, reducing STIs and avoiding teenage pregnancy. "Sex-education campaigns are often still about abstinence," she said. "It doesn't work with sex and it doesn't work with sexting either." By pretending that sex isn't happening, or won't happen if we tell them to "just say no," we are essentially ensuring that girls don't get any good information, and are denying them the opportunity to discuss, with their loved ones, where they are in their lives and in their desires. This gives them nothing to go on when it comes to sexual situations—where they will sink or swim based on information gathered elsewhere. "If you don't teach teens about sex it results in lack of preparation, which means increases in STDs and other risk factors. The abstinence approach is totally ineffective, yet this is how we look at teenagers and sex. We say: 'Don't do it.' Harm reduction would be much more effective. Kids need clear information rather than fear-mongering."

HEAD & HANDS: FROM PORN TO SEX-POSITIVE SEX ED

Thankfully, there are organizations that offer an alternative to the "just don't do it" approach to sex education. Head & Hands is a Montreal non-profit that offers school and community workshops as well as medical, social and legal services. Olivia, an easygoing 25-year-old counsellor, started by telling us about the Sense Project, which aims to bring peer-based sex education to youth between 12 and 25 years old in a way that is not awkward or authoritative, but fun, accessible and thorough. Their open-plan, plant- and sunlight-filled office is in an old limestone building on a main street in Montreal where anglophones and francophones intermingle. There are books piled on every surface, with titles that span pop culture, psychology and queer politics. In this inviting space, we sat on soft leather sofas and spoke to Olivia, whose first piece of advice was to be open with young people.

"We have seen that if you have a negative or shaming or judgmental approach to sex, you will completely cut off a participant from asking their questions—important questions—about their own health and their own protection. Olivia gave us an example, "If you make someone feel bad for asking a question about something like rimming; if you react badly and shut it down, then that kid will still do it but not have the information they need to do it more safely, and they won't ask about it again, or in the future. We see it as less risky to be sex-positive. This helps us to meet youth where they are at in their development, helps us hear what they are up to, and really help them.

"So if a participant asks about condom use for anal sex," she continued, "or they're asking about lube and when to use it and why, that's great. We try to validate them when they ask stuff, because they are curious and want to learn how to do it, and how to feel good doing it; we want to encourage that. So we are starting to develop more content about sex and pleasure because conversations are not usually brought to teenage audiences in this way and, as a result, youth have this idea of sex as something that gives you diseases and causes you to die, and that conflicts with the desires they feel. They want to have sex, and they are seeing everywhere—on TV, on the Internet, in advertising—that sex is a great thing. We want to address the conflicting messages, to make it less confusing for them."

Olivia told us that teaching desire and pleasure is a radical approach for many schools and parents, "because the dominant Anglo-American culture is rooted in puritanical understanding, so our society is pretty messed up about sex." Head & Hands' innovative approach is based on a harm-reduction model, which acknowledges that young people engage in sexual activity, which comes with risk. Their goal is to reduce the consequences of those risks. This means that they provide accurate and accessible information and answers to questions in a way that equips students to make decisions that are right for them in their sex lives, and that are also safe. Then they provide a space for participants to share concerns, desires, worries and positive experiences. This approach supports teenagers to discover what they like, to trust themselves, to communicate what they want and don't want—all of which are linked to empowerment through self-expression, confidence and consent. If this process begins at an age when sexuality is naturally awakening, if young adults are given support, this can lead to healthy experiences of sex that continue into adulthood.

One of Olivia's recent experiences reminded us of how far we are from this ideal. "When I did a sex and pleasure workshop not long ago, we did an 'anatomy of pleasure' exercise. We put pictures up—one of a vulva and one of a penis—and we asked the students to label them. I was afraid that this would be too easy but it was very difficult for both the groups of girls and guys. It was so hard for them to label the clitoris, the vagina, the vulva and urethra. None of the participants knew all the names or where to mark them on the map, whereas the picture of the penis was 80 percent accurate. This was different from what I was expecting. I realized it's a lot harder for people to understand the female anatomy. Our society is sexist and privileges the experience of men over the experience of anyone else."

We discussed how little society generally knows about the female body in light of the fact that it's a subject of visual consumption. It's a surprising fact that perhaps reinforces the notion of objectification— that women's bodies are an instrument for someone else's pleasure. We asked how it was possible for girls to attain pleasure in sexual activity if nobody knows what the different parts of the vagina are or what they do. "It's not," said Olivia.

Olivia told us that a lot of the kids they work with seem to know their bodies well. However, some of them feel uncomfortable and awkward, others feel they are ugly or fat, or that the physical-developmental changes happening to them are bad. Some of them are questioning their sexual orientation or gender identity (approximately 5 percent identify as questioning), or identify as LGBT (approximately 5 percent identify as lesbian, gay, bisexual or transsexual)[15]. "If they don't have the support to share their experience and to know they are okay, from friends or adults, they struggle a lot more with accepting their bodies, with what they look like, with being comfortable and confident in their choices. A teenager who doesn't have support in this has a lot more worries, insecurities and feelings of shame."

The Head & Hands program encourages critical thinking to help teens combat the silence around sex that can prevent positive experiences and to move societal ideas about sex out of the Dark Ages. Through dialogue and engagement, they dispel judgment, myths and fear around what sex can be like.

For example, they might start a discussion by asking participants, "Who has sex?" Instead of focusing only on heterosexual people, they invite answers that cover a broad range of sexual activities. Olivia explained that this type of approach immediately opens up the conversation and creates a trustworthy space where kids can freely think, freely ask and be freed of prejudice around sex. "We say to the kids, 'How do people have sex?' and we brainstorm how—we talk about the physical, emotional and relational aspects. We talk about gender identities and sexual orientations, and we try to normalize a variety of sex acts. Just because someone identifies as heterosexual, bisexual, homosexual or transsexual doesn't mean anything about what kind of sex they are having, whether they are even having sex and whether they are enjoying it. If we make all sorts of relationships and desires seem normal, this invites teenagers to open up, be more natural, accepting, curious and not ashamed, which leads to better experiences."

Olivia gave us an example of where silence and attitudes still block progress. "I notice how girls are worried about being perceived as slutty, and simultaneously feel pressured to have sex while being told that sex is bad. The idea of girls seeking pleasure is just not present, which creates this cloud of shame. For example, girls are not encouraged to masturbate; it's not the same as it is for boys, for whom it's considered normal and funny when they masturbate. Girls are shamed for doing similar things as boys. The double standard still exists, girls are often called a slut if they give someone a blow job or have sex at a party, whereas when the guy does the very same thing he is congratulated and seen as popular and masculine. This is a real concern that I hear kids talking about. I think this is still a barrier to sexual empowerment and pleasure."

Many of us secretly know, and Caitlin Moran's *How to Build a Girl* outright confirms, that "hearty girl wanking" is a big part of the sexual fun and discovery in girlhood. Being more open about and embracing of masturbation dispels old stigmas and offers girls a lot of freedom on the journey toward sexual confidence.

We talked about some of the good education that girls are getting via other girls. Laci Green is a self-identified 23-year-old sexuality geek based in the San Francisco Bay Area. She runs a sex-positive education project consisting of a vlogger series, a live show, a blog, a presence on the university lecture circuit and a peer education network. She also hosts two other web shows: a science news show for the Discovery Channel and a sex-education series for Planned Parenthood. She gets millions of viewers for every vlog that she posts, not just because kids are interested in sex but also because they are interested in safe, consensual sex.

One of Green's fans is fellow blogger Hayley Trimmier, who is also in her early twenties. On Feminspire—a positive community for young women online—Trimmier explains why Green's approach is so vastly popular in teen culture: "In a society run rampant with stigma surrounding sexuality, Laci's goal is to spread awareness about the Sex Positive movement and help inform people about their own bodies. Her videos cover issues of sexuality, relationships, and sexual identity with very little censorship. Laci is known for her blunt and direct approach with her viewers. Because of her candid approach to her own sexuality, Laci has gained a dedicated following of young men and women all over the world."[16]

How is Green's approach playing out? In *Wanna Have Sex? Consent*, for example, she talks about how sexy it is when a guy asks if he can kiss you. It shows that he is down with respect, and also has a bit of sexual communication going on. Easily accessible messages like this are what girls and guys need—and want—to hear.

Girls love talking about sex, and yet there is a fundamental lack of opportunities for having informed, fun discussions beyond their peers.

Not everyone has access to good sex education or trusted advice from people who have more experience with sex and sexual relationships, and are willing to share it. In the US, only twenty-two states require public schools to teach sex ed.[17] Girls everywhere have told us how mentors and good sex-ed programmes were the key for them in learning how to be safe and in becoming empowered. They wanted places where they could share their thoughts and experiences, ask their questions and learn new and relevant things.

Girls who come from cultural or religious backgrounds where sex is taboo, and where abstinence is the rule, are often forced to find their own ways to learn. One of our survey participants confessed that, "In my community, people wear blinders about sex. There's lots of [advocacy for] abstinence, and lots of fake pregnancy scares." Girls get limited information about sex, about risks and protection, and are usually left to piece together knowledge by themselves. According to another survey answer, "You have to ask for what you want [in a sexual relationship]. I wasn't told this early on and it's really hard to do this. We are trained to go and get an education and a job, not to ask for what we want sexually." Another girl wrote, "For me, masturbation is a taboo. Nobody at my high school ever talks about that." Yet another wrote how the Internet is a source of incomplete information: "I spent a lot of time on the Internet and reading *Glamour* and *Cosmo*. I spent hours studying it, how to give a good blow job, stuff like that. But there weren't articles on how to have girl pleasure. I found out by myself."

Some girls (the lucky ones!) told us they had parents who were open and sex-positive and taught them the basics and gave them confidence in their exploration. Girls also enjoy talking to each other and seeking each other's advice. Marre, 16, one of the girls we interviewed in Montreal, recalled the way her sister, who is three years older, tutored her on sex. "She talked about masturbation and for years I told her I didn't like that. I hadn't really tried it. But once I felt so horny and I tried a technique I hadn't tried before and I told her about it, crying, saying that for the first time I had real pleasure while masturbating. She thought it was great news."

Marre's sister also helped her discover how to feel attractive in pictures. "One of my friends had made a calendar of sexy pictures of herself half naked, for her boyfriend. I thought it was a great idea and I asked my sister to take pictures of me just for myself. This day was amazing, really empowering for me, to take pictures, show my body without shame. We had so much fun, laughed a lot, and the result is amazing! Looking at the pictures I really find myself incredibly sexy and beautiful."

We shared these stories with Olivia, and she agreed with us that when you hear the many kinds of experiences that girls have, there is no single way to define a girl's sexuality. This means that talking about it in enjoyable, non-judgmental ways is even more important. The more girls can share their many different experiences, the more they can learn from each other, realize that they are normal, and move their experiences from shame to being self-aware and empowered. If we want girls to have healthy sexuality, to be able to give and receive consent among equal partners, then they have to know what they want. They need to believe that their desires are worthy of respect and fulfillment. Olivia sank deeper into the leather sofa saying, "I couldn't agree more!"

After we left Head & Hands, we walked up the street, past bookshops, shoe shops, cafés and peep show theatres. We talked about how enlightening our glance inside the sex lives of young women had been. We'd seen how girls are experimenting with their bodies and their emotions, and expanding the definitions of relationships, sex and love. Girls aren't necessarily victims of porn culture, and sexuality doesn't scare them. They are showing us what their desires are and how they like to express them. They are using the tools of their era to reshape the sexuality map and make it more navigable, more fun, more subjective and more positive.

Some girls find power in their personal styling. Other girls find it in sports, music and books. Pretty much all girls tell us that they also find power in their ability to listen to themselves and to say yes and no, and in their ability to know what they want. The challenges they've inherited from previous generations are not all resolved, but we see girls' emerging sexual empowerment as inspiring. It's a move forward, even when it's being viewed by some as a step backward, to heightened sexual objectification. But this contemporary sexual revolution is so much more complicated than that. Girls are demonstrating that, far from what the headlines would have us believe, they are not *just* sexy (and that they really do "know it"!). For many, their sexual expression, sexual fluidity and sexual embodiment are essential aspects of their new brand of feminism. They are coming at the world with all their smarts and all their smart phones; with the knowledge that they can be trusted to navigate their teen and early adult years; and with their burgeoning sexuality. They are doing all of this in their very own way—a way that has its unique place in history and seems destined to break down the fear and limits of traditional sexist convention.

SURVIVAL KIT

TALK about the Internet. Tao Lin is a digital-generation fiction writer from the United States. He says that when he was growing up in the 1990s and falling into digital-world pastimes that replaced his old after-school hobbies of shooting hoops and riding dirt bikes his parents were too baffled by the Internet to ever ask, "So, how was your day on the Internet today?" Make no mistake: the Internet is a place. We should be asking our children what they're doing there, who they're meeting and where they're going, so they are not alone in that world.

ARM kids with online street smarts. Stay informed and stay aware. Keep an open dialogue about their activities online and monitor their engagement.

- Reinforce the idea that not everyone is who they say they are online. People can pretend to be older, younger or a different gender.
- Just as you would explain appropriate behaviour in the offline world, the same guidelines should be provided for online activities.
- Discuss the difference between private and public information.
- Explain to girls that they should trust their instincts and block anyone who asks questions online that seem "weird."
- Explain that the Internet is not censored and that they may come across inappropriate content.
- Help girls understand and use privacy settings.
- For more information and tips go to: www.cybertip.ca

CONSIDER YOUR OWN ATTITUDES toward sex. Psychologists say that parenting is an opportunity for learning. Consider and examine if and how you carry sexual shame, and if there is shame, embrace the opportunity to challenge that shame and let it go. This may even be liberating for our own sex life, and it will be truly empowering for our girls.

PRACTISE sex-positive parenting. Find resources at: thesexpositiveparent.com.

ADVOCATE locally and at policy levels for sex-positive sex education in schools. We need sex ed that promotes knowledge about how the body works, how to give and experience pleasure and how to be safe, and that isn't based in shame, abstinence and fear-mongering. Support local sex-education programmes, porn literacy and consent education for girls and boys.

CONNECT GIRLS to sex-positive online resources. Laci Green is an American YouTube vlogger, public sex educator and feminist. She has hosted online sex-education content on behalf of Planned Parenthood and Discovery News. She has resources on subjects ranging from sexuality, relationships, body image and consent to feminism and gender.

BE OPEN to discussing porn and suggesting better porn to teenagers and friends. Check out corporate mogul and entrepreneur Cindy Gallop's TED Talk on porn. Also see her website MakeLoveNotPorn.tv, which brings more realistic and emotional sex to the Internet: www.makelovenotporn.com.

QUESTION your own heteronormativity. Heteronormativity assumes that all girls want is a boyfriend, and all boys want is a girlfriend, and all anyone wants is to grow up and get married and have children. These values exclude the possibility of diverse expressions of sexuality and identity, including gay, lesbian, bisexual, trans and queer identities. They also limit options for girls in their sense of autonomy.

Kids are sexting. We are not going to tell them not to do it. It's new territory; we [youth] can start to make our own morals and ethics around it. Young people need to know how to approach sexting in a healthy way, so they don't feel forced or obligated. They need to know the legal repercussions of non-consensual forwards. But we [youth] have the power to reclaim and define how we are going to use these new forms of media. We have to know what it is, and go forward in a positive way.
Andrea Villaneuva, 18, co-founder of Project Slut

AMY'S TIPS for safe sexting[18]: "We know that some people are sexting," says Dr. Amy Adele Hasinoff. "So if you're going to participate, how can you reduce the risk and potential harm? No sex act is ever 100 percent safe, but there are lots of things you can do to **PRACTICE SAFER SEXTING**." Here is a list you can share with girls:

- **EVERYTHING DIGITAL IS NOT MEANT TO BE PUBLIC**.
- **THINK ABOUT SEXTING AS A SEX ACT**. Learn, use and promote the affirmative consent model in your sexual relationships and among your peers.
- **MAKE SURE YOUR PARTNER WANTS TO RECEIVE A SEXUAL IMAGE** before you send it. Talk or text about it first; don't just assume they want to see it.
- **NEVER COERCE OR PRESSURE ANOTHER PERSON** to engage in any sex act, including creating and sending sexual images. If you ask once and the person says no, accept their answer.
- **CONSIDER SAFER-SEXTING STRATEGIES**. For example: crop your face or other identifying marks out of suggestive photos, delete old photos often and ask your partner to do the same. Consider an app that deletes photos automatically after they've been viewed (but understand that nothing ever really 'disappears').
- Sexts sent under pressure or coercion are much more likely to be distributed without consent to third parties. So, **IF IT STARTS OUT CONSENSUAL AND FREELY CHOSEN, IT'S MORE LIKELY TO STAY PRIVATE**. Sexting someone you trust and who respects your sexual boundaries/needs/desires appears to be less risky.

Here are some additional tips for parents:

- **AVOID BLAMING THE VICTIMS** of privacy violations. We don't blame people who got an STD from a cheating partner, and we shouldn't blame sexters whose trust was betrayed either.

- **BE AWARE** of and work on resisting rape culture, slut-shaming, homophobia and the sexual double standard in your everyday life. It's unfair to condemn and criticize women and girls for it (for example, by harassing female sexters and calling them sluts, or by telling victims of privacy violations that they deserved it).
- **SPEAK OUT** against gender- and sexuality-based insults when you hear them.
- **TALK** to girls about mitigating risk and about how to make informed decisions. Risk taking requires good communication with a partner, trust and a strong relationship.

I would worry less about a photo being taken and shared. I would be more worried about malicious intent. The kids who are mean face to face are the mean kids online. Don't panic about a photo. Teach your kids about respect and the implications of public self-expression online.
Lucia O'Sullivan, a Canada Research Chair in Adolescents' Sexual Health Behaviours

TEACH YOUR KIDS about the criminal consequences of passing on private photos without consent. It is illegal for a person to distribute an "intimate image" of another person without that person's consent.

IF SOMEONE has published anyone's nude photos without consent, it is possibly illegal and you can take steps to have the picture removed from the Internet. This needs to be done as soon as possible after the photo is posted to limit the likelihood of it being shared or re-posted online. For more information go to:

withoutmyconsent.org
womenagainstrevengeporn.com
takebackthetech.net/know-more
needhelpnow.ca

+++

SLUT SHAMING

IS A FORM OF BULLYING

WHO GAVE YOU

THE RIGHT

TO MAKE OR BREAK

SOMEONES REPUTATION?

PROJECT SLUT

INSIDE THE HYPERSEXUALITY HYPE: MARAUDING THROUGH MONTREAL, PART 2

JUST AS WE WERE FEELING pretty good about how this generation of girls is deftly and, for the most part, safely navigating the tricky terrain of expressing their sexuality, our 15-year-old friend Tasha popped by Tatiana's for a visit. She was preoccupied and fidgety and, after a bit of hesitation, launched into a story about her history class that day, and how the teacher had invited the students to volunteer issues for discussion.

Tasha, who is a bi-racial young woman of colour, had wanted to talk about the recent tragedy in India, where two girl cousins were gang-raped and hanged from a tree,[1] but she had not been prepared for the class's response. Everyone had seen the gruesome online images of these young girls, ages 14 and 16, hanging lifeless in their traditional Indian clothing. The conversation, however, veered from this tragic event into entirely different territory—about how a girl dresses and what that means about her sexual availability. One of the boys in Tasha's class said, "If a girl dresses in a certain way, it's like putting meat in front of a dog. Like she is asking to be raped. It's her fault." A rush of excited agreement rippled through the room. Only one other girl in the class of forty grade-nine students was comfortable enough to argue alongside Tasha that what you wear doesn't give anyone permission to violate you. When the rest of the class—and the male teacher—strongly disagreed with that girl, she called them sexist and then she was sent home.

Where the nuances of girl sexuality are concerned, speaking out is not as straightforward as we might hope, nor are commonly held ideas about girls as evolved as we might wish. High schools are increasingly making the news for introducing and upholding conservative dress codes, as are the students who rebel against these codes. In Beaconsfield, Quebec, 16-year-old Lindsey Stocker wore jean shorts to school on a very hot day. Two vice-principals measured the shorts in front of the class, told her they were too short for school and asked her to go home and change. When Lindsey refused, she was asked to leave—without being given a chance to make a case—and was suspended for a day. Lindsey subsequently started a protest about her school's dress code by making posters that directly addressed the fear many seem to feel about girls' bodies and the "temptation" they arouse in boys. "Don't humiliate her because she is wearing shorts," the posters read. "It's hot outside. Instead of shaming girls for their bodies, teach boys that girls are not sexual objects."[2]

This story made news headlines, and led some outlets to cite similar cases playing out in other areas. Students at Morris Knolls High School in New Jersey; Kenilworth Junior High in California; Duncanville High School in Texas; and Stuyvesant High School in New York have all issued complaints about their dress codes, many of which have resulted in full-on protest.[3] A quick search of current social media, magazines and newspapers reveal similar examples breaking out in Europe, New Zealand and Australia. The way a girl chooses to dress—and the effects this is said to have on her, on her peers and on her environment—is a hot topic.

Dress codes exist to greater or lesser degrees in almost all schools. In some—especially in private and religious schools—the codes are very specific and strictly enforced. For example, for girls there can be no short shorts or skirts (some schools give exact measurements; usually that, when standing with your arms along your sides, shorts and skirts must come to the fingertips or below), no crop tops, no spaghetti straps, no visible bra straps, and no "excessive cleavage." Some schools specify no bare arms or shoulders. At Tasha's school, where they wear uniforms, knee socks must be worn to the knee but not over the knee.

Tasha herself has had her long socks confiscated for wearing them too high. Wearing socks too high seems like an anomaly if the codes are about covering up. When we asked Tasha about this, she said she didn't understand it either; when she asked her school's authorities, she wasn't given a satisfactory answer.

As the three of us walked to a nearby café, Tasha told us that she would gladly leave her school if she could find another that was more tolerant and understanding about girls' issues. In the meantime, she said it would be great to get some interesting experts into her classroom who could talk about how dress codes are sexist and harmful—first because they make girls feel ashamed of their bodies, and second because they imply that the mere existence of those bodies dangerously turns people on. She also told us that because of her breast size, she is harassed all the time. "I walk down the hall and the guys are like, 'Hey, Double D.' I tell them to shut up, but it does hurt me. I wouldn't go around calling someone something because of a body shape or size that they have no control over. Judging and putting someone down for a physical attribute is really bad. When it's happening to you, it makes you want to look different from how you are. It makes you feel wrong about yourself. It can make you feel really sad and do things like stop eating or start cutting yourself."

Despite the fact that this verbal harassment happens all the time to her and other girls, Tasha told us the school does not provide help or support. She doesn't feel like she can approach the faculty about being called "Double D"; she worries about being judged, and that a lack of experience on behalf of those in charge at school would make it impossible for them to see her side and support it. "They are mostly just as sexist as the boys in the halls. There's no one you can go to with these kinds of problems."

Tasha said she would love to be a peer counsellor and go into other schools to talk about these topics to classes who don't know her and can't dismiss her as the class feminist. "So many people are thinking critically about dress codes but they're too afraid to talk about it. Girls stay silent because they don't want to get kicked out."

Tasha may not be getting the support she wants or needs at school, but she is finding this support elsewhere. Tasha attends Girls Rock Camp—a programme that started in Portland, Oregon, and has since grown into a global network. As we caught a glimpse of in chapter 1, Girls Rock Camp is a summer camp and year-long choir programme where girls learn to play guitars, bass and drums, create a band and perform in front of an eager audience that includes web, radio and TV journalists. Organized by young women and local artists, the programme encourages girls to find their voice through music and performance education, while also providing social justice and leadership workshops. The camp draws on support from local businesses, artists and university students to connect girls to positive role models.[4] Tasha told us how the weekly gatherings are a source of support for her outside of her school environment. "Rock camp is so much about self-expression and we talk about girls' stuff," said Tasha. "I see these girls once a week. We *need* to see each other once a week. We really need that place in our lives because we are always being put down at school. How are you supposed to discover yourself and come out of your shell if you feel like you are being judged at every turn, including by the authorities at school who are telling you how you can and cannot dress?"

By strange coincidence, the same day that Tasha knocked on Tatiana's door, Caia's daughter, Nova, who was 14, was given the dress code speech at her school.

Nova goes to an inner-city performing arts school that is liberal about how the students dress. A lot of the girls, including Nova, make their own clothes, using them as a way to express their emerging identities. There are experimental versions of Debbie Harry, Joan Jett, Grace Jones and Madonna in her "Like a Virgin" stage gracing the hallways. Their DIY fashion features everything from military uniforms to cyberspace suits to the retro–Cyndi Lauper look where ripped fishnets double as hairbands, and collars and sleeves get shaved off with pinking shears. The teachers encourage the theatre of dressing as part of the spirit of the school, but still, they are required to give the dress code speech.

Nova's class of thirty outlandishly dressed boys and girls were gathered in their homeroom classroom and the dos and dont's of the code were listed—no exposed belly buttons, no "provocative" clothing. Some of the students, most of whom were breaching the dress code without even knowing it, asked why it is wrong for a girl to dress the way she wants to. The female teacher said, "Because if a girl does that she's drawing attention to herself." The kids asked, "What's wrong with that?" The teacher replied, "It's wrong because it's asking for it." When the kids asked what it was asking for, the teacher stated it plainly: "If a girl dresses sexy, she is asking for rape."

~Caia

This made two teachers in two days telling classes of eager-to-learn teens that a suggestively dressed girl is a danger to herself and her community. What is going on here?

The idea that a girl needs to conceal her body so that the boys in her class can concentrate on school work is a loaded statement on several fronts. On the one hand, we have the notion that boys lack an innate ability to focus and are helplessly at the mercy of the tantalizing girls all around them; on the other hand, we have the idea that it is somehow the girls' responsibility to ensure the academic success of the boys, and not jeopardize it via provocative attire. Let's be clear: what we're really saying when we haul out the "asking for it" line is that boys and men are sexually irresponsible, violent and uncontrollable, and that girls are ultimately responsible for their actions. This is an absurd idea, and one that suggests that violence occurs because of girls.

In chapter 3, we saw how girls are confronted with a paradox: an enticement to be sexy, but at the same time being subject to powerful forces of control including surveillance, policing and punishment that try to keep them free from sexual corruption. We also saw that girls are finding strength through sexual discovery and expression, and are pushing back against moral panic and other social reactions, to claim their agency. If healthy sexual development is positive and empowering for girls, why are we so quick to shame girls?

THE HYPERSEXUALIZATION OF GIRLS: THE APA REPORT

While school dress codes are garnering headlines, behind the scenes, they are informed by an underlying social debate over the "hypersexualization of girls." This conversation not only informs school dress codes but also has tremendous influence on the way girls' sexuality is framed and "managed" by teachers, parents, mainstream media and society at large. It is also tangled up with how the commercial world solicits and packages consumer products to girls. While the debate allows us to shine light on important issues related to objectification, it also takes us backwards by giving credibility to the dated notion that girls are vulnerable and in need of being policed and controlled.

This debate focuses on a central concern: that tween girls (ages seven to 12) are increasingly sexualized. As evidence, panicked onlookers point to sexy pop culture idols, the pornification of culture and the proliferation of sexy clothing marketed to girls. For their part, the media and the corporate world spin sensationalized stories that heighten the debate, even as they themselves continue to market sexy merchandise to young girls. And all the while, as we saw in chapter 3 and earlier in this chapter, the so-called depraved prepubescent girl herself is blamed for society's fascination with her, criticized as the problem, and then identified as the source of its solution.

At the cornerstone of this thinking is a highly influential 2010 report produced by the American Psychological Association (APA) following its Task Force on the Sexualization of Girls, created to inform educators, parents and policy-makers alike.[5] The report found that the sexualization of girls leads to self-objectification in tweens, which can harm girls' mental, physical and sexual health. It demonstrated a link between self-objectification[6] and low self-esteem, impaired cognitive and physical functioning, body dissatisfaction, appearance anxiety and issues of mental health.[7]

Sexualized images found in media and advertising were cited in the report as influences of sexualization. The amount of exposure to media that girls get per day (an estimated six hours and twenty-three minutes, including Internet, television, movies, magazines and video games) means "this naturally increases the potential for massive exposure to portrayals that sexualize women and girls and teach girls that women are sexual objects."[8] The report expresses concern with commercial media and advertising, and the importance of girls' relationships with their parents, teachers, peers and others. These relationships can reinforce the idea that sexualization is a normal, natural and unproblematic component of being a girl.

If we take a quick sweep through the cultural landscape, we get an idea of why the APA may be concerned (and why even adults aren't immune). Even before exposure to media sensations such as Katy Perry's cupcake-and-whipped-cream-missile-shooting breasts, younger girls are being primed for sexualization through Disney. The "princess" brand, with twenty-six thousand items comprising every plastic-dolled fairy-tale dream in pink and pearls that a girl could imagine, is the highest grossing toy brand in the world, with annual North American sales in the billions of dollars.[9] Disney teaches girls that all "girl" things come in only one colour (pink) and one aesthetic (the stereotypically feminine), and that it is important to be "the fairest of them all."

Wanting to be the fairest of them all is one of the drivers of hyper-sexualization, according to a recent CBC documentary entitled *Sext Up Kids*. With the best of intentions, this documentary, along with numerous popular culture texts,[10] is an example of how slippery this debate becomes and how easily we can be led down a path of fear and panic.[11]

The narrator sets off alarm bells in the first frames with catchphrases like "from sassy to sexy," "strutting stuff before having any stuff," and, perhaps to turn Freud in his grave, "anal is the new oral." Girls get bored with Barbie by age seven, we're told, and quickly graduate to dolls with "attitude," like Bratz and Monster High—dolls whose anorexic proportions and thong underwear send "bad" messages to girls whose "brains are still under construction." Gail Dines, an English-American feminist anti-pornography activist, author, professor and lecturer, makes an appearance. "You have two choices in a hypersexed society," she says. "You are either fuckable or invisible." In other words, pop culture provides only one way of being female—the hypersexualized way—because, as Dines elaborates, "it is developmentally and socially out of step with adolescence to choose invisibility."

What *Sext Up Kids* and similar media explorations lead us to believe is that today's toys, clothes, media and, most especially, girls themselves, are ruinous. Combined, they raise the issue of the objectification of the girl's body, which then leads to the issue of self-objectification, which creates a domino effect that pulls the whole of society down a treacherous path that ends in gang rape. If we weren't already scared for—and *of*—today's girls, we are by the end of the documentary. And if we might have guessed that there were other culprits in the degeneration of society, we are by now convinced that girls *are* depraved.

Stories and reports like this explain why so many adults are so concerned about their daughters; unfortunately, they also explain why girls like Tasha suffer at the hands of policies that use the "ethics" of dress code to justify their tyranny.

SMARTER THAN WE THINK

But is it real? Despite the claims put forth by the APA report, as well as the fright generated by documentaries like *Sext Up Kids*, the reality is that the image being promulgated by pop culture, and fortified by corporate culture, does not reflect what's really happening in the lives of most real girls. The age and nature of sex is not changing because of hypersexualization; the average age of first sexual intercourse remains 16, as it has been for decades, for both girls and boys.[12] Girls are a little shrewder than we, as adults, may think.

Fashion blogger Tavi Gevinson, herself a tween when she hit media fame in 2008 at age 12, spoke about this issue in a *Newsweek* article called

"Sex and the Single Tween."[13] She argued that despite the social perception that girls are a "mass of pink, selfie-taking, Kardashian clones," the opposite is more often the case. "Not only do I think that a lot of girls aren't like that, but I also think the girls who are like that are maybe smarter than people give them credit for. For as much as there are a lot of awful messages sent out to girls at the moment, I think that they are better equipped to deal with it [than they have been in previous generations]."

In chapter 3, we spent some time with Dr. Amy Adele Hasinoff, who tackles the sexualization issue in her research. Dr. Hasinoff told us that "hypersexualization," at its root, conflates sexuality with sexualization; it confuses girls' actual sexuality with external projections of sexuality from adults or society. It sees girls, once again, as victims, and denies them the capacity to act and think for themselves, make choices or be empowered in their sexuality. It also oversimplifies media effects. While it's smart to be critical of global consumer trends, female consumerism is surely a more complex phenomenon than merely buying into a sexualized message out of delusional thinking. We talked about how the APA report may distract attention from other, more fundamental—and perhaps more intractable—social problems such as sexualized violence and the inherent inequalities of a hypercapitalist society.

Dr. Hasinoff stated that the debate surrounding sexualization often positions girls as both victims of sexualization and the site of intervention to solve the problem, which negates any need for responsibility on the part of schools, corporations, boys, retailers, governments and parents. "Girls are seen as carriers of a cultural disease, 'being sexy,' and therefore must be immunized against it by raising their self-esteem and gaining media literacy skills," said Dr. Hasinoff. "When hypersexualization is linking shorter skirts with depression, eating disorders and self-harm, it conflates the issues of what a girl wears with her mental health," she told us. "What's the impact of sexualization on boys? Possibly committing sexual assault and harassment. And on girls? Maybe a bit lower self-esteem. So who should we be more concerned about, and who should we target for media literacy interventions? Men and boys."

Dr. Hasinoff argues that by thinking we can fix the problem by fixing girls, we fail to take up the cultural issues that create the conditions for sexual violence. "We know that clothing doesn't cause assault, and to blame the victim is the cornerstone of rape culture.[14] Hypersexualization blames the girl for 'what she was wearing and how she was acting' and this just isn't right," said Dr. Hasinoff. This approach to violence prevention ignores the person who commits the act of violence—when, as a society, we should be talking to boys about consent, rape culture and homophobia.[15]

As we sat with Dr. Hasinoff and Dr. Karaian following the McGill conference, Dr. Caroline Caron joined us for coffee to discuss the issues surrounding hypersexualization. Dr. Caron specializes in media, youth and girlhood studies. She, too, has conducted research into hypersexualization, and found that surveillance and control over girls' bodies is more about adults' anxiety than about girls themselves. In her research, Dr. Caron talked directly to girls and young women between the ages of 11 and 20 about their experiences. She found many of them to be like Tasha and Tavi and Nova and her classmates—none of them felt hypersexualized in the ways described by adults and experts. They expressed resentment about being criticized and controlled in the way they choose to express themselves through their clothing.

Dr. Caron explained that the issue of hypersexualization is also understood as the "eroticization of childhood," because it's built on the idea that young people are vulnerable and in need of protection from sexuality—their own and that of others. In fact, says Dr. Caron, this point of view actually objectifies young people and interferes with our ability to listen to what kids think and feel about their sexuality. As a result, these views—especially adolescent girls' views—are being silenced, marginalized and dismissed.

"This is a problem," Dr. Caron told us, "because it assumes that young girls cannot speak for themselves and legitimizes the remedies 'we' as adults have chosen over those that come from their own perspectives, ways of knowing or sets of values."

To get a sense of what those perspectives might be, we asked the girls (most of whom came from a white middle-class background) we met in Whitehorse, Yukon, how they felt about the hypersexualization debate's hottest topic: the dress code.[16]

"I don't think it's fair," said Marion, 14. She was curled up in her dance class sweats on a couch outside the studio we were visiting, along with several of her friends. "It's not about what you're wearing. Guys should just learn not to sexualize us. Girls are blamed for the sexualization issue. I mean, judgment behind what you wear so boys can concentrate? It's ridiculous."

"We have a short shorts rule," Clarissa, 15, added. "Shorts have to go to the middle of your hand. No one wears short shorts [even though they are so in style]."

"If they know you have a bad reputation, the teachers will keep a closer eye on you," said Jo, 14. "We have a rule where you can't show your belly or your shoulders."

"I own so many tank tops," said Marion, "but I can't wear them. Are guys allowed to wear tank tops? Yes."

"They [the authorities] call the girls out, but not the guys," Florence, 14, lamented.

"Yeah, girls have to cover up because of guys. No belly buttons, no boobs, no boxers, no bra straps. It's not a shame that we have boobs and we have to hold them up!" said Brie, 14, and everyone laughed.

"Protect girls? So guys don't get horny?" Clarissa questioned. "I asked my teacher and it's so guys can concentrate more on their work or focus and control their thoughts. I'm not responsible for the boys' actions. I'm not purposely making myself look like a slut."

"We make boys out to be out of control," remarked Marion. "Boys are projected as uncontrollable."

"I want to wear what I'm comfortable in," said Brie. "If that makes you uncomfortable, then too bad."

"We just want to be who we are," concluded Marion.

GOOD GIRL/BAD GIRL

After listening to comments like these, it's hard not to agree with Dr. Caron when she says that the moral panic created by the hyper-sexualization debate is having a negative effect on girls.[17] "It is troubling that good intentions, like protecting girls from being objectified by media and by men, have in fact translated into institutional policies like the strict dress codes that are being enforced and/or experienced by female adolescents as something that is very similar to what feminists have termed sexual harassment in the 1980s and 1990s,"[18] she said.

This harassment—experienced first-hand by the girls in Whitehorse and by Tasha, Nova and Lindsey—creates a vortex of concern. Increased measures of surveillance and control are enforced by school staff and supported by media headlines, corporate advertising, worried parents, confounded adults and both right-wing political platforms and feminist interests. How ironic that these traditionally idealistic opponents—conservatives/Republicans and feminists—join forces over the issue of girls' sexuality. Conservative values are rooted in the belief that a girl's sexuality needs to be hidden and controlled. Some feminists see a girl's sexual expression as a form of self-exploitation that perpetuates sexual objectification, which is something that feminists have fought hard to change. In both cases, these strange bedfellows are advocating for girls to cover up.

Dr. Caron has noticed that girls and young women are participating in these forms of surveillance and colluding with them through using slanderous terms that are "slut-shaming."[19] As Mirabelle used it above, the term "slut" is being commonly used among girls, and among girls and boys as a tool for patrolling the boundaries of gender and hetero-sexuality. Dr. Caron pointed out that young people lack a more positive vocabulary to talk about girls and their sexuality. As a result, the regulating frameworks of the good girl/bad girl cultural script go on unnoticed and continue to operate within society as well as in day-to-day interactions among young people.

Embedded in this cultural script is an attempt to maintain girls' purity by instilling fear. While this panic emanates from the white middle class, the virgin/slut dichotomy cuts across cultural and ethnic boundaries. Aside from being an out-of-date cultural trope desperately in need of an overhaul to catch up with the progress made in other areas, the good girl/bad girl dichotomy leaves girls little room within which to explore and embrace their sexuality in positive, self-affirming ways. The upshot? Girls are trapped. If girls express their sexuality, or are in any way perceived as stepping outside the "good girl" script, they automatically risk the judgment that comes from labels like "slut" and "whore." Sexuality, in this paradigm, is synonymous with "slut." And to be labelled a slut is to be publically shamed. As we saw in chapter 3, this is an area that girls are identifying as a serious concern and in which they are pushing for change.

An extreme example of this puritanical approach to controlling girls' sexuality is abstinence-only sex ed. Closely aligned with right-wing anti-abortion agendas, this approach is a popular movement across the US— one that we've seen manifested in the form of Purity Balls. Most notably found in the evangelical community, Purity Balls are ceremonies that parallel weddings, in which 12- and 13-year-old girls dressed in white gowns take vows of purity and pledge to renounce dating and even kissing until marriage, and thereby symbolically hand over their sexuality to their fathers for safekeeping. Purity Ball advocates consider this ritual an antidote to hypersexualization. But as Jessica Valenti, author of *The Purity Myth*, points out, "By defining girls by their virginity, [Purity Ball proponents] are ensuring that young women will continue to be judged by their sexuality. The [girls] who go to Purity Balls are promising that their bodies aren't their own, but instead belong to their fathers and future husbands."[20]

In addition to reinforcing outdated and harmful ways of thinking, this approach pushes an abstinence-only version of sex education that has proven ineffective in preventing teens from having sex. In fact, multiple studies have shown that teens who vow abstinence *are not* less likely to have sex, but *are* less likely than their peers to use contraception when they do, making them vulnerable to unwanted pregnancies and STIs.[21]

Abstinence, it seems, is a dangerous approach to recommend to teens, not least of all because it insists, under religious oath, that sexuality is shrouded in shame.

As we talked, Dr. Karaian explained how the moral panic around hypersexualization has been focused on white, heterosexual, middle-class, able-bodied girls, and how this maintains them as the "jewels" of the nuclear heterosexual family by elevating their responsibility to maintain family structure, and classist, racist, patriarchal norms. "These are the girls we tend to be worried about," she said, "to the extent that we are panicking about white middle-class girls, we maintain 'the other' (girls of colour and working-class girls) as unexploitable and marginalized and increasingly vulnerable to racism and structural violence." It sends a message about who is valued, who we need to protect, and creates a dangerous dichotomy between innocence and sexualization by casting the oversexualized girls as damaged and pathological.[22] (We will explore this subject further in chapter 5.)

It's clear, then, that the debate over the hypersexualization of girls is damaging in many ways. In their critique of the APA report, scholars Kari Leruma and Shari Dworkin argue that, "By neglecting agency and desire—focusing instead on the dangers of sexual images, metaphors, and practices—everything sexual appears to become (re)stigmatized for girls. This leads girls, boys, women, and men backwards into seeing sexuality as something that should be veiled from girls."[23] When society at large falls into this backwards mode of thinking, the result is that girls are offered little to help them understand the reality of their sexual awakening, and how and why it should be supported.

Even at its most well intended, then, the debate over the hypersexualization of girls is clearly hazardous terrain. Dr. Karaian summed up this disturbing irony: "By obsessively focusing on protecting children, we are saturating children with a sexual discourse that inevitably links children, sexuality and erotic appeal."

MONEY AND THE CORPORATE VALLEY OF THE DOLLS

What about the corporations that rely on the hypersexualization of girls? Corporations have a lot to gain from the economic gold mine of the growing girl market, and they seek profit through targeted marketing schemes. Do girls have power in this? They may, in fact, have plenty.

The Disneyfication of culture has been under way since the early animations of the 1920s, which colonized the imaginations of film and television viewers and influenced the attitudes, behaviours and beliefs of children. With a sentimental sweetness, Disney has been busily recruiting young consumers for generations by offering them fairy-tale gender-specific consumer goods from their very first toys to their most breathtaking costumes and party dresses. This corporate desire to make money has recently found an opening in a fast-growing and very profitable market in Gen Z tweens, who have been identified and groomed as loyal buyers who align themselves emotionally with brands and spread their loyalty through their vast and active social networks.

Despite the fact that many of them aren't even in high school yet, Generation Z is already a driving force in the economy. According to a report by the international advertising firm J. Walter Thompson, over 70 percent of parents in the US say their Generation Z children influence buying decisions about apparel and family meals, and more than half say their children influence electronics and entertainment purchases. Beyond their parents' wallets, thanks to allowances, part-time jobs and a propensity for saving vs. spending—born during the biggest economic crisis of recent times, this is a frugal generation—Generation Z already holds the purse strings to US$44 billion in spending power.[24]

Messages that idealize Western beauty standards and prescribe strict gender norms are everywhere in the imagery we consume daily, and they continue to propagate the codes for what is valued. Girls are especially targeted as a lucrative economic market within this model. Having been identified as powerful influencers over household purchases, kids as young as two are directly solicited in advertising as soon as consciousness sets in; it's expected they will persuade their parents to establish brand loyalty. As girls grow older within this model, they are increasingly groomed to leverage their spending power. Strategies like Kids Getting Older Younger (KGOY) target children as "hot teen" consumers and, for example, seduce younger girls into older-girl desires and attitudes with things like the Abercrombie & Fitch padded-bra swimsuit for eight-year-olds. These KGOY-targeted marketing schemes are a US$150 billion-a-year brand-growing success.[25]

Aggressive corporate targeting has become even more ubiquitous with the evolution of social media. Sarah Banet-Weiser, whom we met in chapter 2, sees all kinds of opportunism working behind the scenes of what appears to be a "freedom of expression platform." "Public self-expression and self-branding is validated by culture," she told us. "This connects gender empowerment with consumer activities and is defining a new set of relationships between young people and corporations. Developing a self-brand on commercial social networking sites means that girls reference brands not simply as commodities, but as the context for everyday living." Sarah believes that this branded context around day-to-day living encourages people—and girls particularly—to craft identities as "products" capable of catching a lot of attention and attracting and demanding feedback.[26] As we've seen, girls compete to get flurries of "likes" for conforming to the commercial model of girlhood. To venture outside of this corporate-dictated image is to be punished and rejected with no "likes." "In the past," said Sarah, "identity development centred around 'Who am I?' Now it centres on 'How do I sell myself?'"

As parents, we have a lot of decision-making power over the access we give kids to all that there is to consume. We can limit their exposure to corporate targeting by not buying products that push a corporate agenda, by putting time or content boundaries around them and by boycotting products or brands that sexualize young girls or have a message we don't support.

If La Senza and Victoria's Secret make thong underwear or padded bras for preteens this doesn't mean we have to buy them. If four-year-old girls are being offered mini-stilettos, we don't have to buy those either, nor short shorts or crop tops for eight-year-olds. We can outsmart dubious corporate marketing schemes by joining efforts to call out corporations, by signing petitions or participating in campaigns and by not buying the products. Initiatives like the Let Toys Be Toys campaign are taking a step in the right direction by encouraging the toy and book-publishing industries to stop limiting kids' interests through gender-based marketing. The UK-based parent-led initiative has successfully influenced large retailers to take down pink and blue signage and to organize toys by theme and function rather than by gender.

We are in charge of what our children consume and can apply critical thinking and common sense to our purchasing power. We ourselves have used this power as parents and gift givers by choosing not to go too far down the road of all things pink and girlie, offering our daughters and other girls we buy presents for many versions of role playing, dress-up, toy and identity play. When Tatiana's daughter, Morganne, was in a princess phase, for example, Tatiana navigated this by diversifying Morganne's influences.

> I didn't boycott everything princess, but I didn't brand her bedroom Disney either. We didn't watch Disney movies, but instead watched great Japanese animation movies. Her dress-up clothes ranged from a princess dress to Spider-Man. It's good to try on different identities and dress-up play is just that—fantasy and fun. By the time Morganne turned five, princesses weren't cool anyway, and Morganne has been more interested in Lego and Pokémon. Now I can't get her to wear anything other than sweatpants even if I really want her to put on a dress. Because we talk about it at home, both my kids are able to analyze ads whether on TV or the Internet and see behind the tactics to seduce their loyalty. They feel good about their consumer savvy.
>
> -Tatiana

It's fun to talk to kids about why the world assumes pink, long hair and skirts are for girls, and blue, short hair and trains are for boys. When we talk to kids about this, especially kids between the ages of eight and 15, they are able to see the stereotypes and gender boxes into which mainstream society wants to put them. Girls, like boys, like to run and play, so they feel great when they can break loose from clothes that hinder them. Sarah Banet-Weiser enthusiastically agreed that toy boxes should include trucks, blocks and superheroes, offering girls a range of experiments and explorations. If they were encouraged as very young girls to take radios apart and play with technology, the way boys are, more girls would grow up to be coders, industrial designers and engineers. In these roles, they could join the emerging girl gaming and toy innovators who are beginning to create more interesting girl characters and more science- and tech-based toys that appeal to girls.

At the same time, girls will emulate their pop idols and their older siblings, whether these are the same or different gender, as well as their moms. Playing dress-up with grown-up clothes, makeup and accessories is normal for little girls *and* little boys. Kids are only sexualized when someone actually sexualizes them; if a girl dresses up in adult clothing, this doesn't mean she is sexualizing herself. Adults need to be held responsible for their own sexual boundaries; if an adult interprets a little girl dressed up as sexual, then the adult can examine his or her own projections of sexuality onto the girl. We don't need to be alarmed by a little girl wearing makeup, nail polish and a standout dress once in a while.

As kids get older, we can introduce them to the concept of conscious consumption. Branding is everywhere and can easily go unnoticed as the powerful influence that it is. It can be strengthening to have dinner table conversations about how and why corporations advertise to kids directly, and how to approach shopping with a bit of cynicism and savvy. We can ask our children to consider where our clothes come from: who makes them, who sells them and who profits from those sales. We can discuss what a multinational corporation is, and ask kids how much they think the seamstress who may be working in Pakistan or China is paid compared to wages in North America. We can also ask them to read up on the toxins that are in the lip gloss they want to buy, and how they think that might affect their health and the ecology of the planet. We can initiate critical reflection on consumption and status by asking kids questions like, "Why do we think brands define us?" And, "Does a brand really define a person?" Or, "What value do we give people when we judge their worth based on what they wear?" Teaching kids that corporate marketing is in the business of cultivating passionate bonds between buyers and products invites them to see themselves as potential drivers of this fast train.

It's very inspiring to know and to tell tweens, teens and young adults that if we ask ourselves these questions and become more deliberate about what we do and don't buy, we have a lot more power than we realize. By using our dollars and social-media followings, we can change attitudes, messaging and spending patterns by bringing corporate interests into closer alignment with our own interests.

In fact, this is already beginning to happen. Girls have been successfully lobbying advertisers and brands to remove products from the market, and are questioning influential ideas that are not in line with female interests. In Australia in 2013, for example, Olive Bowers, a 13-year-old surfer, wrote a letter to *Tracks*, a top surfing magazine, about how they never depict girls actually surfing in their print edition and, on their online platform, only show girls in a special "Girls" gallery where they are wearing bikinis and lying on the beach. Her letter was the subject of national TV and newspaper discussion, and the *Age* (Melbourne) ran it on its weekend cover.[27] To *Tracks* she wrote, "I urge you to give much more coverage to the exciting women surfers out there, not just scantily clad women (who may be great on the waves, but we'll never know)," and told them that she, and everyone she knew, would be terminating their subscriptions. Before her story went viral, the editor of *Tracks* wrote Olive a rebuttal letter that denied her observations and tried to vilify her for the popularity of her views.

In 2015, Tatiana Ruei, a former Miss Malaika beauty contest winner, launched a campaign against skin-lightening creams that were targeting women of South Sudan. Her campaign is part of a growing movement aimed at raising awareness of both the harms and risks associated with skin bleaching. Skin lightening is a huge and extremely lucrative industry—which was predicted to reach profits of US$10 billion by 2015.[28]

Unilever's credibility has come under fire for the hypocrisy inherent in its promoting skin lightening in India while simultaneously running the Dove Real Beauty self-esteem-boosting ads in North America.

Julia Bluhm, a 14-year-old from the United States, took on the girl-magazine media in 2012 with an ambitious survey in which she collected over eighty-six thousand signatures on a petition to end retouching at *Seventeen* magazine. She presented this to the magazine, and it agreed to stop retouching. This energetic effort to help create more realistic images for girls by showing the real-life "imperfections" in the models who represent girl ideals has been widely discussed across social-media platforms as a good example of girls influencing change.

More generally, a recent Kellogg's commercial shows how the girl lobby has begun to infiltrate and change the corporate tune. The #OwnIt campaign responded (albeit opportunistically) to what Kellogg's saw as a desire for more diversity and flexibility in mainstream culture vis-à-vis how girls and women are depicted and celebrated. After hearing what girls had to say to the brand and to each other via social media and networks, the company ditched its focus on dieting, swapping it out for the idea that to be healthy is to own who you are, whether you conform to social norms or not. This is an emotionally powerful commercial. The message, however, goes a step or two further than the product. As a company, though, they are on trend in trying to market to a very power-ful potential ally and a potentially dangerous enemy: girls and women.

WISE WORDS FROM THE SEXOLOGIST

To deepen our discussion of the hypersexualization debate, we dropped in to see Den Temin, an energetic international advocate for sexual and reproductive rights and a practising sexologist. We met at her shared office at the Centre for Social Innovation in Toronto. As she poured us green tea, Den told us that her practice is teeming with parents who are pulling their hair out because they don't know what to do about their daugh-ters and sexuality. She, too, sees how the fears around this topic have come to focus on clothing and shutting down a girl's natural exploration. Den works with parents and young women to reframe the fears they're feeling by putting girls and their needs at the centre of the discussion. "If you are a girl and you and your body are being controlled, it's challenging to question and to have a voice when it feels like the power is in the hands of other people."

When girls are looking to define themselves in their tween and teen years, it really helps them if parents give them agency and trust. "They are scared," said Den. "Girls' biggest worry is, 'Is this normal?' They fear, 'Is what I'm doing okay?' Puberty is a superanxious time. Their hormones are intense, their emotions are up and down, their bodies are changing and there is little room for positive advice. What credit are we giving kids? They are coping with so much—school, peer pressure, emotional transformations. They are confused and they want answers. They want a safe space to ask anything."

Den believes that we need to start by teaching girls about their own pleasure and how to recognize it as a way to arm themselves. If girls understand what they like and don't like in social and romantic interactions, it builds confidence and clarity about everything from self-awareness to consent to desire.

"What tools are we giving kids to understand boundaries, consent and what feels good emotionally? That gut instinct when something is feeling good is emotional pleasure. We aren't teaching kids those things," Den told us. She suggested that pleasure is linked to being "in our bodies," which in turn is linked to sexual and personal empowerment.

Den stressed the importance of approaching this issue from an inclusive perspective, and one that challenges the heteronormative assumptions that get reified in the hypersexualization debate. Den meets with many kids who talk about what it feels like when their desires don't exist in the language that everyone else uses—and that, even if they do, they are often viewed negatively. "They tell me how small they feel, how they want to hide, how much they want to separate themselves from the whole conversation. It's like if you are not hetero, then you are made invisible on the school playground. You shouldn't exist because you don't fit into the narrative of the sexual prowess. You can only be a man if you are looking for sex from a woman. You are only a woman if you are looking to please and be with a guy."

In her workshops, Den finds ways to break down the fear around these insecurities and discomforts. "It would be amazing if we could say to our teenagers, 'Ask me anything,' and really mean it," she said. "When you give your children agency it's very powerful. It's so uncomplicated: the minute you give a human being agency, it makes them visible."

PROJECT SLUT

From Den's, we walked down Spadina Avenue in the crisp afternoon air to meet Andrea Villanueva. Andrea is an 18-year-old university student of Mexican descent who, with two girlfriends, has been busy setting fire to school policy around dress codes. Andrea was waiting for us at a snack bar table wearing a short skirt and a tank top, looking very self-possessed behind her chocolate milkshake. She stood up and hugged us enthusiastically, ready to tell us about Project Slut, the activist movement she co-founded at age 15, along with Kerin John and Erin Dixon, at Central Tech, a secondary school in inner-city Toronto.

Andrea told us how her career at Central Tech started with a bang. "I went to another high school in grade nine," she told us. "But I had to leave; they all thought I was a massive slut. This had started in grade eight when people were saying, 'You are not pretty, but you have huge tits.' This was a confusing time. On the one hand it validated me because I was receiving attention, but people assumed my body was accessible and I was available." Andrea told us that when she was younger, she was a high achiever and her identity had been wrapped up in being smart. When she started high school, she struggled with her identity and confidence. She worked hard to maintain the image and performance of being the "smart girl," but she was also being bullied and harassed because of her body. People called Andrea a whore and a slut and treated her as "less than human," in her words.

"To be called a slut is to be treated with a lot less integrity. Photographs of me [in revealing clothing] were spread around, without my consent. It was an awful time. Some of my classmates made up an Ask.fm about me that painted me as a bad person." Andrea went through a really difficult time. She was bullied to the point where she attempted suicide. Her parents did their best to support her but were at a loss. Andrea decided she wanted to leave her school and start with a clean slate.

When she changed schools to Central Tech the rumours and bullying blew over. Part of her strategy was to cut all contact with her old school and friends, including via social media, so she could start anew. Andrea considers herself lucky. "For a lot of other girls, people don't forget," she said. Having the room to heal and rebuild herself was important, and as she grew stronger Andrea began to understand how common her story was. "It's not just me, I realized. There are lots of girls from all walks of life who become that word, and who people regard in that way. I decided I didn't want to accept that I deserved [bad treatment] because I was a [supposed] whore. No girl deserves to be humiliated in a classroom, to feel like their bodies are wrong."

This experience sparked Andrea's drive to change the dress codes in schools. "When I was in school, I heard a story about a girl wearing a tank top, and the teacher saying, 'What you are wearing is lingerie, you should be totally ashamed of yourself, put a sweater on,' or, 'If you don't cover up, you will be sent home.' After being humiliated in class, this same girl would walk around and people felt free to slap her butt and touch her. She felt like it was her fault, as if she was asking for it, and if she reported the harassment, she would get in trouble." Andrea spoke up. "I started saying we shouldn't have dress codes and that it's not right to humiliate anyone. People make assumptions about you if you are dressing a certain way. People try to tell you to cover up for your own sake. They assume that you have low self-esteem, or that you are trying to get attention. The way people go about this is destructive; it basically shames someone just for being physically present."

A lot of Andrea's friends and peers disagreed with her views. They would tell her that we live in a society where women are objectified and that covering up is better (and safer). People told her she was going about it the wrong way, and that her approach wasn't feminist. But Andrea was persistent; the injustice of it all fuelled her passion and commitment to the cause. Andrea decided to do a survey of teachers. She wanted to know how comfortable the teachers felt working with girls, and in dealing with issues around their sexuality and dress. If teachers are shaming a student because they themselves are uncomfortable, Andrea figured, then there needs to be another approach.

"I wrote the survey," Andrea remembered, "and it was taken away. I was asked, 'Are you a guerrilla terrorist?'" She laughed, remembering this, and told us that she'd been prevented from distributing her survey. Not willing to let the idea go, she, Kerin and Erin built a little army that put pressure on the teachers, but the teachers thought they were being too radical. "We were saying our dress code was problematic; it includes 'we don't show bosoms,' which [as a gross overstepping of personal space and slanderous suggestion] is a violation of the Charter of Rights. It's illegal."

Project Slut was founded from there, to raise awareness around slut-shaming and to support change in this sphere. "The system reinforces those perceptions—it's the fact that a girl gets slut shamed in a classroom that elevates the idea that a girl wearing certain things is allowed to get raped. The teachers argued that dress codes helped prepare kids for the work world and train them to present themselves professionally. To the teachers, we were like, 'You are trying to prepare us for the real world by telling us how we are supposed to dress? Our school is racialized; we are already judged based on race and class—you don't prepare us for that. And anyway, half of the students in the school already have jobs. We know how to wear a blouse; we know how to dress appropriately for work. I don't see why you are challenging our ability to make decisions over our own bodies!'"

Andrea remembered how they made posters that the teachers took down, and how the discussions got heated when more students joined the movement and were saying to teachers, "You have the right to advocate professionalism, but you have no right to humiliate a human being based on your policy." The students agreed that it was acceptable for the school to want to set some sort of standard for presentation, but they discovered in the Charter of Rights that if you detail a certain group of people, this is a form of systematic discrimination.

"Eventually, after pushing and pushing, the teachers listened to us. The school began to support us and teachers began to advocate for us. They connected us to a social justice teacher, they let gender-based violence counsellors come and help us, they let us speak to the teacher body—and together we took down the dress code." Since the summer of 2014, there has been no dress code at Central Tech high school (except for technical safety).

Project Slut is gaining momentum. It has been featured on social media and in *Flare* magazine.[29] The story of Andrea and her friends has influenced students in other high schools across Toronto, as well as at Fredericton High School in New Brunswick. Inspired by the growing numbers of girls like Andrea who are speaking up and taking on this issue, protests are being organized by girls across North America. Armed with social-media networks and slogans like "Stand in solidarity," and "Not asking for it" written all over arms and backs and torsos exposed by crop tops, girls are saying no to dress code policy and yes to political potency.

As we walked back out into the busy evening street, Andrea told us she is now working on changing the sex ed curriculum to include consent, and facilitating leadership workshops in her community. "Race adds another level to the degree you will experience slut-shaming. Women of colour get sexualized on such a different scale than other women and experience more slut slurs. As a Mexican woman, there is also an extra layer of machismo and misogyny in my culture to endure. All women's bodies are different, but when you are under surveillance and monitored and shamed, it makes you feel uncomfortable."

Andrea's experience shows that girls' leadership in this area is both possible and necessary. The more girls are empowered to speak up on their own behalf, and to take control of their own bodies, the more likely we are to see real change—in schools, in communities and in the pop culture and corporate arenas that send such conflicting messages to these young women.

SURVIVAL KIT

DON'T BE DUPED! When we engage in critical reflection while reading the headlines and take moral panic with a grain of salt, we can consider whether we actually agree with what we are being told.

BREAK FREE from gender stereotypes and marketing schemes to seduce girls. Boycott corporate products that are inappropriate. Question targets and trends, and practise critical thinking when it comes to your own purchases. When we make our own decisions about what we want and need, we take a stand against being coerced into accepting what the mainstream deems appropriate.

UNDERSTANDING DESIRE AND PLEASURE is important, especially if we want girls to have a healthy sexuality and to be able to give and receive consent. We need to tell girls that their desires are worthy of respect and fulfillment. Nurture this development in children by engaging in conversations that explore pleasure, even outside of intimate sexual pleasure. Ask: "What is pleasurable to you? Do you have access to that pleasure? How does pleasure feel in your body?" For example, "The sun beating on my face is pleasurable, and feels warm, and like I'm bathing in gold." Or, "I feel pleasure in a hot bath, or after a long run." The idea is to make the connection between pleasure and life experience.

IF KIDS ARE TOO SHY to do the asking, sexologist Den Temin suggests asking girls directly what they want to know about. She encourages parents to talk to girls about their bodies and their body image, and about healthy relationships, sexual health, consent, sexual desires and the notion of pleasure.

FACE YOUR OWN FEARS, shame and taboos. How often do we ask ourselves, "What creates desire and pleasure in my life?" and how often do we deny ourselves these things because we think they're not allowed?

FREE YOURSELF from clichéd extremes like "object/subject," "virgin/whore," "good girl/bad girl." When we embrace the in-between, and the complexity of the many possibilities that we can be, we give girls more.

EXPLORE SITES like www.amightygirl.com to find diversified toys, gifts and books for girls. Encourage variety.

CHECK OUT lettoysbetoys.org.uk to learn more about the UK-based campaign to remove gender stereotypes in toy and book marketing.

WE LIVE IN A DIVERSE world. Language is power. Use the word "partner" instead of "girlfriend" or "boyfriend" when referring to relationships. This sends the message that it's okay to choose relationships with people of whatever gender you like.

TRUST KIDS and see them as agents rather than as victims, as dangerous or as in danger. This can calm the panic and allow us to be sane support systems in their tumultuous lives. They need us!

RESOURCES FOR GIRLS: GIRL SPACES, PROJECTS AND TOOLS TO MOBILIZE FOR CHANGE:

1. Learn more about Project Slut and their work to raise awareness about slut-shaming and dress codes: facebook.com/projectslut
2. Learn more about Rock Camp for Girls: girlsrockmontreal.com
3. Learn more about girl-positive spaces in Canada: girlsactionfoundation.ca and in the US: sparksummit.org

Start Something
Fierce

WHO GETS TO "LEAN IN"

REMEMBER JOYA FROM CHAPTER 2—the 15-year-old who loves reading and theatre and was spending a Saturday morning with her mother and brother at the Venice Beach skateboarding bowl? What we didn't tell you is that Joya and her family are homeless. She told us, almost as an aside near the end of our interview, that her mother could no longer afford to pay their rent and that they had been sleeping on the couches of friends and relatives for months; she was hoping her school friends hadn't noticed that she wore the same clothes every day.

It's always interesting to hear what girls say when you ask what they would change in the world, if they could. For Joya, homelessness is the issue that she would tackle. "The homelessness we have in America, it's scary to look at—all these people that don't have places they can call home. I'm sort of in a weird transition. Technically we are homeless, but we have friends and places to go to where we can stay as long as we want until we get back on our feet. But to know that some people don't have that, they don't have the resources to help them . . . it's sad. There should be more support around. They don't want to be homeless, but they don't have any choices to get out [of poverty]."

When Joya told us more about her family's financial hardship, we saw how economic vulnerability was having an impact on her life. "There were too many of us to stay in one house together. It is hard. And there are things that I hate. I want to go shopping and buy some cute boots, but that's going to have to wait. You want to look good; you want to have things, simple things, like clothes. But I have to wear the same thing every week."

Joya's experience is not unique. In fact, in the US, one in five girls live below the poverty line, and 42 percent of girls live in low-income families—and these numbers increase for black, Latina and Native American girls.[1] Nearly half of all children with a single mother—47.6 percent—live in poverty.[2] The fact that the mainstream doesn't often hear from marginalized girls is cause to reflect on *which* girls the world (governments, the media, dominant culture) cares about and to whom leaders and decision-makers pay attention. Joya talked about the same things that all the other girls we've spoken to talked about—music, role models, cliques, pressures and social life. She is smart, and aware of the world around her and its injustices. Despite her situation, she has a positive sense of herself and nurtures dreams for her future. But how can we expect her to realize those dreams when she doesn't have a home, and when her socio-economic conditions create real obstacles?

The very reality of being a girl is present in all other aspects of a girl's life, and, affect girls' lives profoundly. According to Girls Action Foundation, "These aspects, such as ethnicity, socio-economic status, sexuality or disability, can create specific barriers as well as strengths. For example, girls with disabilities, girls who are or are perceived to be in a sexual minority, and girls who grow up in poverty are also at higher risk of violence and can experience specific forms of marginalization, discrimination and barriers to education, and negative impacts on health."[3]

As Joya and her family walked away, we rolled up our jeans and made our way along the beach, taking in the mosaic of visitors as we reflected on how society wraps all girls into one category called "girl" that assumes all opportunities are available, all successes are achievable in this new "girl world." But there are problems inherent in the singular category "girl," and her assumed "girl power." What happens to this potential power when girls are facing structural barriers rooted in poverty or racism or violence, or all of these together? What happens when girls in these circumstances are still expected to make the "right"— meaning middle-class—"choices" regarding education and career paths and are held individually responsible if they don't "succeed"?

Facebook chief operating officer Sheryl Sandberg's bestselling 2013 book, *Lean In*,[4] argues that outdated belief systems are an obstacle to the advancement of women in leadership. It examines ideas about women in the workplace, and the internalized barriers these women face—including confidence and ambition gaps. It also explores the changes needed to adapt the workplace to women's lived realities, including more affordable childcare and support for part-time work. Sandberg makes a great case for the advancement of educated, middle-upper-class women in the corporate sector; she urges us to challenge the mindsets that create impediments to women's success and careers. *Lean In* is an inspiring read, but as we caught a last glimpse of Joya as she vanished into the crowd, we asked ourselves: "Just *who* gets to lean in?"

THE SCHOOL TRIP: FIRST STOP, TORONTO

Back in Canada, we set out from Montreal on a road trip to meet with girls in their schools. Our first stop was Toronto. Armed with bags of Twizzlers, iced lattes and Hubba Bubba cherry-flavoured bubblegum, we tore along the highway like Thelma and Louise. We arrived at our destination—a suburban middle school—just as the bell rang for lunch. Pulling in to the visitors' parking lot, we saw hundreds of teenagers coming and going through the entrance, and walking and talking together outside on the lawn: girls wearing hijabs with skinny jeans; girls with red bindis on their foreheads and high-top shoes; boys in hoodies and turbans. Natasha Burford, a teacher here, had invited us to spend the afternoon with her grade-seven all-girl class.

Natasha met us in the entrance hall. Together, we walked through the corridors to her room, where the class was gathering after lunch. Natasha told us that she was happy with how the school year was progressing. She felt she had managed to create a strong sense of community in the classroom by working closely with the girls to help them overcome social drama and cut down on bullying among themselves. She asked us to do a workshop on media literacy before her students began the afternoon's work—dance performances, staged in the classroom, as part of their physical-education curriculum.

The girls went up to the front of the room in groups, with iPod speakers and costumes in tow, and proceeded to blast the class with a loud song of their choice (everything from Katy Perry to traditional Hindi music) and a self-choreographed dance. The onlookers hollered and clapped as their classmates twirled and high-stepped and broke into the splits. Each performance was followed by enthusiastic feedback—initiated by Natasha to be constructive criticism about the artistic quality of the work.

When everyone had had a turn, the girls sat back at their desks giddy and open, and in the mood to chat. They talked a little about their pop star and cultural influences. We asked how they see themselves represented in the songs they chose, and how they experience the mainstream media. This question touched a nerve, and they broke into a lively dialogue about identity and how the racist stereotypes they confront in their lives and in the media make them feel.

"People think we all look the same," Samira, 13, said. "For example, they think all boys with a turban eat roti, and black people always have to come from Africa and Jamaica. This guy in the neighbourhood said some African thing to me. I looked at him with a confused face, and he was like, 'Aren't you African. You're black, aren't you?' That's racism."

Tricia, 14, agreed. "The media does that, too. Look at most of the Barbie dolls. They are fair-skinned, blue-eyed, blond-haired. People who have dark-coloured skin are always judged. One thing I don't like is when people see an Asian person and they always assume they are Chinese. 'Oh, you're Chinese, right?' people say to me, and I'm like, 'No, I'm not Chinese.' I'm Vietnamese. That's really insulting. My friend is Filipina; the same thing happens to her. I have another friend who always gets asked if she's Jamaican. She's like, 'I'm from Canada.'"

Shadia, 13, has had this experience, too. "I have a friend who has blond hair, but people say she looks terrible [as if it's not okay to be a black girl with blond hair] and she cries every day. Everyone expects black people to have nappy hair. As non-whites, we feel always judged."

Tamara, a quiet 13-year-old, told the class how deeply this stereo-typing affects her. "When you don't see yourself and when your stories are not told or they are twisted, it makes you feel like you don't exist, that you don't have any value." Samira added, "It makes me feel like I don't belong in the world. I don't feel like anything, I'm just here, doing nothing, just watching them, like I have nothing to do with life." When one of the other girls asked Tamara for an example of how she is left out, she said, "If you want to get a job and you don't look a certain way, [employers] are going to say no. They are going to shut you down."

Tamara's and Samira's comment led to a discussion about media, and how very aware the girls are of how racism in the media translates into racism in their everyday lives. Anthea, 15, told us, "If I was to talk to the media, I would be like, 'Take stories from our lives!' [Media] always puts people in the spotlight that don't look like us and change up our words. The stories aren't true."

Anthea was alluding to the way mainstream culture tends to portray girls of colour in one-dimensional ways, and how the complex realities that girls of colour actually live become invisible through these assump-tions and stereotypes. For example, Latina girls are represented as "the help," or Asian girls are portrayed as "submissive," or black girls are char-acterized as "ratchet."[5] These stereotypes perpetuate the "othering"[6] and dehumanizing of girls' lives. In the words of Marian Wright Edelman, founder and president of the Children's Defense Fund, "You can't be what you can't see." When girls don't see their realities reflected back to them, when they see limited and damaging stereotypes, the world essen-tially limits what they dream and envision for their futures.

When school was over, we stayed behind to talk with Natasha. She told us how racism leads to feelings of alienation, and how on a daily basis she hears confessions of how girls feel depressed and isolated.

"This generation of girls is facing pressures and contradictions and expectations like never before. Pop culture tells us that girls rule the world. But it makes me so upset, because the picture of false invincibility that we are painting is more destructive than good," Natasha continued.

She finds it challenging to watch girls learn this the hard way. Her girl students tell her, "Yeah, I rule the world! No one can talk to me, no one can give me advice because I rule the world!" When these girls encounter troubles, though, it becomes, "Oh wow, I wasn't ruling the world after all." It makes the fall even more painful.

"I work with 12- and 13-year-old girls, some who are already cutting themselves. Through their rebellion, they are reaching out and saying, 'I need help,'" Natasha says, explaining that among other girls, the rebellion is often deemed admirable. "Cutting is seen as cool. Demi Lovato's 'Stay strong' tattoo is cool, it's popular . . . but she doesn't say how she went to counselling for seven years and had a mentor. If they're going to really rule the world, girls need friends and helpers."

Natasha gets discouraged when she sees how this impacts black girls, and she works hard to change that. She told us, "It still often happens that when I ask a young black girl, 'Are you going to go to college?' that she says, 'I don't have to; I'm going to be a hairdresser,' or 'I don't have to; I'm going to be a singer.' How do you change that mindset? When girls of colour see themselves as only valued for the commodification of their bodies, how do we promote more than 'being sexy' as the way to get ahead?" People like Natasha are educating, mentoring and learning from girls in ways that allow girls to critique the messages they see and hear in the media.

One of the ways Natasha helps is by guiding girls to contextualize and acknowledge the discrimination around them. "When we look at Beyoncé, for example," she told us, "what does she use to market herself? Her long blond hair, her light skin. Girls see that and think, 'What are the expectations of me and how close can I get to being in that box?' Girls think, 'What do I have to do to achieve that ideal of beauty?'"

Natasha decodes these messages and names the racist assumptions. She invites the girls in her class to question and talk about why black bodies are expected to be made lighter skinned to be beautiful, and to think critically about how and why beauty products to lighten skin are marketed to racialized girls and women. "Even when you look at

Beyoncé," Natasha continued, "you see that when it comes to racialized women, black is still *exotique*."

Exoticism is the representation of one culture as consumable by another. It is rooted in the Western imperialist desire to consume the exotic non-Western "other." The term emerged in relation to the history of Western colonial consumption of non-Western art and culture, but it also describes the ongoing objectification of racialized women's bodies, casting them as props for sexualized fantasy and commodification. Nicki Minaj and Rihanna are both marketed by playing on sexual motifs, said Natasha, a fact that underlines just how often culture perpetuates the idea that racialized girls are valued for sexual desirability and sexual consumption.

However, there is a movement that is successfully gaining attention by calling out racist stereotypes in mainstream media. The 2013 edition of *Sports Illustrated*'s Swimsuit issue was criticized for featuring white models posing with "native locals" in China and Namibia, for example—who are depicted as exotic aids to the Western imagination. In an article that takes *Sports Illustrated* to task,[7] Professor David J. Leonard, from the Department of Critical Culture, Gender, and Race Studies at Washington State University–Pullman, is quoted saying, "Beyond functioning as props, as scenery to authenticate their third-world adventures, people of colour are imagined as servants, as the loyal helpers, as existing for white Western pleasure, amusement, and enjoyment."

On a recent MTV *Girl Code* episode,[8] the host, Nessa, who is a California native with Middle Eastern heritage, covered the topic of race and interracial dating. The episode defined exoticism and described the negative impacts of this form of aggression. It gave example comments like, "Hey, you're looking exotic, what is your ethnicity?" and explained how this implies that someone is an "outsider" and therefore doesn't belong. The MTV blogsite had twenty-three thousand likes and created a mainstream platform to get youth talking about microaggressions[9] and racist stereotypes. Girl-generated digital activism also took on racism with #NotYourAsianSidekick, a Twitter hashtag that went viral in 2013.

The movement provided a platform for Asian-American girls and women to call out their experiences of being "exoticized" and to name their experiences of being stereotyped as submissive, of facing sexism in their own cultures and of being marginalized in mainstream feminist conversations.[10]

Many of the girls we spoke to for this book—thanks to how they are mentored by peers, in arts and sports, or in classrooms—are able to decode racist stereotypes and then play an active role in transforming them by talking back and speaking out. But not every girl has the critical tools and support required in order to talk back safely. When educational systems fail to equip kids with media- and political-literacy skills, harmful stereotypes are perpetuated and can become internalized.

When Natasha's student Anthea called out how the media misrepresents girls, with few checks and balances, she gave us a great example of girls talking back. Natasha, though, is very aware of how hard it is to combat mainstream media messages when a deeper analysis of power structures is absent and oppressive constructions of race go unnoticed and unquestioned in popular culture. Girls are continually negotiating and often resisting external and internalized racism, sexism and classism, and resisting it at the same time. These are just some of the tensions and contradictions they live with.

SECOND STOP, NEW HAVEN

We left Toronto in evening traffic and drove south into New York State, and on to New Haven, Connecticut—home of Yale, the famous Ivy League college, and one of the wealthiest cities in America.[11]

Early the next morning, we set off to visit a high school in one of New Haven's wealthiest neighbourhoods. It was the last day of school before summer holidays, and when we arrived, there were squad cars stationed around the entrance and uniformed security guards patrolling the doors and the hallways. When we asked about this at reception, we were told that these are regular security measures. There were also metal detectors and scanners at every entrance, and active surveillance cameras throughout the building. We learned, too, that there is a daycare on the grounds so that teenage mothers can continue their education.

New Haven is a city with a small-town feel. The population is 122,000. There exists both extreme poverty and a lot of wealth. At this school, they told us, there is a visible divide between regular-level students who face economic challenges (and who are bused in from other areas of town), and the advanced-placement students, who are typically local, white and affluent. We could see this economic divide as we walked around the school and through its hallways.

On this last day of studies, six girls from Hispanic, Latina, African-American and Italian backgrounds stayed after their exams to have a party in their science classroom. They invited us in to share their pizza and chat about their school and life experiences. To get them started talking, we asked, "What do you feel is the difference between girls and boys?" Shy at first, they began to tell us a little about what their lives are like.

Manuela, a 15-year-old girl born in Mexico with long black hair and a luminous face, told us that she's always been taught that, unlike boys, girls look beautiful when they are quiet. "But I am not quiet," she said, and everyone laughed. Manuela is loud, vivacious, opinionated and very bright. When we asked how she deals with trying to be "beautiful" by being quiet, Manuela said that she stands up for herself sometimes but also finds it challenging. There are many of these kinds of contradictions in her life. She is told, mostly by her parents but also by the social codes of her peer group, to be the opposite of what she experiences as her authentic self. She gave us a touching example: "I keep my hair long even though it's a pain because my mom likes it long. She likes to brush it and treats me like her Barbie doll. It makes her happy, so I let her, because she's had a hard life." Manuela's family came from Mexico when she was a baby and there is a lot of pressure on her to do well at school so she can earn a scholarship to attend college, which her family can't afford otherwise. They are hoping she will get a job that will lift the family out of poverty. When we asked how she manages these combined pressures—to do well academically and also to be quiet—she said, "It's hard to be a girl."

Simona, 15 added, "People tend to underestimate us, they don't think we are as intelligent as males would be. They think we do a lot of sexual activity with boys when in fact it's not true."

Echoing what we heard in Toronto, Natalia, 14, told us that there are few realistic representations and role models for girls of colour in pop culture. "They just think we're ghetto and ratchet because we're black and Latina, no matter how many manners we have, no matter how polite we are."

Maya, a 15-year-old Latina girl, said, "Look at the people that TV shows and magazines and movies cast. They are all tall and skinny and white with perfect skin and no zits who have somehow already gone through puberty. That's not what real American high school girls look like."

These girls have plans for college and university. They want to be a veterinarian, a physical therapist, a teacher, a guidance counsellor and a forensic scientist. They play soccer, hang out with friends, talk on the phone, read and love books like *The Fault in Our Stars*. They don't go to many parties and if they do, their parents have a tight rein on where they go and with whom. A few of the girls expressed how they felt surrounded by people who care about them and they can talk to, while a few told us they felt isolated and it was difficult to find spaces to talk about their feelings and struggles.

When we asked them more about their school life, Marina, 15, said, "The girls here have fist fights that are bloodier and more vicious than the boys' fights." According to their teacher, "The boys' fights are all for show. You can pull them back and they will stop their fighting. The girls, they are in it for their pride. It often has to do with boys."

While on the topic of boys, the girls launched into details about what they have to put up with, and how they don't really feel respected by boys. "They treat us like we are lower than them," said Maya, "they don't treat us like we are human. They always talk about sexual things. They call us 'thots' ('that ho over there'). Boys act like we are worthless. If you have a big butt, they will go and smack your butt and say, 'Oh, you got a fatty,' or, 'Oh, you got the cake.' It's disrespectful. They go around touching girls' butts. They try to touch your boobs, they touch you inappropriately."

"They don't do it to me," Tynice, 15, interjected with enthusiasm. "They know better. If they say something, I go off. I will punch them in the face. They know not to mess with me."

This group told us how some of the girls live in neighbourhoods that can be unsafe. "There are lots of shootings," Manuela said. "Kids getting shot; parents, siblings and friends being killed. It's mostly gang-related shootings. There's also kidnapping, raping, girls getting killed, girls running away. There are a lot of little kids by themselves."

Sabrina, 15, feels angry about the multiple crossfires that she and her friends have to navigate every day. But she doesn't blame herself. She launched into a sober critique of the system at large: "Society has all this expectation for girls and the economy, when there is a real struggle to live, there is so much poverty and homelessness—we don't have people really thinking about other people. In the US, we are selfish. We are historically horrible. Basically, the conquerors who came here killed the Natives for their land and enslaved a whole other race [black people], then said, 'We're independent and free and equal,' and then they treat girls, women, immigrants, Latino and black Americans unequally, and they're not even American—'Oh, you are from a different country!' No one is American except Native Americans, who are definitely not treated equally."

Sabrina, also of Mexican heritage, showed us what we've seen in a lot of girls—that they are savvy and articulate about the world around them. Sabrina is part of a social justice book club and this is where she was able to discover and discuss these issues of American history that offered her both a broader political context for, and a deeper understanding of, her own life experience. When this history is not taught as part of mainstream education, many girls miss out on understanding the historical legacies that still inform their experiences of being overtly and covertly discriminated against and "othered." Race and racism are then internalized as individual problems without any context, which often leads girls to feel responsible both for being in their situation, and for having to get out of it.

When we met Dr. Nisha Sajnani at a café near the Yale campus after our visit with the girls, she gave us added perspective on the realities playing out in the school. Dr. Sajnani teaches mental health counselling at Lesley University in Cambridge, Massachusetts, and has worked with schools and students in New Haven. She told us that New Haven is a city characterized by elevated levels of economic and social distress. The secondary schools are challenged by high dropout rates, low standardized-test performance, and behavioural problems requiring significant disciplinary action. "Full-scale efforts are being made to address these problems," she explained, "but the daily stressors many children are exposed to at home, in their communities and in the city, add to the challenges facing the educational system. These include poverty, parental unemployment, racial prejudice, substance abuse, community and domestic violence and child maltreatment." Many of the students' day-to-day experiences constitute toxic levels of stress, which contributes to poor academic performance and can lead to challenges later in life.

Dr. Sajnani told us about a girl she calls Shae. Shae is 13 years old. Dr. Sajnani met her when the school administration referred Shae to a therapeutic theatre programme Dr. Sajnani created—not for fun but as an intervention: Shae was hanging around people known to recruit girls for prostitution. When she began working with Shae, Dr. Sajnani discovered that Shae had been sexually abused by an uncle who still lives with her family (Shae's mom is a single mother and the uncle is a source of financial support). Although Shae has developed strategies to avoid her uncle, his presence in her home means she is not safe. As a lot of teenagers do, Shae engages in sexual activity. She also gets into trouble at school because the administration suspects she is selling sex; this (discriminatory) assumption means that Shae is being fast-tracked toward criminalization.

"Recently, Shae was picked up and questioned at school by the police for possible prostitution on school grounds," Dr. Sajnani told us. "Even if this isn't true and she isn't engaging in the sex trade, it is a frequent occurrence that kids in this school are questioned by police. Now that

Shae's been picked up, she is starting to get stigmatized for it, which gives her a sense of not being liked. With Shae, we are dealing with the ripple effects in her behaviour of what has happened to her in her early life. This has everything to do with her negotiation of her own body and her authority as a person and her ability to make decisions in her own life—and how all of these have been compromised."

Hearing about what goes on behind the scenes for some of these girls as their economic realities take hold alongside the emergence of their young womanhood really illustrates the ways in which society fails them. Deep poverty and violence, such as what Shae is living, create conditions in which a girl's safety is compromised. How then, do we expect Shae, and the many girls whose experiences are similar to hers, to "lean in"?

THE SCHOOL-TO-PRISON PIPELINE

We wandered across the street to sit in the sun, and talked with Dr. Sajnani about how in America, as it is with Indigenous girls in Canada, racialized girls are over-represented in the juvenile system, and these numbers are increasing. In the United States, black girls are suspended six times more often than white girls, while black boys are suspended three times more often than white boys.[12] Girls who are suspended face a greater risk of dropping out of school. They are also more likely to face underemployment, low wages and contact with law enforcement. On the boys' side, harsh disciplinary policies are a well-known risk factor, and a good deal of research has been dedicated to understanding the school-to-prison pipeline.[13] As for the girls? The number who are facing trouble in school is increasing, yet there is precious little research that examines the intersection of race, class and gender. The result is a lack of understanding about the inequities that girls of colour face.

A 2014 report published by the African American Policy Forum and the Center for Intersectionality and Social Policy Studies set out to fill this gap. *Black Girls Matter: Pushed Out, Overpoliced and Underprotected*[14] investigates the unique challenges and experiences of black girls in the school system. Black girls, it seems, deal with specific factors that push them out of school, including criminalization, stereotypes and sexual assault. They feel undervalued in their academic achievements. They are punished much more severely, frequently and in disproportionate measure to their behaviour, than are their peers. The sexual harassment, bullying, criminalization, punitive measures, trauma and violence they often deal with in their everyday lives spill over and impact their sense of security and safety at school. The report makes several recommendations, including providing equitable funding to support girls as well as boys, revising policies that funnel girls into the juvenile justice system and creating responsive programmes for girls that take experiences of trauma and victimization into account.

In *Race, Gender and the School-to-Prison Pipeline*, a report from 2012, Monique W. Morris, Ed.D., writes that punishment for these girls comes directly out of "their fight to be seen in a world that does not favour black girls who speak their minds, and raise their voices to be heard." While the in-school behaviours that get black boys punished tend to be associated with perceived threats to public safety, Morris states that, for girls, punishable behaviours are related to stereotypes of a perceived moral deficit, or their non-conformity with notions of white middle-class femininity.[15] For example, black girls are penalized for the way they dress, the way they talk, any confrontation with authority and any profanity they may display in the classroom. This research suggests that black girls are being criminalized "for qualities that have been associated with their survival as black females"—their ability, for instance, to defend themselves verbally and, if necessary, physically.[16]

Dr. Sajnani has seen this dynamic at work in New Haven. "A lot of these kids are survivors of trauma," she said, "and punitive responses to racialized girls do not take this history into account. If somebody goes through a difficult event, it changes the way they see themselves, the world around them and their relationships. Their world is no longer safe, the people around them are no longer safe, so they operate from this supposition."

From a clinical point of view, she told us, you could call this response a cognitive impairment—this person is now seeing everything through a lens. "They think, 'I'm skeptical of you, especially skeptical of authority dynamics, because it's usually always a person of power who has hurt me,'" she told us. "The kids will operate from this position, they think, 'I am going to do what I need to do to stabilize myself.' This can be a ritual that they participate in like cutting, isolating or medicating themselves, or in public displays of emotion. A defence could also be in the way they dress, the way they speak to their teachers and parents and the police if they are involved, and the way they take out their anger among their peers."

Dr. Sajnani gave us a fictional example based on things she has seen in her work. "Imagine there are kids in a classroom," she told us, "and one of them gets out of a chair, and some other kid sits in her seat. She comes back and says, 'Get the fuck out of my seat!' The other girl says, 'Just sit over there, it's no big deal,' but the angry girl shouts, 'No, I'm not going to sit over there. Get the fuck out of my seat!' The reaction is potentially elevated by past experiences of displacement and reflects the inner turmoil experienced by the angry girl. [But] what is going to happen is that a teacher will come with a control action—'You need to leave the classroom; your behaviour is not appropriate.' Or, 'Just sit down. What's wrong with you? You are not behaving right.'"

Given the current preference for zero-tolerance responses in these kinds of situations, the reaction will most likely be that the teacher will call the security guard in the school. The cops will arrive, and the girl will be handcuffed and taken into custody. "The simplest incidents like this can start a lifetime of prison sentences for a vulnerable girl," said Dr. Sajnani.

This calling in of authorities is an illustration of the zero-tolerance policy that North American schools are using as their prime disciplinary measure. So seriously is this being taken that there are cases in the United States of zero-tolerance responses with five- and six-year-old African-American girls. In April 2012, for example, a six-year-old black girl had a temper tantrum in a Georgia kindergarten classroom. She was removed from her classroom, handcuffed and dragged out to the police station in front of all the other children and staff, and suspended for the rest of the school year.[17] In 2007, in Florida, a five-year-old black girl was arrested and led out of her kindergarten classroom in handcuffs for having a similar tantrum.[18] In 2014, a 12-year-old in Georgia was caught writing the word "hi" on a locker room wall; she faced expulsion and criminal charges while a white female classmate who was also involved faced a much less severe punishment.[19]

So where does all of this escalation leave us? If girls in schools like the one in New Haven have strong voices, and justified strong reactions to unfair treatment, is there a way these voices and reactions could be supported and transformed into a source of power rather than criminalized and punished? As it turns out, Dr. Sajnani has been trying to do just that.

WORKING UPSTREAM:
RESTORATIVE AND TRAUMA-INFORMED RESPONSES

As we sat together at the cafe, Dr. Sajnani explained her alternative to an escalated response. She co-created a trauma-informed, combined theatre and civics curriculum programme called Animating Learning by Integrating and Validating Experience (ALIVE) that has been used by several schools in the New Haven public school system. Rather than call in the police, a trauma-informed approach focuses on what has happened in kids' lives. "You can ask a very simple but still somewhat radical question like, 'What happened?' or 'Has this ever happened before?'"

Trauma is rooted in experiences of loss, abuse and neglect. There are also collective traumas like slavery, racism, homophobia, human rights abuses and attendance at residential schools. The students in New Haven's school populations experience trauma because of racism, sexual abuse and losing loved ones to gang warfare and other forms of violence, which leave them in states of fear and mourning.

Dr. Sajnani described the way simple incidents can be managed effectively with her method.[20] "We treat kids who act out with the idea that we can help them see that not every relationship will be a direct re-enactment of the initial traumatic events. We find out what else is going on that is getting them so upset. Rather than discipline them or call the police, the teacher or a counsellor in, in this approach you could say something like, 'Wow, that was pretty upsetting. What about all those other times your spot was taken?' Then, if they feel safe, they may go into the other times in their lives when their place was taken, their agency was taken, their body was violated, they were neglected, removed from their home, or worse.

"This helps kids to tell the difference between the original trauma and the current situation, which allows them to stay present with their teachers, the group, the class and their whole school environment," she continued. "You can't get there by cognitive force alone. There are some physiological techniques—things like focused breathing, counting, known methods of calming the system—that then open up to the thinking piece, the analytical piece, where in this case the girl whose seat was taken can disassociate her feelings from the current event and see it more clearly and in a less traumatic light. This restores functioning or decreases distress but also gets at deeper healing."

The assistant principal at the New Haven school, Ann Brillante, is successfully using ALIVE's trauma-informed methods in the classroom. "Suspension and criminalizing of student behaviour is not something I do," she explained when she joined us. "We want students to want to come to school, to be engaged and to learn. I learned very quickly that wielding power over students doesn't help kids to become confident learners."

For the past year, Ann has also been mobilizing restorative justice methods in the school.[21] She believes this approach has allowed teachers and students to redefine the power dynamic and foster more engaging relationships. "Kids feel safe and supported with this approach," Ann explained. "It creates a space for them to talk about what happened. They can acknowledge who they harmed and, if they have been harmed, imagine what possible outcomes could make it right. What usually happens is a new understanding. The student realizes, 'Okay, so my teacher didn't mean to hurt me,' and once the teacher understands the circumstances behind the student's lashing out, they are like, 'It makes sense that this happened and I don't have to take their reaction personally.'"

What Dr. Sajnani and Ann Brillante are demonstrating is that alternatives to escalation do exist. Trauma-informed and restorative approaches give teachers more tools to deal with scenarios where they find themselves viewed as "the face" of the trauma. They are then able to see that the incident is not about challenging their authority, but rather finding new ways to move forward that are constructive and positive—where everybody wins.

After just one year of the ALIVE trauma-informed approach, this New Haven school has jumped to a 95 percent passing rate and the suspension rate has lowered to 7 percent. "The important thing is finding enough adults who understand how to work with kids in this way," Ann concluded, "to surround them and attend to them before behaviours escalate."

THE ROLE OF CARING ADULTS

As Natasha Burford told us in Toronto, and as we heard again from Ann Brillante and Dr. Nisha Sajnani in New Haven, the number-one contributing factor to resilience in teenage kids is an adult who can pull them up, build their trust and "have their back." Natasha is a strong advocate of mentorship in general because there is a lack of responsive supports for racialized girls. So many of these girls fall through the cracks in destructive and hard ways, she told us. "There is more violence around girls and women than ever, and this increase is accompanied by pop culture messages that tell girls of colour that their only value is in sexual objectification and commodification of their bodies. How do they deal with this without systems of support? Girls who overcome these barriers will all tell you that there was somebody important in their lives who mentored them. People don't always share how they made it; they sometimes forget to say, 'I actually did get help.'

"When I work with young women, I see that there is confidence there," she continued. "Our girls are confident, resilient and keen to be out in the world involving themselves, not being afraid to learn. Young black women have that ability to bounce back. They just need someone to encourage them and be there for them as they do it." In fact, according to the Girl Scout Research Institute in the US, African-American and Hispanic girls have higher leadership aspirations than white girls. In their recent nation-wide study, *Change It Up! What Girls Say About Redefining Leadership*, they found that, "African-American and Hispanic girls were more likely than Caucasian and Asian-American girls to view themselves as leaders. Also, African-American and Hispanic girls aspired to leadership more than Caucasian girls and had more frequent and more positive leadership experiences. In addition, they rated themselves higher than Caucasian girls on key leadership indicators such as overall self-confidence and quali-ties such as creativity, caring, and problem-solving."[22]

Natasha understands that working with youth in an effective way requires special tools, including the willingness to put adult-centric views aside. "Sometimes we, as adults, want to lead and teach youth, but we know that doesn't always work," she explained. "The girls might memo-rize and regurgitate curriculum, but they don't really learn. We need to learn with and from girls, so that their experience and expertise is valued and engaged. It is by not being afraid to fail, by asking questions and by allowing girls to lead," said Natasha, "that we can support them to be empowered in their learning."

We spoke to SooJin Pate, a professor and educator in Minneapolis, Minnesota, about this same topic. "I exercise my passion for change through education," she told us, "my picket line is a classroom." It was during her studies in graduate school that she woke up to the transforma-tive power of education. "The classroom can be a site of colonization, but it can also be a site of decolonization. I chose the latter." She explained how people of colour are not used to experiencing institutions as a place *for* them; they don't see themselves reflected in the material they learn. As a way to counteract this, her curriculum holds the lives of her students at its centre: "I start every class with an assignment about identity. 'Who are you and where are you from?' I do this because it's important for me to have my students realize that their identities matter in my classroom and that their experiences hold certain kinds of knowledge that we need in order to make our world a better place. It's imperative to me that my students leave my classroom realizing that they are knowledge producers. So my classroom becomes an alternative space of learning where they have the power to not only receive but also *produce* knowledge. And with that production of alternative knowledge, they can shape the world and transform minds. When my students realize, 'Oh my goodness! My experience, my opinions matter; my history counts,' they become much more invested in their education and their learning takes off. They're able to see that participating in the production of knowledge is a very powerful act. They get to define and determine for themselves what is valid, what is credible and what constitutes their past, present and future. Inevitably, they begin to see themselves as agents rather than victims of history. Knowledge truly is power!"

When students take ownership of their own education, they begin to show a confidence that is both contagious and empowering. "They realize that, 'Yes, maybe this space wasn't originally made for me, but I have a say in what matters *now*,'" said SooJin. "And once they realize their own individual agency, a shift in consciousness happens where they begin to think about their connection to their ancestors and to their larger community. They become eager to pass on their learning in the hopes of raising the consciousness of others. The students who commit to decolonizing their minds are the very students who think about the larger picture, about giving back and about serving their community in ways that bring about healing and social transformation [not just for themselves but for others, too]."

SooJin also sees girls leading the way and taking up the larger social issues of the day because, oftentimes, they are the ones most harmed by these issues and policies, which are usually created by men in power. "We, the community, know how to heal ourselves better than anyone else, better than any outsider with a PhD or an MD. But we don't make the policies. Matter of fact, we're not even consulted most of the time," she said. That is why she emphasizes the importance of cultivating self-care and self-love in her teachings. "Girls are socialized early on to take care of everyone else. The moment they begin to think about taking care of their own self, they are branded as being selfish." It was reading Audre

Lorde's *Sister Outsider* that made SooJin realize that self-care is neither selfish nor a luxury, but rather but a necessity, "if women of colour are to live out their full potential. Not only is it a necessity, but Lorde goes on to say that self-care is a radical act because the systems and institutions we live in aren't designed for people of colour. In fact, they are designed to harm and destroy our lives in various ways. So the very fact of our survival is revolutionary. Taking care of myself becomes truly radical in this context. And I teach my students, especially my female students, just how imperative it is for them to love and take care of themselves."

SooJin talked about how children intuitively know what they need and how important it is to nurture this self-awareness early on rather than obstructing it or closing it down. She explained that practising self-care means asking for what you need and taking the space you need. "Ask yourself, 'What makes me feel good about myself? What feeds my body, spirit and soul?'" she said. "Make a list based on your answers. Carry it with you because when we're down, it's easy to forget about the things that nurture us, and we end up making unhealthy choices."

SooJin also stressed that taking care of yourself means being open to receiving other kinds of knowledge, like the knowledge that resides in your body. "Our bodies are constantly communicating [with] us. Instead of ignoring or suppressing the messages we receive from our bodies, we need to learn to listen, and respect their limits." SooJin added that expressing your emotions and not feeling ashamed of how you feel is also a crucial act of self-care: "I don't know how many times I've heard girls apologize for the tears that bubble up when they talk about a particularly painful event. When this happens, I tell them what I tell my eight-year-old daughter: 'It's healthy to cry. It's your body's natural response to feeling something intensely. Let it out. Let it all out. Your body still needs to process the pain, and crying is its way of releasing it. So let the tears flow, baby.'"

In all kinds of ways, adults can play an important role in girls' lives by being an ally. We can practise self-care and teach it to others. We can take action when we see that someone is facing discrimination, and we can speak out against hurtful or inappropriate comments or conduct when we witness them. An ally supports the rights of marginalized people, and actively reflects on discrimination and marginalization, and how these relate to privilege. We can all practise how to unlearn our own biases, and respond to and intervene in stereotyping, discrimination and harassment.

Pointing out and opposing racism and the clichés of "normative behaviour" that discriminate against racialized communities can take many forms. Eighteen-year-old Kyemah McEntyre of East Orange, New Jersey, spoke out in June 2015 via her prom dress, a stunning, vibrant, red floor-length dress inspired by traditional African prints. She designed it herself after a long history of being bullied about her ethnicity and her "anger." The photo she took of herself wearing the dress—with goddess-like neck and headpiece—was sent out into digital world with the tag, "I'm Kyemah McEntyre, I am 18-years old and I am undoubtedly of African Descent."[23] The photo went viral, which allowed her thoughts to go viral, too. On Instagram, Kyemah explained, "We stunt our collective spiritual growth by allowing assumptions and stereotypes to cloud our mind and thus our physical reality. We let these negative ideas get the best of us, and in turn a world of isolation is manifested by our lack of sensitivity and desire to sympathize with each other. I would like to take this moment to say that you have to understand who you are because if you leave that space open, you leave your identity in the hands of society. Don't let anyone define you. Beautiful things happen when you take pride in yourself. #blackgirlsrock #kyebreaktheinternet." Kyemah's dress and her message struck a powerful chord: she was crowned prom queen and, more important, got her class, her school, her community and the world talking about racialized bullying and black pride.

The supportive peers and caring adults who work with girls on their terms make a difference in girls' lives, and by association, in the lives of others. There are a few caring adults in every chapter of this book, who have opened doors for the girls whose voices we have documented here. Having the support of adults can also arm girls with the kind of assertiveness and self-love that can transform them from victims of a flawed system to transformers of that system.

ALL GIRLS ARE NOT ALIKE

On the long drive home to Montreal, we thought about Natasha's grade-eight class in Toronto and the girls we ate pizza with at the New Haven school in Connecticut. Our "school trip" had shown us how incredibly varied girls' lives are today. To spice up the miles of highway ahead of us, we took turns driving and reading out some of the anonymous replies we received to our online survey that asked, "Who are you?":

- I'm a black girl, straight, who loves art, music, films and travel.
- I identify as a straight, white girl but not one who drinks.
- I am a 21-year-old girl, self-identified member of the Mi'kmaq community.
- I am a black girl. Afro-Caribbean.
- I am a girl in grade 9. My favourite colour is green, I like to read and write.
- I'm a brown (Indian) girl.
- I'm a white girl from France, middle class, hetero.
- I'm North American, biracial, upper-middle class, culturally fluid, strong.
- I'm Asian, white personality, social norm.
- I'm an atheist with Jewish culture, female, pansexual, generalized anxiety disorder.
- I'm Black, African, Ugandan, queer, awesome.
- I'm a Native bisexual.
- I'm white with blue hair.
- I'm a Lebanese tan girl who loves music.
- I'm mixed Persian and Hispanic. Black hair, brown eyes, 5'4".

As these self-identities illustrate, and as the girls we met for this book corroborate, girls can't simply be divided into those whose success is achieved thanks to effort or good choices, and a minority who fail and need to be "fixed." The impact of material resources, cultural capital and racism is erased in the faux philosophy of "opportunity for those who work hard." If we don't take these structural issues into account, we make a lot of girls invisible.

Girls are not a monolithic group. When we listen to the many voices that define girls' reality, we expand the narrative and include more girls. The gender divide has historically been defined in terms of male and female. However, those on the front lines of social justice, along with leading thinkers in black and Indigenous feminism—like Angela Davis, bell hooks, and Patricia Hill Collins—recognize that girls' experiences are deeply affected by intersecting aspects of identity, such as race, class, ability and sexual identity. In order to care for girls and to respond to girls, we need to understand their diverse cultural contexts and consider the realities of poverty, violence and racism that impact the daily lives of so many of them.

What would the world look like if all girls had access to resources and support? Imagine if all girls were free to contribute their gifts to the world? We've observed determination and resilience in the girls we've met—many of them, privileged or not, are ready to take up the challenge of leadership. If we are serious about supporting their leadership in communities, boardrooms, C-suites and politics, we will have to work harder to acknowledge and respond to their true realities, and, in the process, provide the tools they need to flourish.

Like the "Lean In" proponents, we want to encourage girls and young women to grow past limitations, to be more assertive and to take on positions of influence. But if we truly aim to empower *all* girls, we need to keep our eyes on the ball of broader systemic change. When, as a society, we take responsibility for the many systems that have an impact on girls' lives, and shift the old models to accommodate them, we will then have created conditions in which *all* girls can achieve their greatest potential.

SURVIVAL KIT

THINK CRITICALLY about the stories being told about girls in the media. Ask girls if they can relate to these stories, and talk about their experiences. Do they agree or disagree with what's being said? How does this make them feel and think? Do they feel included or excluded in their own lives? Read media headlines with girls and reflect on them: Why are white girls in the news more often than girls of colour? Who does this serve? Whose voices are privileged? Whose voices are missing?

SUPPORT MEDIA that tell real stories by real girls. Support girls and young women in becoming the storytellers across the media they are interested in: writing, video or the arts. A good example of the power of storytelling is found in Belissa Escobedo, Rhiannon McGavin and Zariya Allen's performance of "Somewhere in America" in front of thousands in America. The young women are part of the LA-based non-profit Get Lit.

SEE THE BIGGER PICTURE. Recognize that racism and poverty are the most important factors contributing to criminalization. Challenge assumptions and be a part of the solution; take a stand against stereotypes that perpetuate discrimination.

SUPPORT KIDS to understand and name racist, sexist and homophobic violence, and then support appropriate responses when these types of violence happen. When we ignore the systemic structures of violence, we give permission for their continued existence.

LEARN MORE AND ENGAGE in anti-racist movements led by young women

- Read content at these Twitter hashtags: #BlackGirlsMatter, #solidarityisforwhitewomen, and #BlackLivesMatter
- Watch Asha Rosa's inspiring TED Talk on Mass Incarceration in the US at: https://www.youtube.com/watch?v=x-IntDWD1hA

- Follow Charlene Carruthers, national director of Black Youth Project 100 at: http://byp100.org/about/
- Follow Franchesca Ramsey, activist, actress and host of *MTV Decoded* @chescaleigh

ADVOCATE FOR TRAUMA-INFORMED, culturally relevant and gender-responsive integration into schools and systems of care; juvenile and foster care systems. For information and resources go to:

www.justiceforgirls.org (Canada)
www.centerforgenderandjustice.org (US)
The ALIVE programme: traumainformedschools.org

SUPPORT GIRLS' LEADERSHIP. Read *The Resilience Factor: A Key to Leadership in African American and Hispanic Girls.* www.girlscouts.org/content /dam/girlscouts-gsusa/forms-and-documents/about-girl-scouts/research/ resilience_factor.pdf

LEARN TO BE AN ALLY. An ally supports the rights of marginalized people, acts when individuals face discrimination and speaks out against hurtful and inappropriate comments or conducts.

1. Learn about stereotypes, prejudice, discrimination and the barriers facing marginalized communities.
2. Reflect on discrimination, marginalization, and privilege.
3. Practice how to unlearn your own biases, and respond to/interrupt stereotyping, discrimination and harassment.
4. There are lots of resources on allyship. To get started, check out our friend Chelby Marie Daigle's blog and her suggested 'ways to be an ally' tips here: https://chelbydaigle.wordpress.com/2015/03/17 /how-to-be-an-ally/

TAP INTO GIRL-POSITIVE WEBSITES

www.blackgirldangerous.org
blackgirlnerds.com
www.blackgirlscode.com

CHECK OUT the Radical Monarchs. This group, creates opportunities for young girls of colour to form a fierce sisterhood, celebrate their cultures and contribute radically to their communities: Find them at http://radicalmonarchs.org/.

SELF-CARE TIPS FROM SOOJIN PATE

1. Ask for what you need and take the space you need.
2. Make a self-care list and keep it handy.
3. When a child or a teen needs to cry, don't tell them to stop. If you need to cry, don't stop yourself. Crying is your body's natural way of letting what needs to come out, out; do it as long as you need to.
4. We encourage the self-care process in ourselves and others by not shaming ourselves or each other for expressing what is needed.
5. Listen to your body. Your body holds so much valuable information. Listen to the physical cues.
6. Do these things daily—don't wait till you're down!

For more tips, check out SooJin's article on the radical politics of self-love and self-care: www.thefeministwire.com/2014/04/self-love-and-self-care

TWERKING IN DETROIT:
NAMING THE UNNAMED, PART 1

AS WE FLEW INTO DETROIT, we were doing a bit of research. The media students we'd met in Los Angeles had mentioned a news article about disturbing e-mails from students at Georgia Tech college in Atlanta.[1] We found a CNN news report on the story: "An e-mail from a Georgia Tech fraternity member to his Phi Kappa Tau brothers came to light this week. It was about how to 'succeed at parties,' or more specifically 'luring your rapebait.' It came with repulsively detailed instructions about how to scope out a target, weaken her defenses with alcohol, grab her and—you get the idea."[2] It was distressing to read another headline pointing to the normalization of sexual violence in North America. How is it that we live in a culture where this level of violence against women persists?

With this on our minds, we met with a number of high school girls in Detroit. Many of them told us that sexual harassment and other forms of sexual aggression and unwanted attention are part of their everyday school lives—a refrain we'd heard at every stop on our tour. Based on their personal experiences, girls are telling us—loud and clear—that sexual violence still exists in epidemic numbers. The statistics bear this out: one in four North American women will experience violence by a partner at some point in her life.[3] Fifty-six percent of American high school girls experience sexual harassment.[4] In Canada, forty-six percent of high school girls report being the target of unwanted sexual comments or gestures.[5] But despite the fact that harassment and sexual violence are happening consistently and relentlessly, and that it makes girls uncomfortable and unhappy, our discussions with girls across North America revealed an astonishing fact: it turns out that neither girls nor boys have the language to name it and many fail to recognize it as sexual harassment when it happens. Instead, sexual harassment is largely understood to be a normal part of their lives.

In Detroit, we hung out with high-performing athletes and heard about how volleyball fulfills their passion and opens doors to their aspirations for the future. They told us about social media, gave us twerking lessons and demos and had a great time exploring issues of pleasure and desire. But our fun and lively conversations took a serious turn when the topic dove into boys and power and where and when girls don't feel respected. Being in Detroit, we were aware that it would be all too easy to stereotype inner-city black girls who are steeped in hip hop culture as poster-child victims of sexual violence. But the girls we spoke to here—just like the ones in Whitehorse and LA and everywhere else we travelled—are living complex lives, and they all have one thing in common: they are undeniably contending with sexualized violence on a regular basis.

NAVIGATING SEX, POWER AND AGENCY

Detroit is a city in the midst of being reborn. Decades of economic challenges have led to a drastic decrease in population, high unemployment rates, high crime rates and an average household income of less than half the national average.[6] This social and economic devastation has reached a tipping point, making room for opportunity and creativity in a dynamic city struggling to rebuild. The city's 2013 bankruptcy claim fostered a lively entrepreneurial culture that is incubating start-ups, experimental business models and community-led initiatives.

It was amid this exciting air of renewal that we met with Michele Lewis Watts, volleyball coach to a group of local girls who are transitioning, too—from girlhood into young adulthood, in an atmosphere where creativity embraces change. We visited these girls during their school gym classes and, on our first night, spent a fun few hours with them during volleyball practice at a downtown community youth centre.

We sat on the bleachers and watched the girls practise—diving for balls, smashing them over the net and high-fiving each other. Michele was playing *and* coaching, chiming in with positive feedback as she volleyed and bumped. There was a lot of energy on the court. Some girls were getting frustrated and hitting the ball too hard. Others were noisy. All of them were sweating. They talked strategy, and we could hear Michele blending advice about personal development along with strength-training tips and game tactics. The girls readily soaked up her wisdom and experience.

When the practice was over, the youth centre manager gave us a room beside the gym where we could talk quietly with a few girls who wanted to stay and chat. We laid out early dinners of salads, smoothies, cheese, chips, fruit and candies. Mula (14), Agnes (15), Solange (13), Daria (13), Chivonn (14) and Oriana (14) sat with us around the table. They picked at the food, and were shy at first. But when we asked what they gained from playing volleyball, they told us how the sport is their community; it's an important part of their lives. They were all really good players— highly competitive and very committed. Some explained how volley-ball keeps them busy and out of trouble, or from being bored. It gives them confidence, too, they told us, and it relieves stress and keeps them focused on academic achievement. The girls explained that they all come from different schools and different backgrounds; the volleyball team is their second family, and Michele a surrogate big sister.

The girls also talked about Detroit. It is teeming with entrepreneurial energy and they feel both the opportunity and the ongoing pressures of needing to make something of themselves. They talked about the many expectations they feel—from pressure about their self-image to body pressure, social pressure, performance pressure in school and volleyball, and boy pressure.

It wasn't long before the topic turned to relationships and romance. The girls shared entertaining stories about parties, and talked about navigating power in relationships. There was lots of sex talk, but when we brought the discussion around to actual sexual activity, they admit-ted that they hadn't really done much.

"My mom says she knows it's going to happen, so she prepares herself for it," said Daria, assuring us that her mother prepares her for it, too.

"My mom tells me to make sure you are ready mentally and physically," said Mula. "A lot of stuff comes after [you start having sex], like is he going to talk to you again? What's going to be different? Will he treat you the same? Will you be in a relationship?"

"That's why people have bad breakups," said Oriana. "It's because mentally they aren't ready. You have to be prepared. The boy is going to talk. He will tell his friends. Everyone is going to know."

"If you don't want people to know, why would you do it [have sex]?" asked Agnes.

"The reason people do it is because the more boys you have, the more popular you are, because the more experience you have," Solange declared.

"Yeah, but boys, they brag about it, they compare one girl with another girl," complained Daria.

"It's like boys think they can do whatever they want to boost their ego," Chivonn told us.

"Giving him sex and friendship will keep him, but he still won't appreciate it," said Oriana. "He's gonna cheat. Most girls are hurt after they find out he is cheating, they think, 'I'm not enough for you.'"

It was interesting to hear, from a girl's perspective, about the pressures and assumptions inherent in monogamy—the unwritten dating script, the double standard, the hopes and expectations of commitment, exclusivity and friendship from a guy. When they told us about the strategies and decisions they use to keep a guy's interest and avoid feeling used or getting hurt, we asked them where they thought girls could assume more power in their choices and decisions.

"Some girls have sex for love," Mula said, almost quietly.

"But boys like to collect trophies," concluded Agnes.

"Boys think that they have to have power," said Oriana.

"I think it's all about sex," said Chivonn. "Some men act like boys. Boys mature slower, girls mature faster. I wish they would understand how girls feel," Oriana concluded.

"People think I'm sexually active because I have a big butt, but I just like to eat," added Daria, revealing that many teens believe sex makes your bum muscles bigger.

"Boys want girls with big butts and big boobs," added Agnes. "They want medium-size thighs, big butt, small waist and big boobs. How is that possible? It would look weird on me. I've been this size my whole life."

"Girls look up to people [popular and famous role models] like Kash Doll," Oriana offered. "She had a butt shot, so her butt isn't real. She got illegal butt surgery to look like Nicki Minaj."

"I gave up trying to grow boobs. I just stopped!" Oriana added, and we laughed, pretty sure that she was happy in her body.

"Some girls have sex because they think their bodies will look better," ventured Mula.

"Some girls just like doing it!" said Solange, telling us about a friend of theirs who is self-assured in her desire for and enjoyment of sex. "She just owns it and she doesn't care." Solange said this with admiration in her voice, but they all looked at one another quizzically.

Solange noticed her friends' confusion and shared a personal experience of hooking up. There is an assumption that "hook up" automatically means sex, but Solange clarified that for a lot of girls, "hooking up is going out, chilling and cuddling; it's not always about sex. Maybe it's kissing and maybe it's more." Solange said that hooking up is fun for her, and she seeks it out with boys who have a higher level of maturity than the boys her age.

"I feel like I have power if I decide I have power," she declared. The other girls agreed, and told us that whether they were in a monogamous relationship or not, they felt strongly about making choices for themselves.

We asked if there was a lot of pressure to conform to heterosexual and heteronormative codes. "I think it depends," Oriana said. "At my school we have a lot of lesbians. I have bi friends."

That's when Mula said she had a confession to make. "Actually," she said, with a grin, "I have a girlfriend." She hadn't told anyone else yet.

"We started talking in November and dating in December. It's not that I want to be with a girl. It's just that I met her and started talking to her—and I just like her. I want to be with her. She makes me smile."

Mula told us that people at her school suspect that she and her girlfriend are a couple and they seem chill about it. The girls who were with us were happy for her and said it's okay to be bi, especially because boys "like it." Mula made it clear that she isn't in her relationship to interest boys, but we talked about how videos like Shakira and Rihanna's hugely popular "Can't Remember to Forget You" portray same-sex attraction as a male fantasy. We talked over how pop and porn culture message that it's cool to be gay if you're a girl, but only if it's to turn on a guy. We asked them if they thought this kept us all stuck in a time warp, still hanging on to a world in which the hetero male gaze rules the world.

They talked about this in the context of their school lives and mentioned that their schools do raise awareness about homophobia and try to create environments where kids can "come out" and be open about their sexual identity and preferences. They shared that Gay-Straight Alliance clubs and anti-homophobic campaigns are reaching more communities through social media. When it comes to sex ed, though, they told us that they get the condom demonstration, but nothing about any of the things they see through porn, or anything about safe sex between girls.

To get to know more about the power dynamics in their sexual relationships, we asked those who are sexually active if they were able to ask for what they wanted from their partner. They responded with an absolute yes, but when we asked them if they experienced pleasure, we were met with silence. After a bit of prompting, they revealed that they don't actually have sex, and they don't have orgasms, either. We weren't surprised, knowing that most girls are not having sex at this age, in their early teens, and certainly not having sex in the ways media portrays and fears.

We smiled at their chutzpah and initiated a Girl Pleasure 101 discussion. We explained what an orgasm is and encouraged them to go home, learn how to masturbate and practise. There were lots of giggles at first, but their curiosity quickly gave way to questions: "How do you masturbate?" "How do you have an orgasm?" "Where is the clitoris?" We gave them an anatomy lesson, saying that it's normal for girls to have these questions and concerns and telling them that bodies respond differently to sexual stimulation. We encouraged them to get to know their own bodies and told them how important it is to find out what makes them feel good so they are able to eventually ask for those things from their partners. We talked about the fact that while girls might know better how to please each other, many guys do want to give pleasure to a girl but may not know how. When sex includes a girl's pleasure, we stressed, it equalizes the power dynamics.

Daria spoke about her English class, and how her teacher talks about girls' empowerment. "We are reading Shakespeare and discussing how women's roles were dictated by society," she said, and then mentioned Beyoncé's song "Flawless" and the TED Talk, "We Should All Be Feminists" that features writer Chimamanda Ngozi Adichie. She looked it up on her iPhone and read a few lines from the speech for us:

> "We raise girls to see each other as competitors—
> not for jobs or for accomplishments,
> which I think can be a good thing,
> but for the attention of men.
> We teach girls that they cannot be sexual beings
> in the way that boys are.
> Feminist: the person who believes in the social,
> political and economic equality of the sexes."[7]

"Everyone is talking about how Beyoncé's songs are so sexual—but why can't she be sexual and feminist?" Agnes wondered. "People say it's the way it is, but why? I like this song; it makes people think." Like the girls in LA and elsewhere, the girls in Detroit navigate the contradiction of reinforcing stereotypes and enacting sexual empowerment.

By now, the girls were playing the song on their iPods and singing along, which got them talking about having fun and dancing. "There are more dances now than when we were younger," said Oriana. "It's really great. We do the Hustle, the Cupid Shuffle, the Electric Slide, the

Nae Nae, the Yeek and the Two-Step." They showed us how to "do the circle." Agnes put her phone playlist on speaker and showed us her twerk moves. The other girls got up, too, and dared us to give it a shot. Daria put her hands on our hips and coached—"No, like this"— trying to get us to feel what really happens when your butt vibrates. It was a memorable evening!

SPORTS AND SOCIAL INNOVATION

Michele picked us up at our hotel the next day and drove us to meet the girls at one of the schools where she coaches. She took us through the downtown core, across 6 Mile Road into the neighbourhood where the school was located. She told us about 8 Mile, where Eminem grew up and wrote some of his best songs, and how until recently people living on either side of 8 Mile Road didn't ever cross the line between the two communities. It's the mental and physical divide between the suburbs and the city, and the racial divide between the white and black communities. We drove by lots of vacant homes, and past Michele's in-laws' house. As she drove, she told us that she sees the girls several nights a week and on weekends, too, and often drives her teams to tournaments across the state and even out of state. She does this hoping to give them the best possible chance to show their talents and potentially be scouted by colleges so that they can get the scholarships they will need in order to have access to higher education.

Michele, who is completing her own PhD on girls and sports, believes it's important to offer girls more than just academic help. Her dream is to expand her volleyball coaching into a programme that also builds economic and business skills. On the surface, it seems as if Detroit is a perfect place to do this. Social innovation and enterprise are thriving here, with city-wide workshops and a new Detroit Social Enterprise Alliance community. But there's a catch. "There are a lot of non-profits in Detroit," Michele told us. "When the Big Three car manufacturers stopped giving [monetary donations], non-profit organizations were scrambling." These days, it's a challenge to get funding for programmes, and Michele finds it hard to continually go out and ask for money. She worked with the Michigan Women's Foundation and, through them, was introduced to the field of entrepreneurship. "Black women make sixty-four cents for every dollar a man makes," she told us. In a city like Detroit, which is open to change and where new businesses are just starting to grow, it can be valuable for girls to learn how to start their own businesses and be the boss. "I want to help girls figure out what they want to be good at," Michele said. "If I can provide them with business tools and make them competitive, this will give them an edge in this new market."

Michele believes that sports for girls are crucial as part of this skill development. "Through coaching, I've found my way into the girls' space," she told us. "I see who they are and what they are up against, and I can give them a lot there. *I* grew up feeling strong, feeling comfortable with my body. This came from sports. I don't see a lot of girls walking around comfortably. I want to see what playing sports can do for them."

We stopped at a café and continued to talk over breakfast. "I coach girls differently than I coach boys," Michele said. "I always have to remind other coaches, 'What was the first gift you gave a boy? A ball. What about a girl? A doll. And now you want her to be tough and rough and competitive and aggressive?' This may be a generalization," Michele explained, "but it illustrates how we teach a girl how to be a mother, but not how to use her body in an athletic way. Sports are a safe place to do that. For some of these girls, it's all they have. If they weren't playing volleyball, what would they be doing? Sports fill up their time in a positive way, and give them a chance to develop health, strength and confidence. Sports give them a place to experiment with what it is to be a girl and how to be competitive. It's also an outlet for anger and frustration."

We talked about our own experiences with sports, and named some of the tools we acquired from playing, things that we still apply to life— like how to speak up, how to collaborate and how to fight to win. "If we don't raise girls to be competitive," Michele continued, "and then we throw them into competitive games expecting them to just do it, they can start having doubts and drop out. I try to do competitive drills that force them to go against each other so they can experience what it's like to lose, and feel how you are supposed to act. I tell them, 'Take it out on the ball. It's okay to be mad, take it out on the ball.' Without this kind of constructive outlet, anger [whether it's sports motivated or the venting of deeper feelings through the medium of sports] comes out in negative forms; it gets internalized or it may come out inappropriately in relationships. It's okay for boys to show anger, not for girls."

Michele believes that we need to introduce girls to these situations earlier than is currently the case. "I have a niece. Everyone says she is so pretty. I say, 'Oh, she is so smart!'" she said. "The language we use in the way we talk to and about girls has an impact on them. Boys, too. The four-year-old boy knows he is not allowed to play with pink stuff. If you go into Toys"R"Us, you know right away which section you are in. What you are supposed to play with and what you are supposed to enjoy is very quickly defined. Action figures for girls don't really exist."

Although participating in athletics is not a complete antidote to life's problems, Michele believes they offer empowerment and important life skills: "There is a team context around sports. Volleyball teaches about the mechanism of the team, which is a good lesson about community, sharing and helping, and not letting each other down."

NAMING SEXUAL VIOLENCE

When we arrived at our next school, six volleyball team girls were waiting for us in a conference room. They were already chatting about their plans for college and for starting businesses. They talked about how the entrepreneurial energy of Detroit has changed the city and created both new opportunities and new pressures.

Maeva, 14, who wants to go to business school, told us, "Everyone starts young. *Everyone* in Detroit starts a clothing line—there are at least five in my school. I think it's creative. But everyone is starting younger. There's more stress, I guess, to be a start-up instead of going to college." The other girls told us about their dreams of becoming scientists, physical therapists and marriage counsellors. Their chatting moved quickly from the pressure to plan for the future to the pressure to stay on top of trends. Maeva and Scout, 14, told us how the challenge to conform is a burden but they try to stay original and creative rather than following the latest fashion.

We talked about their social lives and where they find trust and friendship. We also talked about social media and, contrary to what we so often hear, they told us that it doesn't rule their lives. They don't spend too much time online and are too busy to be consumed by social media. "I can't take a selfie every day!" said Rachel, 15, but they all post pictures from time to time, mostly when they go to parties. They discussed Snapchat,[8] how Facebook is "old school," and how Vine[9] and Twitter are better. "My mom spends a lot of time on Facebook!" added Rachel. "I don't spend much time on Twitter though," said Maddy, 15. "It keeps people in your business and starts drama. It's like having two different lives." While these girls were clearly not controlled by social-media platforms, they did give us a sense of how much sex plays out online. They talked about video "hos" and how some girls see social media as a path to popularity and money. "Instagram makes people feel like they are famous," Scout said.

"Yeah, we see freaky pictures and videos everywhere," said Maeva. "Then boys expect their girlfriends to do exactly what's in them."

"I think what those video hos do lowers their self-esteem," Maddy said thoughtfully, "which makes them try harder."

"Some girls like sending pics or videos to guys," Rachel observed. "That's what girls believe is popular—getting exposed."

"Some boys record having sex [with a girl] and the girl doesn't even know," Flore, 15, said. "[But then] some girls do know and they think it's going to make them famous."

We asked if they'd experienced sexual harassment, and they said no. Then we asked if they felt boys were respectful to girls. "Boys are not respectful at all," said Flore. "I have to hit boys at school for touching my butt. They think it's okay, but I'm like, 'What are you touching me for?'"

"At parties, guys try to get you to twerk on them," Maddy told us. "I remember one guy did that to me and he followed me all night, he was tugging on my belt. I had to get somebody to get him away from me."

"They think they deserve it. They're like, 'What are you coming to a party for if you aren't going to dance?'" said Scout.

"Some girls don't like that but that's not sexual harassment," Maddy said, as she finished off the rest of her cola.

"We go in pairs and threes to the dance floors," Flore said. "They are so aggressive. They are really big boys and they talk about you when you say no."

"Stick with your girlfriends, don't leave the pack, if you leave you are in trouble," Maeva told us, looking around—all the other girls nodded in agreement. She went on to explain that girls are getting "ran on" at parties all the time. "Four guys passing a girl around, they all have sex, in the same room at the same time. Some girls agree to do it, but some girls don't know and don't like it." They explained to us that getting "ranned" can happen even when you think you are alone having sex with a guy, and then four of his friends jump out of the closet and expect to have sex, too.

In a second interview in the conference room, over the noise of the bells and endless announcements over the intercom, we asked the girls directly about sexual violence. Their answers echoed the sentiments of our earlier conversation. "No, it doesn't happen here," said Clover, 15, and, "No, not to me, but I've witnessed it before," said Jules, 16. They told stories about boys getting aggressive, grabbing arms, slapping and pushing girls. Some of them said that they didn't put up with violence in their personal relationships.

Although it came out most spontaneously in Detroit, almost all of our interviews revealed that sexual harassment and other forms of aggression and unwanted attention are a normal part of everyday school experiences for girls. Cultural factors may influence how the harassment is displayed (whether overtly, in public or behind closed doors), but whether a girl attends a Detroit public high school, a private middle-class suburban school or a privileged college, this continuum of violence is simply a fact of life.

In Whitehorse, we heard stories about dancers being harassed and called names. In inner-city Montreal, Tasha told us about how the boys at her private school call her Double D. In the Montreal suburbs, middle-class francophone girls complained about how the boys call them names like slut and whore. The girls at the University of Southern California talked about clubbing and being touched in ways that made them uncomfortable, and in San Francisco, girl group leaders alerted us to how girls as young as nine and 11 feel pressured for sex. In Kingston, even the boys told us how their hockey and football team friends harass girls to send them naked selfies, and in Ottawa, another set of boys (whom we will meet in chapter 10) revealed how guys get girls drunk on purpose at parties to try to get laid.

All these cases reinforced what we saw in Detroit, and indicated that sexual harassment is indeed a problem for girls and young women. Most disturbing, however, was how "routine" the behaviours had become: girls, it seems, do not have the language to name these experiences. When we asked them what they thought these aggressions might be called, they mentioned bullying and teasing; it was annoying, they said, but boys will be boys.

But this is not bullying or teasing. Ranning, unwanted touching, teasing about the size and shape of body parts, pressure to perform a blow job, not accepting no as an answer—all of these are violations, and yet, when asked, none of the girls classified them as sexual violence. Without the language to name these behaviours, or the critical lens to call things what they are, and without the tools to combat them, girls lack the support needed to get help, to be legitimized in their experience and to find a way to make it stop. Is it really any surprise, then, when these same girls say that reaching out for help is not an option? Fear of judgment or backlash, of being seen in a "negative light" or not being taken seriously, keeps them quiet. They don't feel they have the ability to change these unwanted situations.

+++

Later in the afternoon we met twins Delray and Deliza in their school cafeteria. At 13, they are two of the youngest but strongest athletes on the volleyball team. Michele has been raising money to help them play in higher leagues, hopeful that success in the sport will give them access to a bright future. They do well at school, help their aunt sell afford-able, locally grown produce on weekends and are close to their mother, who runs their household on her own with a low income. They were sweet and soft-spoken when they huddled beside us to tell us their story, which turned out to include a lot of angst over the boy situation.

"They say ignorant things like, 'She sends pictures to so-and-so,'" said Deliza. "It makes it very hard to [talk] with guys. I let it get to me, and I get irritated."

Delray agreed. "Guys always ask me to send a picture—I say no, and they stop talking to me, they cut me off."

"I will send pics with clothes on, then I stop talking to them. I don't need them," said Deliza.

"We were outside the other day standing around with some friends," Delray recounted, "and a boy came up to us and said I sent a pic [with-out clothes on] to his cousin, and he said his cousin said, 'You have a nice body.' He said this in front of my friends and it's not even true. My friends looked at me different. I told them, 'I didn't do that,' but my friends still looked at me different. I'm actually trying to figure out who my real friends are."

Faced with yet more evidence of the rampant, daily sexual harass-ment today's girls face, we took the opportunity to ask Delray and Deliza some more pointed questions about what it makes them think and feel, and what they can do about it:

Does anyone tell you it's not right, what the boys are doing?
They [teachers and adults] just say that they are childish.

They are actually harassing you—did you know that?
No, I didn't know that. They think they can touch you—in
the hallway. You want to hit them back but everyone [male and

female peers] will look at you and ask, "Why are you like that?"
They will blame it on you—they think you are crazy. So you
don't want to snitch, you don't want to say anything.

How does it make you feel?
Mad and irritated. It's like, "How do you know I want to be
touched? Don't touch me." If girls [touched boys like that], you'd
be [called] a ho. Boys get to do what they want but if the girls
did it, you be nasty.

Is there pressure to have sex?
All the time. The boys [she knows in her school] text me:
"Can I come over so we can have sex?" And I'm like, "NO." I'm
not sneaking a boy into my house. At the movies, they want to
do stuff, like finger us. When we say no, then they [say],
"Man, you are lame."

Oh, that's harsh. What else are they pressuring you to do?
Blow jobs. They want to come over and have sex. The first
thing they ask you is, "Are you a virgin?" They ask, "What's the
freakiest thing you have ever done?" Sometimes I want to be real
rude, just cut them off, but that's not my personality, so I try to
answer the question with another question.

That's brave to do on your own. Does anyone give you support?
I can handle it. It does bother me. I try not to think about it. I
want to talk about it with my friends but I'm afraid they won't
understand [they won't see or take her side]. My mom trusts me.
We tell her a lot about boys and what they do. She is a really
important person to talk to.

It's really great to have a mom you can talk to. How would you say your relationship with boys affects you?
Sometimes I answer their questions because I want to fit in.

I want somebody that's popular and I think is cute. I want to go along with it, sometimes. But I know they gonna pressure me. [When] you like them so much, they expect you to go too far. Guys are pressuring for photos and for everything else. I feel like I've lost a lot of boys as friends and boyfriends because of this. It's irritating. I stopped having feelings for boys. Now it's like, "I don't care if I lose him, it's whatever." I don't want to talk to somebody I don't like.

Do they talk about this stuff in sex ed?
They taught us about condoms and saying no to drugs. They told us to use excuses to say no to guys but sometimes they don't work. They taught us that "you want to stay a virgin," which would not work either. Boys are demanding and hard-headed; they won't take no for an answer.

Telling you to use excuses and "stay a virgin" are a little flimsy as advice and education. What kind of additional support would you like?
How to deal with all this stress. I wonder how different it is in other states. I want to hear from other girls about how they are coping.

We told them that girls say that a lot, that they love hearing advice from one another and imagining the future based on one another's observations and advice. We talked a bit more about boys and how we think all kids need to be taught that what's happening *is* sexual harassment and that girls have a right to say no and to not be violated. After all we'd heard, we couldn't stop thinking about how society condones violence against girls. It's so strong that even girls themselves justify and minimize the trauma of their experiences. How is this ever going to change if we continue to protect, privilege and promote the status quo?

+++

After these interviews, we talked with Michele about sexual harassment, partner violence and other forms of unnamed pressure and aggression. We wanted to see what sorts of connections she was making about it with the girls on the volleyball court. "When I talk about girls playing sports," said Michele, "I talk about being strong, I talk about knowing how to confront, how to protect yourself. I don't want to freak people out but I do talk about things like, 'If that boy grabs you, are you able to push him away?' Ninety percent of the girls I coach know someone who has experienced violence, it's happening to them, they need to know how to deal with it." We agreed that without strong role models, it's harder for girls to understand from a young age that they are strong, too, and can act on—and have an influence on—the world.

Michele also organizes a volleyball event called Volley against Violence. It's a campaign to raise awareness and funding for issues of sexual violence. "While sports make girls strong, it isn't enough," she said—and she emphasized how important it is for girls to have the language to express what is happening in their lives. "The girls don't have the words to name what is happening, and no one is really changing the language," Michele said, echoing what our discussions with the girls had revealed: girls don't connect with terms like "sexual harassment" or "domestic violence," which are often seen as adult terms for adult experiences. As no colloquial words are rising up to define these issues in a tangible, relatable way for young people, Michele is doing her best to make a change.

+++

When Michele drove us to the airport, Delray and Deliza came, too. They put on Angel Haze, their favourite girl rapper, and sang happily in the back seat. We were sad to leave Detroit and to wave goodbye at the departure gate but we left inspired by the spirit of this transforming city and the force for significant change that is living and breathing in the young women we met there.

SURVIVAL KIT

NAME VIOLENCE for what it is: Sexualized violence should not be confused with bullying and aggression. Sexual harassment, date rape, intimate-partner violence and sexual abuse are violence and require appropriate responses. Sexual harassment, the most subtle of these, can include a range of behaviours such as pulling at a girl's clothing, rubbing up against her, grabbing or pinching her, making sexual comments or jokes and spreading sexual rumours. Sexual harassment is so common and so often goes unquestioned that it has been called a form of "everyday violence in the lives of girls."[10]

ADVOCATE for peer-led and culturally relevant violence-prevention education and programming in schools and communities. Find violence-prevention resources here:

- Girl-led campaigns like Project Slut advocate for girls' rights and raise awareness about dress codes, rape culture and slut-shaming. www.facebook.com/projectslut
- Find resources, tool kits and research for violence-prevention programmes at Girls Action Foundation. Their guide *From the Ground Up* includes practical resources and activities around power, gender, healthy relationships and violence: girlsactionfoundation.ca/files /from_the_ground-up_final.small_.pdf
- The National Aboriginal Health Organization created a sexual-health tool kit that covers traditional views on sexual health, healthy relationships, sexuality and sexual abuse: www.naho.ca/documents/fnc/english /2011_Sexual_Health_sexuality_relationships.pdf
- *Crossing the Line: Sexual Harassment at School* is a publication by the American Association of University Women (AAUW) that sets out evidence and strategies for educators, parents and students to address and take action on sexual harassment in schools: http://www.aauw.org /files/2013/02/Crossing-the-Line-Sexual-Harassment-at-School.pdf

- Also check out the AAUW's *Drawing the Line: Sexual Harassment on Campus* for the same on college and university school campuses: http://www.aauw.org/files/2013/02/drawing-the-line-sexual -harassment-on-campus.pdf
- INCITE! is a US based activist organization working to end violence against women of colour: www.incite-national.org/page /dangerous-intersections
- INCITE! offers resources on street harassment: www.incite-national.org/sites/default/files/incite_files /resource_docs/6378_street_harass_pamphlet.pdf
- METRAC provides resources for education and tools for raising youth awareness about sexual violence: www.metrac.org
- The Chicago Taskforce on Violence Against Girls and Young Women offers resources and education on gender based violence, reproductive justice, and teen dating violence: http://www.chitaskforce.org

TITLE IX is a federal civil rights law in the US that prohibits discrimination on the basis of sex, including on the basis of sex stereotypes, in education programmes and activities. All public schools and any private schools receiving federal funds must comply with Title IX.

- Useful information related to sexual harassment in grades kindergarten to twelve and Title IX: www.aclu.org /gender-based-violence-harassment-your-school-your-rights
- Girls for Gender Equity based in Brooklyn, New York, has worked to address sexual harassment in schools. In 2011 they published a guide for others interested in doing the same: *Hey, Shorty! A Guide to Combating Sexual Harassment and Violence in Schools and on the Streets* (Feminist Press, 2011): http://www.ggenyc.org/publications/

ENCOURAGE programmes that include boys: Excellent violence-prevention resources and programming can be found at the following sites.
The Good Men Project: www.goodmenproject.com
White Ribbon Campaign: www.whiteribbon.ca

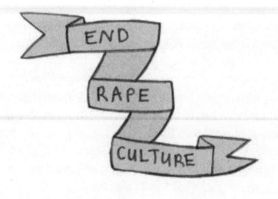

BLURRED LINES AND GREY ZONES: NAMING THE UNNAMED, PART 2

OUR DISCUSSIONS IN DETROIT left an impression. Much of what we talked about on the way home and in the days afterwards focused on what the girls in Detroit had told us. When we shared their stories with Dr. Robyn Diner, a progressive gender, media and pop culture scholar who teaches at Vanier College in Montreal, she wasn't surprised. She confirmed that there is definitely a grey zone of behaviour among teens when it comes to sexual interactions. "Kids don't connect to 'sexual harassment' because it's considered a 'workplace thing,'" she said, "and many boys don't connect to issues of rape because they think, 'I'm not that guy.'" We acknowledged bumping up against this grey area in many of our interviews and told Dr. Diner that we found it disturbing that bullying—a hot-button issue of the moment—had become a catch-all for many forms of abuse. When working with a grey zone like unnamed sexual violence, having a one-word label for all kinds of ugly experiences is too simplistic a response, especially given the many deep-seated and systemic issues that one word can mask.

THE REHTAEH PARSONS CASE

Many of us know the story of 17-year-old Rehtaeh Parsons, who died in the hospital on April 7, 2013, three days after she attempted suicide at home by hanging. This tragic end came after seventeen months of harassment that began when she was allegedly gang-raped, and photos of the ordeal were shared around her school, the community at large and on social media. Prior to the rape, Rehtaeh was a happy, popular girl; after, she lost her friends and became the victim of public shaming and threats. She even changed schools because of the relentless attacks. She reported the assault, and the police initially told her that they had a lot of evidence and would soon be laying charges. Then everything changed.

Glen Canning, Rehtaeh's father, is a photojournalist and writer. He was gentle and open when we spoke to him, for nearly two hours, via Skype. Glen told us that over the course of the year-long investigation following the assault, the police looked into everything about Rehtaeh, including her phone records, her sex life and her alcohol use. There were hundreds of texts that were exchanged between kids at her school about the event but the police never interviewed witnesses, and never once questioned the accused boys or seized their phones. Finally, the police decided not to lay any charges.

In contrast, Glen explained how the investigation and system failed Rehtaeh. He told us how even though there were hundreds of texts and shares of the photo of the alleged sexual assault, three of four accused boys were never interviewed because they declined to be questioned by the police and the option to come in for questioning was voluntary; their phones were not seized, although the police attempted to access the data via the service provider; and attempts to conduct in-school interviews of students involved in the exchange of the photo were thwarted by the school. After a full year of investigation, the Crown advised that there was insufficient evidence for sexual assault charges and erroneously advised to not lay child pornography charges (the only charge that exists yet to deal with sexual cyber crime).[1]

Glen told us that everything was worse after they sought medical help and support for Rehtaeh and she didn't get the care she needed. The one-size-fits-all mental health ward exposed her to "troubled" teens who "taught" her how to harm herself. He also alleges that she was put in isolation and strip-searched by two male guards. The hospital denied the strip-search of Rehtaeh by male guards but admitted that in some cases clothes have been removed from patients deemed to be at high-risk of harming themselves.[2]

In short, both the health care and justice systems failed the Parsons family and, not long after this, they lost their daughter. An independent review into the police and prosecution response to Rehtaeh's case was conducted. It concluded that the system did not work in the way it should have, there were unacceptable delays and it failed to respond and adapt to a cultural context steeped in new technologies. Several recommendations were made to address the police and Crown errors and missteps in the case including the length of time the investigation took, the need for specific training and clarified policies for sexual assault investigation as well as safeguards to prevent what was erroneous advice on the law of child pornography.[3]

The failure of the mental health system to support Rehtaeh prompted a review of the youth mental health services in the Halifax regional municipality. The first recommendation coming out of the review was for the IWK (the Children's Hospital where Rehtaeh was treated) to fully "implement trauma-informed care (TIC) across the IWK MHA program and in the CDHA Mobile Crisis Response Team."[4]

Following her death, Glen posted a moving piece on his blog: "Rehtaeh Parsons Was My Daughter"[5] that went viral. Anonymous— an international group of vigilante hacktivists—got involved, as they do when they see individuals standing alone against an unjust situation. The group exposed the ongoing and escalating verbal assaults and threats against Rehtaeh and her family to try to help bring about some form of legal justice.

Years after her death, Rehtaeh's story still resonates. How is it possible that cultural attitudes and beliefs continue to accept this type of incident as normal? How can a community accept and sustain the alienation and shaming Rehtaeh lived through before deciding that she couldn't take anymore?

"Rape culture" is a term currently being used to address the cultural practices that excuse, tolerate and perpetuate sexual violence. Rape culture is not explicit; in our cultural consciousness we despise the idea of a rapist. Instead, rape culture is implicit in attitudes, behaviours and beliefs. Examples of rape culture include blaming the victim, asking a woman what she was wearing or if she was drinking when she comes forward to report rape and shaming victims by posting photos of their victimization online. Rape culture is perpetuated when we teach girls and women how not to get raped instead of teaching everyone that sexual violence is not acceptable.

Rehtaeh's story—which garnered international attention—has allowed us, in some important ways, to highlight the ongoing and pervasive issue of sexual violence. However, there is still a lot to do, especially when it comes to understanding the root causes of this issue. Following Rehtaeh's death, for example, and in cases similar to hers, mainstream media and government responses have focused on addressing bullying rather than on tackling sexualized violence.

"Bullying gets attention over sexual violence," Glen told us. Although he is still mourning the loss of his daughter, he is armed, as a journalist, with evidence about Rehtaeh's case that he is using to advocate for deeper change. "The hurtful part of this was the sexual assault, but people ran with bullying. It almost seems, especially when you deal with young people, that society goes with an angle they can understand—people can't understand young boys raping young girls. I wish the press had run with the consent issue rather than cyberbullying. We now have new federal policy to take on cyberbullying, as a response to Rehtaeh's life and death, but we are no wiser as a society about rape."

To address what has been missed in this international conversation, Glen works hard to bring attention to the need for education about sexual assault, violence against women and healthy sexuality and consent. In doing so, he hopes that the real reasons for his daughter's death can be illuminated and addressed—and be avoided by other girls and boys and their families and communities.

Bullying and cyberbullying are frequently conflated with sexual violence. Both online and offline, sexual violence—including sexual harassment, rape, revenge porn and slut-shaming—continue to be perpetrated and still go, to a large extent, unnamed and unreported. As we saw so clearly in Detroit, girls often don't even have the language to name these experiences as violence. And boys don't either. We learned from Glen how after Rehtaeh died, one of the boys whom she claimed had raped her, reached out to Rehtaeh's mom on Facebook to tell her his version of what happened and to clarify that he believed he hadn't raped her. He described how he and his friend had sex with her and took the photo while she was so drunk that she was unable to walk on her own and was vomiting out the window. He explained how the other two boys at the party also had sex with Rehtaeh after she had passed out and was carried to another bedroom. He told Rehtaeh's mom ". . . I cannot lie to you and say we all did not rape her, I can tell you for sure that I did not rape her . . ." This new information[6] became grounds to re-open the case and file charges only for the making and distribution of child pornography.[7]

SEXUAL VIOLENCE: A (SAD) FACT OF LIFE

If we've learned anything from cases like Rehtaeh's, and from our countless conversations with girls across North America, it's this: most of today's young men and women don't understand consent. They don't know what consensual sex is; they don't know how to go about asking for consent; and they don't know that consent is a legal prerequisite for sex. They also don't know that non-consensual sexual acts—be it butt-smacking, unwanted touching in the hallways or surprise gang rapes at parties—are serious offences with specific names, offences that can destroy victims' lives and are punishable by law.

Sexual violence, in its multiple forms, is a blatant fact of girls' lives. A culture of normalized violence overtly and subliminally tells girls that they occupy a subordinate place in our society and are not valued. Countless girls have told us that they are touched by boys in school, pressured for sexual acts—and then leered and sworn at by both the boys and the girls who "hate on them" for being sexually objectified. Girls are rarely offered a place to go for help when they need it. As Leila, a 14-year-old in Detroit, told us, "What am I gonna say? 'Principal, a guy keeps licking his lips at me when I walk past him in the cafeteria and it really creeps me out.' I'd get laughed right out of the office."

As if dealing with these issues at school, at work and socially is not enough, sexual harassment jumps the barrier between real life and the digital world. Online harassment takes the form of exploitation, luring, trolling, non-consensual distribution of photos, unsolicited sexual comments and stalking, and is used as a tool to control girls.[8] From coast to coast, girls told us how slut-shaming, body shaming and rumours are as damaging online as they are in "real life." And yet, in this space that adults find difficult to control and monitor, these activities are rarely named and condemned as sexual harassment. Mia Matsumiya, a young professional violinist based in LA, recently launched an Instagram account called @perv_magnet to showcase the kinds of unwanted, unsolicited sexual messages she routinely receives (often from men who don't know her). In the first three weeks of her awareness campaign, Mia's followers jumped from one thousand to sixty-seven thousand; she went viral on Facebook and garnered ample press coverage.

Because of her newfound visibility, Mia Matsumiya has now opened the call for all girls to send her the racist and sexualized "creepy messages" they've received from strangers too, so she can post them on @perv_magnet in an act of solidarity. Not only does this show the world what girls and women cope with on a regular basis, it also highlights how it is all too often ignored as a serious form of harassment. At the time of writing, her latest post is from a man who wrote, "Anyone ever tell you how sexy you are and how bad they wanna let you face fuck them and would love to watch you suck their long cock as you make it all slimy and play with my balls while togging my asshole." It ends with a happy face.

The numbers speak volumes about the prevalence of these unnamed aggressions. We learned earlier that one in five North American women will be victims of sexual assault in their lifetime. Young women under the age of 25 experience the highest incidence of intimate partner violence, sexual violence, and criminal harassment (stalking).[9] In Canada, girls experience sexual assault at much higher rates than boys—82% of all victims under the age of 18 are female.[10] Approximately one in three adolescent girls in the United States is a victim of physical, emotional or verbal abuse from a dating partner.[11] In an extensive study in Ontario,

27% of girls in Grades 9 through 11 reported having been pressured into doing something sexual that they did not want to do.[12]

The potential impacts for girls who experience sexual harassment include dropping out of school, developing eating and other disorders, experiencing fear, self-consciousness and anxiety, an inability to concentrate, a lack of self-esteem, and depression and isolation. Despite these facts, and the knowledge of how poverty and racism negatively impact girls' experience of violence, there is still a tendency to make girls feel they are the cause of the harm that has been done to them. This is especially true in the context of violence against Indigenous girls.

Kim Pate, executive director of the Canadian Association of Elizabeth Fry Societies, a group of organizations that work across the country to advocate for girls and women in the criminal justice system—and one of Canada's foremost advocate for Indigenous women and girls—told us that: "In cases of sexual assault, the same thing is presumed. The victim is lying, the victim is inviting the assault, the victim is encouraging the assaulter to victimize her, the victim made it up, the victim brought it upon herself, the victim is blame-worthy. When Indigenous families report that their loved ones are missing, they are often told by police that the missing person must be out partying."

FIGHTING BACK

While sexual violence and cyberviolence are clearly realities in girls' lives—as Mia Matsumiya's campaign so vividly demonstrates—the Internet may also turn out to be a useful weapon when it comes to fighting back. Through social media, girls themselves are forcing society to bring these issues into the light. Rehtaeh's story and the stories of others like her continue to be a call for justice and action. In the summer of 2014—in a story that is now well-known thanks to the social-media mayhem that followed[13]—16-year-old Jada from Houston, Texas, alleged she had suffered sexual abuse at a house party. Jada alleges that after her drink was spiked, she passed out and was stripped and raped while unconscious. Photos of her lying naked on the floor after the attack were posted on the Internet. A social-media craze began when the posted images incited thousands of people to take photos of themselves in the same position. These copycat photos, a send-up of Jada's horrific experience, were posted under #JadaPose for likes and re-tweets.

But rather than remain silent, Jada fought back. She created her own hashtag—#IAmJada—and spoke out on her local radio and TV channels. Her very public position, which highlighted the fact that rape is a serious issue that should never be mocked, started a counter–media craze. Thousands of people tweeted their support and the cyber disputes that ensued ignited a national debate around rape culture. Jada's advocates began demanding accountability. In seeking justice online, and in instigating social-media pressure, Jada herself ensured that her case received proper legal attention.

Jada's case is just the tip of the iceberg. The last few years have seen an emerging movement through social media and in schools and colleges across North America that is naming and calling out rape culture and the legal and institutional policies and practices that fail to respond to sexual violence. While social media has provided a platform to share stories and raise awareness, the public has shown, in great part via responses on hand-held devices, that it is prepared to wrestle sexual assault and rape culture out of the closet.

Annie E. Clark, 25, and Andrea Pino, 22, political science majors from the University of North Carolina–Chapel Hill, are examples of the progress being made in this area. They have collaborated with a network of activists across the United States to help educate young women about their Title IX rights. According to the American Civil Liberties Union, under Title IX, "Discrimination on the basis of sex can include sexual harassment, rape, and sexual assault. A college or university that receives federal funds may be held legally responsible when it knows about and ignores sexual harassment or assault in its programs or activities. The school can be held responsible in court whether the harassment is committed by a faculty member, staff, or a student."[14] At the time of writing, seventy-eight American colleges—including Harvard, Princeton, Dartmouth, Berkeley, USC and UCLA—were under investigation by the Department of Education's Office for Civil Rights.[15] *The Hunting Ground*, a documentary film about Clark and Pino's fight to eradicate the rape on campus epidemic debuted at the Sundance Film Festival, was aired on CNN, nominated for several awards, surrounded by controversy and features two songs by Lady Gaga—one, "Til it Happens To You," which was introduced by American vice president Joe Biden at the 2016 Oscars and was performed live by Gaga with many campus rape victims joining her on stage. It was such a powerful performance, and proof that this issue has finally arrived in the limelight, that the Hollywood audience was moved to tears and gave Gaga and the rape survivors a standing ovation.

Emma Sulkowicz's story has also been pivotal in bringing rape culture awareness to the mainstream. In September 2014, Emma, in her final year at New York City's Columbia University, launched a performance art piece entitled *Carry That Weight*[16] after the sexual assault she reported to have sustained in her dorm in her sophomore year went unpunished. (Columbia's internal inquiry into the allegations found the accused "not responsible" without getting the police involved.) Two other female students filed similar charges against the same accused male, and Columbia again cleared him of responsibility and failed to involve police or expel him from the school. Now the poster child for the growing North American college and university anti-rape activist movement, Sulkowicz dragged her fifty-pound mattress everywhere she went on campus, including to her graduation ceremony in May 2015, as an act of solidarity with all girls and women against sexual violence. Sulkowicz's protest has been highly praised internationally as an important work of art, and a social justice project of power and influence.

The year 2014 was also transformative in the Canadian landscape: the Jian Ghomeshi scandal became the catalyst for a viral campaign that shattered the historical silence and shame typically experienced by victims of sexual assault. Ghomeshi, a high-profile journalist with the Canadian Broadcasting Corporation and a cultural icon, was accused by three women of sexual assault and choking. The charges were taken seriously by the police and the CBC—despite a huge following of people who wanted, in keeping with chauvinistic tradition, to blame the victims and save their hero—because a critical mass of women supported one another's stories. Soon, women not connected with the case were coming forward with their own stories of sexual violence. Led by long-time *Toronto Star* reporter Antonia Zerbisias—and posting under the hashtag #beenrapedneverreported—the stories sparked a national debate.[17] The non-guilty verdict delivered on March 24, 2016, caused protests in Toronto and leaves a volatile public unresolved but awakened to this issue.

Meanwhile, a campaign to introduce the concept of consent into Ontario's sexual-education curriculum was spearheaded by teens Tessa Hill and Lia Valente. The February 2015 issue of *ELLE* Canada magazine featured these two Toronto eighth graders in an article entitled, "Meet the 13-Year-Old Girls Changing the Sexual Consent Conversation."[18] Hill and Valente first learned about rape culture after choosing it as a topic for a school social justice project. They were so moved by the stories that they created a twenty-minute documentary, which in turn led them to the idea that they needed to fight to have consent education taught in schools to help combat rape culture. The girls gathered over forty thousand signatures on a petition, and convinced Ontario's Ministry of Education that consent education needed to be added to the province's sexual-education curriculum.

Consent is "a voluntary agreement to engage in sexual activity . . . it means communicating yes on your own terms."[19] As stated earlier, "a person cannot give consent if they are being forced to participate, if they are incapable of consenting, if they are afraid of the person who is asking them to consent, or if consent is obtained through the use of threats or fear of force. The Supreme Court of Canada has ruled that silence is not consent."[20]

Consent curriculum, where it is practised in high schools, creates a dialogue that explains rape culture and provides a map for both boys and girls to develop healthy relationship skills. And consent can be taught to kids at even younger ages. We can teach kids that their body is their own, and that no one has the right to touch them in ways that make them uncomfortable. We can teach kids that other people's bodies are their own, too, and that nobody has the right to touch them in ways that make them uncomfortable either. In this way, they can learn about respect (for their body and others') and about appropriate boundaries, in the crucial stages of development where these ideas naturally take form.

The advancements in awareness that we're beginning to see—thanks to mighty girl activism—represent an exciting opportunity to go deeper, to uproot cultural norms that keep us stuck in a world of misogyny and violence. This is an important first step, but we need to keep pushing forward. To lay the foundations for a world without normalized sexual violence, we must expose the links between permissiveness around sexual harassment and the abuse of girls and women. It must identify the systems that currently condone this, and accept the fact that change cannot wait any longer.

In important ways, this is already happening. Beyond the justice system, which so often fails the victims in these cases, there are many movements working to respond more positively and collectively to sexualized violence. These movements are often under the radar of mainstream media and public attention. Indigenous communities and women-of-colour collectives like INCITE!, for example—a Chicago-based nation-wide network—are developing educational initiatives that respond to the realities of violence experienced by women of colour. Projects like those facilitated through Girls Action Foundation, the organization co-founded by Tatiana that has dynamic outreach to diverse communities of girls across Canada, provide resources to educate youth about intimate partner violence, healthy relationships and consent.

Andrea Simpson-Fowler, a girl-empowerment leader in Whitehorse (we will speak with her more in chapter 8), told us about how when girls started reporting date rapes and sexual harassment in her community, she began a "Not Datable" list. Every guy she heard about who was not treating girls well was posted on her list—a public website where full names and details were disclosed. When girls responded by avoiding the first "Not Datable" guy, turning him down and ignoring him en masse, he approached Andrea and asked what he could do to get off the list. This initiated a sort of "harassment rehab" where he learned what harassment is and how to change his behaviour to ensure that nobody gets hurt and every act of intimacy is consensual. Andrea's "Not Datable" list is now infamous in Whitehorse. Thanks to it, the community has been able to engage in healthy discussion, awareness-raising and informal education about what sexual violence is and how to not perpetuate it.

Stories like Andrea's and Rehtaeh's and Mia's all reveal an interesting and vital point: the same system that is failing girls is also failing boys. If we hope to effect meaningful change in this area, boys need to learn about rape culture and consent. Schools can play an important role in teaching adolescents about sexual harassment, healthy relationships, media and porn literacy—and, most important, about what it means to obtain affirmative, ongoing consent from a sexual partner. We do a great disservice to both boys and girls when our education systems, and our society, turn a blind eye to these thorny issues.

But in the midst of all that is so worrisome about the lives of young girls today comes some positive news. Thanks to concerted efforts by concerned citizens and girls themselves, these topics are coming to mass public attention and this, in turn, is inspiring a whole new generation of passionate kids to get involved. We are at a fruitful moment in the evolution of gender and cultural norms—and girls and young women are leading the way.

SURVIVAL KIT

UNDERSTAND CONSENT: Before you talk to youth about sexual consent, make sure you yourself understand the topic. What is sexual consent? Here is a paraphrased summary from teenhealthresource.com:[21]

- Consent in sex means saying "yes" to sexual activity and receiving a "yes" from your partner.
- Everyone has the right to decide if they want to do something sexual or not, and everyone is allowed to change their mind at any point.
- Consent is an agreement given in words, which means to have consent you must *ask before you do anything*, even if the person you're with has agreed to other sexual activities.
- Your sexual partner must be within the age of consent. The age of consent laws are different around the world but most in North America set the age range between 14 and 18.
- Sexual consent should be given for *any* sex act—from kissing to touching to vaginal or anal penetration—*before* it happens.
- Consent may also come with terms such as yes to sex but only with a condom, in which case to maintain consent you must abide by these terms.

FOR MEDIA, EDUCATION AND TRAINING resources check out femifesto, a Toronto-based feminist organization that works to shift rape culture to consent culture at Feministo.org. They produced "Use The Right Words," a guide for journalists reporting on sexual violence in Canada.

FOR TIPS AND RESOURCES on how to deal with and prevent cyber harassment:
- Speak Up and Stay Safe(er): A Guide to Protecting Yourself from online harassment at https://onlinesafety.feministfrequency.com/en/
- #takebackthetech Campaign: takebackthetech.net/be-safe /self-care-coping-and-healing

TALK TO KIDS—BOYS AND GIRLS—ABOUT CONSENT. Don't be afraid
to introduce ideas of consent and respectful interrelating to kids even before
they get to school age. Modelling consent through respectfully interacting in your
adult relationships is the best backup to these discussions. Here are some tips
from the Good Men Project on teaching kids (ages one to 21) about consent.[22]

Talking to kids aged one to five:

- Teach children to ask permission before touching or embracing a playmate.
- Help create empathy within children by explaining how something they have
  done may have hurt someone.
- Teach kids to help others who may be in trouble.
- Teach kids that *no* and *stop* are important words and should be honored.
- Encourage children to read facial expressions and other body language.
- Never force a child to hug, touch or kiss anybody.
- Allow children to talk about their body.
- Talk about "gut feelings" or instincts.

Talking to teens and young adults about consent:

- Education about "good touch/bad touch" is very important.
- Build teens' self esteem, self-knowledge and self-expression.
- Nip "locker room talk" in the bud.
- Explain changing hormones.
- Talk honestly with kids about partying.
- Keep talking about sex and consent with teens as they start having
  serious relationships.
- Mentor teenage and college-aged boys and young men about what masculinity is
  [see more about this in chapter 10].

FIGHT FOR CONSENT EDUCATION IN SCHOOLS AND COMMUNITIES.
You can find good consent campaign material and educational resources for
youth and educators in the following places:

- Laci Green is a sex-education activist living in the San Francisco Bay
  Area. On her YouTube channel, Sex+, she covers topics ranging from
  sex education to healthy relationships. Check out Laci on consent at:
  www.youtube.com/user/lacigreen
- Consent is Sexy is a consent campaign coming out of the UK:
  www.consentissexy.net
- There are numerous resources on Title IX and ending sexual violence on
  campuses in the US. For example: End Rape on Campus
  http://endrapeoncampus.org/title-ix/ and the AAUW Sexual Assault Tool Kit
  http://www.aauw.org/resource/campus-sexual-assault-tool-kit/
- Teen Health Source is a sexual-health information service run by youth
  for youth through Planned Parenthood. For more information on consent
  and other sexual-health resources, visit: www.teenhealthsource.com

CUTTING IS NORMAL:
MEETING "LEAPING FEATS" IN WHITEHORSE

OUR PLANE LANDED IN WHITEHORSE at dusk. Andrea Simpson-Fowler, a friend who runs a local dance studio, met us at the arrivals gate. Dressed in a down jacket and furry boots, she looked every bit the northern-outpost hostess. As we piled into her car, the late-day sun smeared the sky with colour, illuminating the foxes and other wild animals that darted alongside us as we drove.

Andrea, her partner and their two teenagers live in a bungalow on a quiet street set against a backdrop of snow-topped mountains. Leaping Feats, the dance studio Andrea founded, is just a few blocks away—and because there are always visiting dancers, young dance teachers and breakdance troupe members hanging around, Andrea's kitchen, living room and basement were full of raucous teens when we arrived. When we sat down to eat, they all stayed. Andrea's house, it turns out, is like Grand Central station—housing not just her family's food, laundry and dance equipment, but also that of all the visiting dancers and friends.

Over the next few days, we met a number of the girls in Andrea's life. Either around her kitchen table or on the site of her latest project—a community media arts space and games room adjacent to the dance studio headquarters—girls sat around in threes and sixes and eights, talking to us about their ambitions and challenges, their ups and downs and trials and triumphs. The dance studio was painted in bright colours—reflecting the bright energy exuded by the many young dancers we met. The girls, who were mostly white middle class, shared intimate stories about life's pressures and how they cope with these to survive and thrive. It's a theme we'd encountered many times on this tour. Girls from all backgrounds and classes told us they feel a relentless drive to succeed that is linked to their own hopes and dreams as well as to the expectations held by their parents and peers. This drive is reinforced in competitive environments and present in every aspect of their lives, be it academia, sports, social leadership, career planning, personal aesthetics or on- and offline popularity. The result, they say, is a pressure-cooker kind of life, where these everyday stresses can boil up, creating a quiet, internalized pain that, for many, is acted out in moments of violence against themselves.

DAY ONE WITH PRESSURE

Hannah, a gregarious girl in grade ten, explained that her eating disorder started because of social pressure. She felt she had to be cool, and to sustain her status once she was cool. Then, of course, came the many and complicated challenges associated with being cool, and the negative rumours, which sometimes start up even without a shred of truth and which are impossible to control. And there was no way to ignore the alienation so often interwoven with all of this—not just in her actual school day but online, too, where her cyber identity had to be managed and upheld. It was too much for her, she said, so she "stopped eating" [substantial meals] for a whole year in an effort to exercise some personal control over her frighteningly hectic existence. "It was a messy year," she told us, "but I got out of it, alone." One day she woke up and said, "Enough! This is stupid," and started eating again.

When Hannah told us this story, Maria, 15, who was sitting quietly next to her, made a confession as well. "No one knows, but I cut myself," she said in a timid voice. Her self-harm, Maria told us, stems from her poor relationship with her parents (they think her sister is perfect and she is imperfect). She doesn't like the fact that she cuts; it's a secret she keeps deeply hidden, not a cry for attention. In fact, she cuts her thighs so no one will see. "It releases my feelings; it gets the stress out," she said, "but I'm okay."

Cecily, a sweet 14-year-old with a happy smile, told us about her experiences with pressure and self-harm. "Lots of my pressure comes from my family. I can't talk about the stuff that goes on at school with my family. I can't talk about my family to my family. I don't even tell my school counsellor about my family. My family aren't bad people, and it's mostly my fault [that things are tense] because I don't really get along with my mom. We clash a lot and she says things that really hurt me, and then I go into a dark time. I'm good at not showing it. I don't tell anyone because I think people are going to judge me, or think I'm doing it [self-harming] for attention." Cecily cuts her arms and wears long sleeves to cover up.

Cecily, it turns out, is under a lot of pressure to perform. "I try to please my mom," she said. "I do as much as I can. I take lessons for six different instruments. I dance. I did a robotics fair project. It's so hard; I don't get support from my family. This has been the most stressful part of my life. My family just tell me that I'm not working hard enough and I'm not worth anything [because I don't always get the highest marks or win the competitions I'm in]. When I did get recognition at the national robotic fair, I loved it. It was like I proved them wrong."

These experiences have left Cecily with emotional scars. "I feel like I'm not good enough," she said. "I'm always compared to my sister, and everything I do isn't as good as what she does. I don't think my family realizes that I'm not the only teenager who has a messy room, and I'm doing well for my age."

Cecily shared these feelings in front of a small group of her dance studio girlfriends. They seemed to understand exactly how she felt, even her sense that the problems with her parents are all her fault, and they broke in with some stories of their own—sharing other stresses and preoccupations that leave them feeling negative and bad about themselves.

"You always want to impress the boys," said Catherine, 15. "You always want to do what they like, to make them like you. Sometimes you kind of lose a bit of who you are. I can see some of my values slipping. It's upsetting. There are some things I said I'd never do but I've done them. I got Facebook, I go to dances, I drink and go to parties."

Megan, 15, agreed. "Girls are always trying to impress other girls. Girls are always trying to impress boys, too. And teachers and parents. Girls judge themselves so much; they want to fit in."

"You want to be the girl that everyone likes," said Cecily. "Every girl worries about what people think, especially boys. But if guys like you, girls won't like you. If girls like you, then guys won't like you. You can't be [liked by] both."

"That's true," said Megan. "Guys will think you are boring if you have lots of girlfriends [because you will be caught up in "girl drama"]. To build your identity you have to perform on all these levels and find a way to be popular with as many people as possible."

This comment started another round of confessions. Fourteen-year-old Jackie told us, "I used to not like my body. I used to spend all my time thinking about it. I would look at everyone else and think, 'I'm not as skinny as her, and I don't have as much muscle as her.' I looked up to the older girls; they were so perfect and skinny. I didn't have good friends to talk to. My mom started finding out that stuff wasn't going well, so we talked. I didn't need to tell her too much, but it got better. Before that it was a competition [with myself] to see how little I could eat."

"I don't talk about it at all, but I cut myself sometimes," said Manon, 14. "It scares me to say it. I don't want anyone to know at all. I do it because I get really stressed out. I feel like I'm not good enough. Once you are in the moment, it provides release. I don't feel good enough, but when I cut myself, I feel something. After you do it, you know why people do it. I do it on my hips, so no one can see. I'm not suicidal. I would never want to kill myself. It's a coping method. When I'm really stressed out and I have too much to do and my parents are making me feel bad about myself, when I'm at my lowest points, I just do it. Then I go two weeks and I will do it again. I'm mad at myself. I'm punishing myself. I feel like my problems actually mean something when I cut, like someone actually feels them even if it's just me."

When we asked these girls if they knew that self-harm is often an internalization—or an "acting in," as opposed to an "acting out"—of their troubles within broader social issues, and that it's important to understand that they are not the problem, they told us how often they feel that they are the problem, and that they are all alone. "There's no place to talk about our problems and worries. There's nothing to really do about it," Manon said. The girls felt strongly that there were few (or no) outlets for their pain or anxiety.

When asked what they would say if they could act out and show their feelings, Cecily jumped in with an answer: "I would tell people how I feel, scream a loud scream. I would yell at my parents, I would say what I want them to hear: 'I'm doing okay, I'm normal, and there is more stuff I'm dealing with than at home, so the stuff you are saying to me makes me feel stupid—it's not helpful!' If I say something to my parents I get into more trouble; it's always all my fault! Which isn't true!"

Maria was very careful to let us all know that she's not telling anyone about her self-harming—a refrain we heard more than once in confessions about this type of activity. It's almost as if this lack of attention-seeking is thought to reveal something about character. Girls who harm themselves are often accused of being drama queens looking for headlines. Maria's "but I'm okay," was a powerful statement; it seemed to exemplify not only a girl's need to express herself, but also her need to be able to make mistakes and even fail.

As the girls set off and we packed up our recording devices, we talked about this harmful world we've created—a world where girls need to shrink, hide and manage the expression of their negative emotions by turning inward and, sometimes, hurting themselves. A world that simultaneously acts as if something is wrong with them, something that needs to be "fixed" by parents, schools and health professionals. If so many girls share this experience, surely it can't be all about the girls themselves. Are we suffocating girls with impossible expectations? Is the accumulation of high-pressure performance, unnamed violence, public policing, surveillance and control driving girls into quiet violence against themselves in much greater numbers than what is seen in boys?

Recent studies show that the number of hospitalizations for self-harm has increased by more than 85 percent in the past five years; girls account for 80 percent of young people admitted for self-harm injury.[1]

Instances of depression and anxiety are also increasing, and girls are twice as likely to experience these than boys. The dissatisfaction and decline in girls' happiness is marked by diminishing self-confidence and struggles with depression, body image, self-harm and suicidal thoughts. Girls' mental health suffers as they move through the years between grade six and grade ten.[2] Additionally, 31 percent of girls admit to starving themselves to lose weight,[3] 34 percent of high school girls have symptoms of depression and about 18 percent of all high school girls report that they have seriously considered attempting suicide in the past year.[4]

Taking a global look at this issue, Candis Steenbergen, a girlhood academic and professor of humanities, philosophy and religion at Concordia University, told us, "In the redrawing of the trajectory of fear in all these negative ways around girls' sadness, never once does anyone stand back and say, 'What's wrong with the system? What's wrong with our [Anglo-American] culture?' Why are we allowed to make this a personal problem rather than a cultural one? Making it personal keeps it tidy."

Perhaps we need to see activities like cutting, self-starvation and drinking (which we'll explore later in this chapter) as dangerous survival tactics—for coping with a world in which girls feel limited in their ability to act and to be in control of their own lives. Perhaps these are strategies girls use to get through their challenges and hardships, rather than pathological behaviours that need to be shamed and contained. If we can see these self-harming acts as signals from girls that they need help to navigate their experiences, we can try to change the road map. How can we give girls more room to move? What do girls need to take space, to speak out, to try on different identities and to push the limits on their very public road to self-discovery?

DAY TWO WITH PRESSURE

After our first day of Whitehorse interviews, we stayed up late talking about what we'd heard and how it fit in with our experiences elsewhere on our tour and in our research. A few things were glaringly obvious: girls today feel tremendous pressure to perform at very high levels (to be supersmart, superattractive and superpopular), and they try their best to respond to these desires (which are often covertly and overtly imposed).

The following day, we walked in the early daylight to the dance studio for another round of interviews—in which a new group of girls shared more about the external stressors at work in their lives. Sitting on the long retro couch in the media arts room, Sam, 15, told us that high school was the hardest thing she'd done so far. "It's like reality slapping in you in the face," she said. "Academically it's hard. Socially it's even harder. I don't want to hang out with anyone. I hate everyone at my school." Fourteen-year-old Marley added, "I feel like I could be doing so much better. I'm so exhausted, I can't even open my eyes; I can't even wake up in the morning [because I'm working so hard and staying up so late to try to do better at school]." Katia, 14, simply said, "I'm lonely."

We passed around some lemonade as the girls continued to talk about social pressure. "For girls, there is also pressure to look a certain way, to dress a certain way, to act a certain way," said Gloria, 16. "We have to act strong but also be nice. But if you're nice people call you fake, and then if you are quiet, people call you rude and judgmental. It's really hard to find a happy medium where people aren't judging you that much. I used to get really upset when people didn't like me, because I wanted everyone to like me. It's hard when you hear that someone doesn't like you."

"In grade eight," said Sharlene, 16, "it was a crazy year. All my friends were really popular, and I was always trying to keep up and do stuff to make people like me. But this became kind of the opposite. If you try to dress nice, then other girls are going to be jealous. If you only listen to the haters, then you are going to think you are really not a good person. Then you are basing your values on what other people think. You have to find reasons as to why they are wrong."

"I'm pretty sure that 90 percent of girls are called sluts sometime in their lives," said Alison, 15. "I've been called a slut, but it's really stupid because I know I'm not."

Tanya, 15, one of the top dancers and a proud tomboy, told us, "Out of all the girls in my school, I was probably called a slut the most—and I'm the most square, if you actually know me. It just seems really stupid.

I think it's because I have a lot of guy friends. The word gets tossed around so much, it doesn't mean anything anymore."

"But it can still destroy your reputation and make life very bad, though, because people judge you. They spread rumours and then exclude you," said Alison.

The idea of shaming and the policing of girls by girls and boys turned the conversation in a new direction, and the girls discussed alcohol, sex and partying as other areas where they experience a lot of pressure. "A lot of girls get drunk and have a lot of sex at parties because they are drunk," said Sharlene. "We sort of know that you shouldn't mix alcohol, sex and drugs, but again, there is a lot of pressure to do this. There are guys who are all about sex who really push this."

Chelsea, 15, told us, "Because my friends are really popular, we started hanging with older people and now there is so much pressure to drink and go to parties. This has made me so depressed. I don't feel ready. I was really down for awhile about this; it got really bad to the point where I didn't eat for a few months. I've never talked about it before. I don't think I felt overweight. I just felt so hateful of myself for not being into it and up to it with the older crowd. I felt I didn't deserve to eat. So for a few months I was anorexic. I was really scared of getting caught but there was just so much stuff going on, so much drama, too much pressure. I couldn't take it anymore."

Gloria put her arm around Chelsea. She said that even being depressed is a tricky situation because it carries a coolness factor and can be a way to get peer attention. "Some girls post all over Facebook, 'Oh I'm so depressed,'" she said. "They tell everyone. The people who actually seem really depressed never talk about it because they are ashamed."

Some of the girls mentioned Demi Lovato, one of their favourite pop icons, and how she has endeared herself to tween fans by publicly disclosing how she suffered depression as a young, high-performing girl. Like so many girls, she lived through years of self-harm, in her case with bulimia and drug abuse. Since coming out of rehab in 2010, she has been on a path of active role modelling, staying in close contact with her fans via Twitter and promoting self-acceptance in various ways—like posting selfies while wearing no makeup, cheering fans on with positive messages like, "You're beautiful just the way you are," and speaking about the fact that her grandfather was gay and so is she. She is admired by many of the girls we've met, not just because she's Latina and successful, but because she's so open about her struggles and is using her fame to initiate awareness about the lesser-known side of the girlhood experience and about female self-harm.

"The media makes it feel like every girl has some level of depression," Gloria continued. "So if you are not depressed, you are like, 'Wow, there must be something [I can] find to make myself depressed, because I can't be happy because no one is happy.'"

"Every girl goes through not liking herself," Alison told us, "but if you get to know other people and learn about what they are feeling, too, you become kinder."

We talked to the girls about the fact that the higher rates of depression, self-harm and low self-esteem among girls are linked with their limited coping channels, which means that girls are more likely to internalize their troubles, while boys are more likely to externalize theirs.[5] Boys are encouraged to take their aggression out "on the field," or in the gym, where girls are generally not encouraged in the same way. Expressing strong negative emotions is not what we expect, or accept, of girls—something numerous girls have told us. The girls in Whitehorse agreed that they feel the pressure to maintain the "good girl" image. Girls who rebel or don't meet this standard are often met with dismissal, judgment or punishment, rather than support and affirmation.[6] This simple but powerful "good girl" stereotype prevents girls from acting out in the way boys do and puts girls at higher risk of the harmful side effects of internalizing their negative emotions and frustrations, including participating in heavy alcohol use and substance abuse, dropping out of school, low physical activity, intentional self-harm and being victims of dating violence.[7]

When the girls left for dance practice, we walked back to Andrea's under an early moon in the crisp night air. We discussed how at a time when girls are feeling so much pressure to lead full and productive lives, they are also faced with contradictions, double standards and social pressures that keep them constrained and controlled by outmoded societal attitudes. How can we assist girls to become aware of these constraints? we wondered. How can we make sure they have effective coping strategies along this tumultuous journey, so they have choices beyond self-harm?

WHY DO GIRLS CUT THEMSELVES? A CLOSER LOOK

Our discussions about self-harm with the girls in Whitehorse made us remember a story a little closer to home, one that we followed up as soon as we returned.

> While dropping off Morganne at her soccer practice, I ran into her teammate's mom, Adrianna, who confided in a moment of grief that her 15-year-old daughter had been cutting herself. She looked at me in that instant of shared concern, hoping for any way out of the desperate fear and helplessness that a parent feels when confronting the dark reality of their child's self-harm. I told her about our work and the research we were doing, and we promised to talk further. We got together and she shared the story of how her daughter progressed from cutting herself to being hospitalized with an eating disorder.
>   ~Tatiana

Adrianna is trying hard to understand how today's youth see themselves, their bodies, their feelings and their world. Like many of the girls who turn to self-harm, Adrianna's daughter, Lili, who is 16 now, seemed fine on the outside—sociable, talented, beautiful and smart. But underneath her smile, and the scars accumulating on her arms, she is also battling an eating disorder and suicidal thoughts.

"In primary school my daughter was extra-high-performing," Adrianna told us when we sat down for a chat after our tour. "She was the academic superstar, the last person you could imagine would act this way. Back then I thought she'd be a breeze."

We told her about some of the stories we'd heard at the dance studio in Whitehorse, and how the pressure those girls feel can lead them to self-harm. "You can't just be average these days," Adrianna added. "Pop stars sing about how they'd rather be anything than ordinary. There is incredible pressure on kids, especially with social media, because they all have to broadcast themselves and get 'likes' and have some kind of public persona. Even if you reject the 'superskinny' version of stereotypical beauty it's like, 'I've got to be really good at curvy and bodacious, then.' It has to be one extreme or the other; it has to be extraordinary."

Adrianna has had to take a leave of absence from work to care for Lili. This includes monitoring her food intake and overseeing visits to psychologists, psychiatrists, emergency ward nurses and medical doctors.

We met with Lili to hear her story, and to try to gain insight into how this sort of thing happens to girls. Lili is tall and beautiful, with long brown hair and soulful eyes. She was wearing her school uniform the day we met her in a buzzing café on her private-school campus, where Sia was crooning from speakers in the background. Lili told us about her life a few years ago—she was popular among her social group and at the top of her class in a highly competitive school where affluent kids are driven to perform at the highest levels, on their way to some of Canada's top universities for degrees in law and medicine. At first it felt good to be an elite among the elite, but the pressure to stay on top required a lot of things that Lili didn't feel good about. Socially, her friends were catty, constantly backstabbing, criticizing, betraying and humiliating others, a practice at which she, too, was expected to be proficient. Academically, she worked incredibly hard but felt no passion for the subjects. These pressures mounted until she began to feel very unhappy. She started reaching out to other kids to make up for the bitchiness, and to search for friends who were more like her on the inside. She was tired of maintaining the image that was required for her to stay on top—always happy and perfect when in fact she was struggling to be, and to find, herself.

Soon enough, she lost her old friends and her marks slipped, and Lili's unhappiness became unbearable. She started cutting herself, and because this relieved some of the pressure she was feeling, the practice became an addiction. But when one of the girls in her class discovered her secret and word got out, other girls started cutting, too. In this highly competitive high school, cutting turned into a competition over who was the most authentically sad. "I got called an attention whore," Lili remembered, for unintentionally starting a "craze" that to her was very real and very private. "I wanted to disappear." Lili began to starve herself. She was medicated for depression, and the hospitalizations that her mother described above started. "Cutting to get the pain out of your head, not eating to forget that you're sad, forget that you're losing friends, forget that you're not doing what you like, avoiding the issues, not accepting that you are sad"—this is how Lili described her attraction to self-harm.

Two years later, Lili is in recovery. "I was scared to fail but I had to lose everything to want to get it back," she said. "I had to crash to get back up. [For awhile] I really wanted to die. I wanted to free myself from it all—it was so exhausting."

Today, Lili feels that her harrowing experience helped her discover how to express herself. "Now, when I'm sad, I don't stay in my room. I will come out and tell someone about how I'm feeling," she said. She also told us that she's found a gift for art, and in the process learned how good it makes her feel to express herself this way—none of which was obvious to her while she was battling for survival in her high school's competitive pressure cooker. This crisis brought her to her true interest and her true self. "I don't cut myself to get through bad feelings anymore. Now I turn to music, drawing, writing, singing, acting, dancing. It's such a good feeling. I've always loved singing; this is one part of myself I will never doubt. It's mine."

We asked what advice she had for other girls who turn to self-harm to deal with life's hardships. "Girls are taught to be very reserved, but we have so many emotions—we think a lot," she said. "Everybody expects us to be the best at everything." She stressed that this competitive drive applies even to negative situations. "We want to be the saddest, the skinniest, have the most cuts. I want to remind girls that they are all unique.

The more you want to be like someone else, the worse you'll feel; you never will be anyone but you. Stop focusing on what other girls have. Focus on what you have. Keep on doing what you love and what you are good at. Be proud of what you have, instead of comparing yourself. And dare to be different—have different styles, different ways to think, and then bring these differences and qualities together with your friends. Help each other."

It was great to see Lili beaming her strength. She said she was happy, that she has good friends and that she loves her dance programme. She is proud of her healing, realistic about her nature and optimistic about how to manage these issues over the long term. "I know that I will always struggle with not feeling satisfied, so I focus on what satisfies me instead," she told us as she prepared to head back to class. "I focus now on what makes me feel good."

Following our meeting with Lili, we sought out Dr. Nancy Heath, an international leader in the field of self-injury and a professor at McGill University. Dr. Heath sees self-injury as a way for girls to claim ownership over their bodies and express overwhelming negative emotions. "The reason they are having negative emotions is that they feel they have no power or agency to get their needs met. They internalize self-hatred and self-criticism, and there is very much a feeling of not being good enough. They think, 'What is wrong with me, why can't I do better?'" Dr. Heath told us that in her work with girls, she asks them how they can take control and fight back. "What girls need is self-determination," she told us. "Do they feel they have some say in life? Are they supported in their environment? Or do they feel they are hitting their head against a brick wall and they have no control?"

Dr. Heath's advice to parents is to take the signs they see or hear from their daughters about unhappiness or self-harm seriously, without either over- or underreacting. "The main issue is that they don't feel close to someone. Listen, understand what listening does; let them speak," Dr. Heath said. She noted that in cases like these there is often a history of feeling invalidated. "We can react without reacting in a way that undermines girls' realities. For example, when our daughter comes home from school and tells a negative story about friends that affects her and we say, 'I'm not sure if she meant it, maybe you are overreacting; I'm sure she wasn't trying to be mean,' this downplays or devalues her experience and invalidates her feelings. It does not create autonomy or support. As parents, we want to problem-solve. We need instead to let them say what they are feeling and have faith that they will problem-solve on their own, or ask them if they can."

DEPRESSION, RESILIENCE AND NEW IDEAS FOR COPING

Sitting on Andrea's couch after our second day of interviews in Whitehorse, with her houseful of visitors teeming around us, we wondered about the links between the relentless pressure girls are feeling and the increasing amount of attention society seems to be paying to depression. Is depression really on the rise, or is this new focus the result of a society that pathologizes girls? The answer, in fact, is both.

Due to the rapid social and technological changes we've experienced over the last ten years, today's teens live their lives much more visibly than ever before. While there are certainly positives that come along with this—the accessibility of information, platforms for diversified self-expression, connectivity and the ability to participate in world events—this increased visibility makes it more difficult for them to establish a secure sense of self and identity. When we were in Toronto, we met with Dr. Nancy Poole, director of the British Columbia Centre of Excellence for Women's Health. Dr. Poole is an author and leader in women's health and policy research; one of her areas of focus is alcohol and prescription drug use in girls and women.

Dr. Poole began our chat with a thoughtful question: "How do we support girls' resilience in the face of all the pressures they are contending with and what are the things we need to do to strengthen their ability to manage?" She explained that the institutional response to teenage depression is a quick diagnosis followed by a plethora of pharmaceutical drugs. "If we understand the pressures girls are under, supporting them to be strong and resilient in managing these instead of diagnosing this normal struggle with depression would be more helpful," Dr. Poole said. Girls and women are twice as likely to be prescribed mood-altering medications such as benzodiazepines than are boys and men.[8] "The massive amounts of medication being prescribed to girls for depression, as opposed to the amounts prescribed to boys, is a real concern. I don't want to diminish the fact that there are girls who are in danger while depressed. Medication can be important, but we are filling girls' bodies with antidepressing chemicals. I think we are paralyzing them and preventing them from finding an authentic self and a sense of resilience."

Two years ago, the *Diagnostic and Statistical Manual of Mental Disorders* (DSM) was updated to include fifteen new disorders specifically aimed at conditions girls are experiencing, including depression, premenstrual syndrome, binge eating and mental disorders linked to emotional stress. While doctors claim that having these added to the manual gives them more room to try to find relief for their patients, in the wake of the changes, profit margins for pharmaceutical companies have gone up 20 percent in the US alone.[9] This trigger-happy tendency when it comes to medicating (and overmedicating) girls has an economic underbelly—a fact that Dr. Poole tries to highlight by raising awareness of gender stereotypes in the medical field.

"It's not only about the differing levels of depression," she told us, "it's also about the gendered responses to depression. Girls are seen as emotional and boys are seen as needing to go and work out in the gym." Dr. Poole argues that these stereotypes result in girls having fewer options for coping, and therefore being prescribed more medication. "It is quicksand that girls are standing on. Who are they supposed to be? On the one hand, they are expected to be and act empowered and liberated, and on the other they are still seen and treated as if they are the softer girls of the past." Socially, girls are left in the impossible position of having to be cool, have sex and drink, yet not be "sluts" or struggle with addiction or depression.

While social media has meant so many good things for girls, Dr. Poole pointed out that, as with the advent of anything new, change also requires us to look back at all that's been supplanted and consider whether there are "old ways" that should be woven back into the new fabric. "Kids need reflection and time off," she said, "and we as a society need to be critiquing how structured girls' lives have become. In many cases they don't actually have any free time. They don't have time to consider what they want to create or what they want to be and do, or how they might spend their time in a way that makes them feel good inside." She described how girls can be overpraised for performance and overmonitored; the quiet, unplugged, reflection and free outdoor-play time previously available to them is now either gone, or has been made public. The result, Dr. Poole noted, is that we have taken away their opportunities to develop resilience through making mistakes and experiencing failures, and having the privacy and the time to reflect on these. "We have to give kids space, and permission to go through challenges to find their own solutions. This is part of the act of knowing themselves and being a strong human being."

Dr. Poole reiterated that girls know what they need and can articulate it when they are approached in the right way. Rather than panic and rush to medicate girls, she suggests that we engage more with them and seek their advice. "A great start would be to ask, 'When you get upset, how would you like us to respond?' And if we say, 'Go ahead and make choices and know that it's okay if it doesn't turn out or if you get upset,' this is a powerful signal that we are there for them and that they won't be turned into victims for struggling in life."

BINGE DRINKING AND SUBSTANCE USE

As we continued our conversation, Dr. Poole pointed out that girls as young as 13 are using alcohol excessively, and that in a recent international study, Canada was identified as one of the countries with the highest rate of girls drinking to extremes. "What's troubling is not only that they are starting to drink at a young age," Dr. Poole continued, "but that they are drinking at binge levels." Girls are using alcohol at an earlier age and in greater numbers, and in some jurisdictions adolescent girls and young women are just as likely as boys and young men to engage in "binge" drinking (drinking more than three to four drinks per sitting). Over 85 percent of Canadian girls ages 15 to 24 drink in excess of Canadian low-risk guidelines.[10]

Dr. Poole is concerned that we just aren't talking about this issue and, as a result, aren't equipping girls to be safe. She wonders if the stigma associated with the topic prevents us from tackling the issue openly and effectively.

The girls we met in Whitehorse told us that drinking and drug taking are big social pressures—and we heard this in several other contexts, too. Substance use is also one of the chief go-tos for dealing with the pressure of high performance. In our online survey, 49 percent of girls reported they deal with stress by using substances.

Recent studies conducted by the Johns Hopkins Bloomberg School of Public Health found that adolescent girls are increasingly targeted by alcohol marketing, and that girls are more likely than boys to be overexposed to alcohol advertising. The Canadian Medical Association ran an editorial piece that found that this increase in exposure was associated with increased alcohol consumption in adolescents.[11] "The advertising industry knows very well how to secure new, lifelong clients," the story concluded, "The type of alcohol advertising being directed at young women suggests that an attractive body and a successful, trendy life will be the result of using any particular product. Many of these ads also suggest that men will find them to be a more desirable sex object." Covering this topic in the *Globe and Mail* in 2013,[12] journalist Susan Krashinsky spoke to 15-year-old Brayden, who confirmed why these ads are effective: "At my school, [the students] definitely support drinking. They see it as fun and cool and trendy . . . You see the ads and [the teens] all look like they're having fun, and they're on a private jet and stuff." These stories shine light on the fact that while girls and women are drinking to keep up with and surpass boys and men, this new-found equality is having an unequal impact on their bodies. Women have higher risk for liver, brain and heart damage than men do who drink comparable amounts, and gender-specific risks include breast cancer, osteoporosis, violence and unwanted sex and pregnancy.[13]

Dr. Poole shares this concern. "The impact of drinking on girls' bodies is really problematic. We don't have enough data, given that we haven't seen the long-term health impact of drinking younger," she said. She elaborated by telling us, "If alcohol is the recreational panacea to teen angst and social experimentation, anxiety medication and pain medication are the drugs of choice for girls. The combination of alcohol and antidepressants, and other medications, has negative impacts that we don't yet fully understand. Early alcohol use may result in fertility problems for girls, and long-term alcohol and substance use can also cause damage to the liver and kidneys, as well as create a compromised ability to manage pressures and accumulated stresses."

Dr. Poole emphasized that she wasn't being moralistic or judgmental, but that she wanted to help girls be healthy—to think through what they want to do, where they want to go in their lives and what their relationship is to alcohol and other substances. By doing so, she hopes to create a context in which girls can be safe. She defined her approach to educating girls about alcohol and substance use as "harm reduction." This acknowledges that while girls do drink and experiment with substances in their teen years, risks can be reduced when girls are coached about how to avoid them. "Hospitals are seeing toxic overdose all the time," Dr. Poole told us. "Yet we are not talking about this. We need to be open." She believes that it's very important to discuss and publicly debate alcohol and its associated risks, and to give girls lots of healthy choices that counterbalance their social lives, things like sports, resilience-building, eating well and practicing mindfulness or other alternative methods for relaxation and awareness.

Dr. Poole recognized that it's not easy to broach this subject with girls. "If we come at drinking and its effect as a discussion about body parts, it isn't going to work," Dr. Poole said. "Girls will learn about alcohol through sharing their experiences. It's essential to build trust between teens and adults and to create an open dialogue."

How can adults offer support on this front? We can help girls analyze how they are targeted by the commercial alcohol industry. We can teach them how to drink safely and to understand the risks associated with binge drinking. We can encourage a buddy system, where girls learn to stick together with a friend or group of friends that they trust when heading out on party adventures. And, perhaps most important, we can avoid making them feel bad for satisfying the natural curiosity of adolescence and instead encourage chats about risks and responsibility with alcohol and drugs. If girls know that it's okay to come to adults whenever they have questions, or to call if they're in trouble—even and *especially* if that's late at night at a party and they're drunk or high—then we will truly have brought this topic out of the closet.

DAY THREE WITH PRESSURE: RESILIENCE

On our last day in Whitehorse, we gathered girls around Andrea's kitchen table and asked them to describe their resilience, and how they've come by it. Over the course of the three days with these girls, we found that providing a space in which they could share their experiences and vulnerabilities allowed them to discover that they were not alone, that they were not the problem and that they had advice and good strategies to give one another. In this spirit, we asked them to tell us what they've learned from their experiences and what more they feel they need to help them through the tough times.

Melodie, a graceful 16-year-old, told us, "I have the ability to do what I want. I'm strong. It's usually myself in mental struggle, reminding me to stay strong."

"Me, too," said Annabel, 16. "I feel confident. I'm not ashamed. I feel if I want to do something, I'm comfortable. I can go after what I want."

Seventeen-year-old Sasha said, "Because I'm a dancer people don't know that I do weight training four times a week, and that I'm also creative and imaginative. I'm independent. I don't need people's approval."

Maddison, 16, said, "Having a sense of who you want to be is important," and she told us that she wants to travel and study to be an engineer.

Lucy, 16, who survived the sadness of a death in the family, told us, "You are going to be sad and feel worthless and you're going to feel bad. You will have things happen, and you have to keep going. That's what makes you confident. Resilience builds confidence. Every time you go through something you think you can't handle, and you do, it just shows you that you can get through. It makes you stronger every time. It's totally true."

As we ate the cookies baked in Andrea's kitchen by the breakdancers, the girls told us about the importance of friends. "You need to surround yourself with people who make you feel better," said Olivia, 15, remembering how when she went through a difficult period she decided to spend time with only the people who build her up.

"Part of overcoming pain is having support," Thalia, 15, agreed. "You have to change yourself. My best friend and I both had an eating disorder; we were helping each other through it. We were like, 'I have this problem and I know you do, too.' There was a lot of leaning on each other's shoulders. It really helped to have friends to support me."

"There should be a class in school where you learn to be supportive and loving," said Olivia, "where girls can get past drama and being mean."

Perseverance was also a theme. "You have to be prepared to sacrifice things with an end goal in mind and work through tough times to succeed, which can be hard," said Sasha. "It's hard to pass up the fun stuff, like drinking and parties, to get though the nitty-gritty daily stuff to get to that point where you're on the other side. You have to be confident enough to say no to the things that distract from your goals."

Annabel talked about how crucial dancing has been. "Sports and dance and gymnastics are really important. Through these you learn from a young age that if you want something you have to work at it. Sports gave us that."

Olivia said that having one another and having Andrea has made these difficult years manageable, even enjoyable. Not feeling alone, and having good advice and trustworthy support has been crucial. "Andrea is a role model. She notices when you are having a bad day. We actually hang out here, and also at the studio. We get close with the dance groups."

The other girls were a chorus of consensus, demonstrating the importance of both peer support and support from sympathetic adults. "I love hanging out here, too," said Maddison. "If I have a bad day at school, it's a good place to get away. It's a place where people can come and hang out and be free to do whatever they want. The studio built a big huge table for teens. This one guy has been there all summer, drawing. Andrea is creating a space where we can be ourselves and no one cares."

"We get a lot of information from Andrea. She answers all our questions. She shows us books and pictures and stuff about sex things. She's really good with it; she is not awkward," said Lucy.

With Andrea, they talk about all the things they want to know but are too shy to ask others. "She is our own personal teacher," said Melodie. They go to Andrea when they have a question, when they need birth control, when they're having trouble with their families or friends or partners. They trust her and she inspires them with good advice.

+++

When the girls had gone and Andrea returned home, we sat and watched videos of her son, Riley, breakdancing with Kiesza at the Juno awards, and her daughter, Grace, putting a whole roomful of male breakdancers in Norway to shame. We ate the rest of the cookies. Then, over tea, we returned to our discussion of pressure and self-harm, and what we had heard from the girls in Whitehorse.

Today's girls, it seems, are suffering the consequences of some long-standing systemic problems, many of which we have covered so far in this book: limiting gender binaries, sexist stereotypes, double standards and cultures of violence that are considered normal. This is the back-drop of girls' lives. Add to this high performance expectations and the pressure to be "supergirl"; gender differences when it comes to ways of coping with that pressure; and a basic unwillingness on the part of society to address the root causes beyond the individualized "problem" of a girl. All of this is combined with a new world in which life is lived as if in a fishbowl, and where peer and parental judgment are all too often swift and harsh and rationalize new opportunities to lock girls down. The results can be toxic. Self-harm in the form of cutting, eating disorders, binge drinking and drug use may seem to be more prevalent than ever before, but part of the problem could be that these behaviours—and the reasons for them—have been festering in silence for far too long, and that it is finally time for them to be addressed, by all of us.

It's outrageous and terribly sad for girls to be secretly cutting and puking almost as a rite of passage from girlhood to womanhood. Our rites of passage should celebrate girls—their voices, their gifts, their potential—and arm them to nurture these special qualities so they can thrive. We can do this by supporting girls in the ways they've told us they'd like to be supported: by helping them locate their internalized pain within broader social issues; by nourishing their friendships and trusting relationships; by fostering their self-determination and autonomy through choices; by being open and honest with them about alcohol and substance use; by encouraging sports and the building of resilience; and by being sincerely open to hearing their feelings and having faith in their solutions, no matter how much we want to step in and problem-solve. If self-harm is happening, the best way to counteract it is not by judging it and freaking out, but by listening.

Girls may internalize both their own problems and the collective problems around them, but it's the external contexts we need to address to stop this internalization from morphing into self-harm. It is society that needs to change, not girls themselves. In the words of Camille, who is 12 and cutting, "I don't want to be treated. I want to be heard."

SURVIVAL KIT

HELP GIRLS LEARN ABOUT THEIR BODIES IN POSITIVE AND FUNCTIONAL WAYS. Validate their strengths and abilities. Break out of the usual "appearance-focused" way of talking about girls as pretty and cute. Instead, notice how fast she runs, how strong her muscles are and how good she is at kicking a ball.

HELP GIRLS DEVELOP RESILIENCE. Research shows the fastest way to develop resilience in young people is to help them develop confidence, critical thinking and connection.[14] Here are some ways to do that.

1. Focus on something that is special about her and reinforce that for her regularly.
2. Don't put yourself down in front of her or talk about how fat you feel or look.
3. Let her lead, let her take risks, validate her experience and provide fair and consistent structure for her daily life so she has a safe space in which to grow.
4. Give her room to make mistakes, to fail and to do her own problem-solving.
5. Recognize the cultural dimensions in girls' lives that may support or hinder resilience.

BE CALM ABOUT SELF-HARM. If your daughter is harming herself, don't blame anyone, don't get angry and don't worry hysterically. But don't underreact, either. Take it seriously, even if it's only happened once. Listen to her. Ask her what she wants to say and how she would like to deal with this issue. Let her speak.

ENCOURAGE SAFER DRINKING. Talk to girls in their late-teens about drinking safely and responsibly. Refer to Canada's Low-Risk Alcohol Drinking Guidelines. Here are some tips:

- Drink in safe settings.
- Drink slowly. Have no more than two drinks in any three hours.
- For every drink of alcohol, have one non-alcoholic drink.
- Eat before and while you are drinking.
- Always consider your age, body weight and health problems that might suggest lower limits.
- For more information on girls, depression and alcohol visit: http://girlsactionfoundation.ca/files/alcohol_depression_1.pdf

BUILD A DIALOGUE around and promote the practice of self-care.

- Encourage her to take time out from her regular routine, go for walks, do exercise or meditation, have massages, or soak in a bath with a good book—all ways to practise mental health promotion.
- Model this by making self-care a priority in your own life.
- Encourage some activities (like those listed above) that girls can do on their own. Alone time fosters self-knowledge, self-investment and self-reflection. Girls learn to build confidence and resilience in the face of challenges by forging a loyalty to themselves.

EXPLORE ALTERNATIVE APPROACHES to mental health and wellness. Learn about youth-led and girl-centred groups and programmes in your area. Explore alternatives to medicalization, like naturopathy, homeopathy, counselling, osteopathy and acupuncture.

HELP GIRLS CHANNEL NEGATIVE EMOTIONS OUTWARD through sports, art, media creation and activism. Support girls to express themselves and to think critically about why they may be feeling self-destructive or why they may be feeling down. These kinds of activities stimulate reflection and help girls develop action strategies for coping with and transforming external influences.

ENCOURAGE PHYSICAL ACTIVITY. Physical activity in general offers important opportunities to positively influence mental health by providing a range of benefits, including enhanced mood, increased confidence and resiliency, decreased stress, improved body image and improved working memory and concentration. If team sports don't suit your daughter, encourage her to try a solitary sport like running, cycling, skateboarding or walking. Self-defence classes like martial arts or boxing also add confidence to a girl's experience. Check out FitSpirit, an organization that helps teenage girls discover the fun of being active and healthy with friends.

CHALLENGE YOUR OWN EXPECTATIONS, PRESSURES AND SUPERHERO ROLE. Practise what you preach and call yourself out when you see that you are modelling a quest for perfection that your daughter, niece or friend may try to follow. Talk about this with her and tell her about your own insecurities and hardships. This will give her permission to have failures, feel disappointment and be realistic in her goals, as well as strong in her ability to take both the good and the bad in stride.

POWER PLAYING:
ROLLING WITH THE DERBY GIRLS

WE WERE ON OUR WAY to a roller derby game in Montreal when we started to think really deeply about power: how girls deal with their place in a wider power structure, but also how they wield it against each other. At a time when there is a lot of attention given to girl "drama" and bullying, our mission was to examine "girl power" dynamics and gather information from girls about how they are accessing power and exercising it affirmatively and positively.

As the neon, sequined and tattooed audience poured into the stadium to witness this derby extravaganza—a women's game that takes place on roller skates and is both ultra-athletic and aggressive, not to mention populated by players in fishnet stockings and glamarama short shorts— we thought over the various ways that girl power has manifested itself in recent years. Perhaps one of the most prevalent incarnations, if not necessarily a positive one, is the "mean girl." Ever since the film *Mean Girls* illuminated the world of "The Plastics," and the sitcom *Gossip Girl* invented bitch-face air kisses, the mean girl has become an infamous cultural prototype that feeds into, and amplifies, popular anxiety about girl bullying.

The idea that girls are becoming more aggressive and violent gets a lot of airtime.[1] As with the saying "boys will be boys," this social dynamic is trivialized by the catchall description "girl drama," and packaged into an overarching problem of girl bullying. We see regular sensational headlines about mean girls, gossip girls and girl bullies, but the truth is (as you'll see later in this chapter) girls are no more violent today than they were in the past. So why is this even a newspaper-selling topic? Is it because the way we monitor and respond to girls is changing? Is it that girls police each other differently than they used to?

As the roller derby teams faced off and began rushing around the track, jamming and blocking at high speed and getting fishnet burns as the crowd cheered, we thought about how today's girls are told that they are empowered—and yet they come up against systems, structures, attitudes and judgments that limit their ability to exercise power. Girls are expected to be nice, to accommodate others and to not "rock the boat." At the same time, girls also experience daily encounters with injustice through surveillance, dress codes and sexual harassment. Girls are led to believe that they have only one path to power—popularity. And to be popular and successful, as we've seen, girls are expected to meet the requirements of idealized femininity, which, above all, are to be pretty and white and a conspicuous consumer, dressed in the latest brands that mark social status.

Power, it seems, is a minefield. In today's competitive, high-pressure and very public world, what forms of power do girls actually have access to, and what constraints bind their actions? On the roller derby track, it's clear that power, strength and bravery are admired and applauded. But what happens when the game ends and the congratulatory high fives and embraces are done?

Given our society's emphasis on individualism and choice, girls are often on their own when it comes to figuring out the power structures within which they are operating, how to live within these limiting dynamics and how to cope with issues of aggression, conflict and violence. Girls are also largely on their own to make sense of and manage their own knots of power, anger and rage. Who is guiding today's girls with these struggles? Where can they turn to learn the strategies they will need in order to be powerful beyond the tropes of popularity contests and meanness?

In looking for answers to these and other important questions, we talked to girls, moms of daughters and experts on bullying. We also arranged to meet with some of the roller derby players. Who better to tell us about breaking the rules and redefining the power-playing game?

WHERE GIRLS ACCESS POWER

The Montreal roller derby team is one of the first and best international roller derby teams in the world, and a subcultural space in which there is a lot of room to experiment with self-expression and leadership. We met Alex, Mel and Sami in a taco bar. Chill in snowboarder tuques, trendy sweats and sporting a mix of long and semi-mohawk hairdos, these late-twenties derby veterans—all players and coaches for the younger girls—had a lot to say about power. Around a table laden with drinks and vegetarian Tex-Mex, near a swing door that let in music from the adjacent band venue, the three of them talked up their pasts and the journeys they took to become the confident, assertive, powerful young women they are today.

They told us how they grew up in small towns where sports were one of the best pastimes available. Alex and Sami played hockey; there were no girl teams so they played with the boys. Mel was a snowboarder. She would go for weekends on the hills with the other snowboarders—also boys. "It was a little weird in the locker room," Sami remembered about her hockey tournaments, where she would change in the equipment room. "But the boys were so supportive and their dads would congratulate me like one of the boys after every game; they all protected me and gunned for me," she said, which is how she first discovered the feeling of camaraderie and team membership.

"This is one of the biggest things we teach the younger derby players," said Alex. "Teamwork and sisterhood. I like the idea of girl gangs. Derby is a girl gang. There is a big difference between a clique and a gang. If you're a gang with a goal, you're inclusive and directional—you support each other, defend each other and celebrate what's great about each other. Instead of looking for approval from outside of the circle, the gang helps you get what you want and need from inside, so it's not so risky or so lonely."

Mel agreed. "If you're in a gang and you're working as a group toward tangible goals, one of the things you learn is what everybody's strengths are, and what your own strengths are, and not to step outside of your boundaries and limits."

Roller derby is an aggressive sport,[2] and one whose contemporary athletics-oriented incarnation was spearheaded by women, where most sports have been originated by men. "It's rough, but we don't hit each other until we have bloody noses," said Mel, "that's not our thing. We are all so different, but we maintain a sense of humour. Our derby names are funny and we wear neon from head to toe. Even at the highest-calibre competitions, if there is a time out, we are always dancing." Roller derby provides an interesting case study for observing how power, aggression and competition come together in a positive way through collaboration and a shared goal.

"You learn to trust yourself, and to work together. It's super empowering to think, 'How can we build each other up?' and celebrate each other's qualities and skills," Alex agreed. "It's about, 'I'm going to try to focus on the positive, one thing I like about her, and help her bring that out.' When you are building something together, you have to find each other's strengths and make those glow." Alex explained that this is not about comparing and feeling bad. "If everyone agrees that every girl has something special about them and each of us points it out and encourages it to get stronger, then we are all benefitting because we all feel good, we all feel special and we are all pooling what's great about us to create a winning team."

"I think you need to differentiate good competition from bad competition," said Mel. "Bad competition is taking someone down to make yourself feel better. Good competition requires collaboration and recognizes people's strengths."

"Instead of seeing people as threats," said Sami, corroborating the derby girl mantra, "we see them as a challenge to better yourself. I still do that and I tell girls younger than me to do that, too," she told us. "Find someone you admire and follow them on Instagram. Find out what they do to be that thing that they're good at and that you admire, and try doing it, too."

"People are attracted to people who are doing things and being themselves," said Alex. "That's how you find your gang. Girls often gravitate to passive roles when they could be active doing things. Ask yourself,

'What's going to challenge me and make me passionate; what are my goals?' instead of looking to the outside, waiting for others to tell you what your qualities are."

Girls have so few opportunities to learn and really hone these skills. Many of the girls we spoke to complained about, but also revelled in, girl drama, bullying, gossip, exclusion, slut-shaming and the ups and downs and ins and outs of popularity. They emphasized the importance of "like" culture, boys' attention and sexual competition. While these social relationships are grounds for learning, they can also be a daily struggle that fuels the constant threat of slandering, alienation, harsh and public shaming, exclusion and, in extreme cases, social annihilation. Relationships with each other are very important to girls, and take up a lot of their time and energy.

"Girls are still socialized to gain value and attention through external approval—get good marks, please the world, get approval, get a guy," said Sami, reiterating the messages girls receive from the world. "We need to educate girls better when they're younger. We shouldn't have to wait until university and women's studies [classes] to discover that being sweet and winning the guy isn't the only narrative."

DEBUNKING THE BULLY: BAND-AIDS AND ROOT CAUSES

Bullying has gained a lot of attention in the digital age. Private lives now have a public platform where everything is evaluated. Bad news and scandalous behaviour gather sensational crowds on social media, often with public, passionate and negative reactions. Among a digital generation raised on violent immersive video games, pornography and reality TV—where careers and reputations end when contestants are slandered and voted off the show by viewers on their smart phones—public shaming is woven deeply into public behaviour as a socially sanctioned blood sport.

As focus has shifted onto this dynamic by both bullying-awareness campaigns and social-media publicity, adults have made attempts to understand and fix this increasingly public "girl problem." While girls seem to talk about it and accept it as part of growing up as a girl, the popular response to the stock image of the mean or violent girl is one of fear and anxiety. Teachers are looking for support, especially as parents pressure them to help deal with daughters facing social exclusion. Education leaders and policy-makers try to quell the problem with bullying policies and programmes that are largely generic. But bullying is about power, and a one-size-fits-all approach is doomed to fail.

In our online survey we asked two questions about bullying, not just to hear more about the nature of girl bullying but also to differentiate between bullying as a generality and the many forms of discrimination that bullying entails. Our questions were: (1) Were you ever bullied? (80 percent of our respondents answered yes); and (2) Were you ever bullied as a form of discrimination? Below are some of the responses:

> I was called every name in the book that had to do with a woman giving herself away—worthless, stupid, whore, etc.—for what was at the time kissing at age 12. I was always a little out there, very sexually curious, but it was always something private for me. I'd tell my friends and they'd spread it around. At the time of the bullying I lost all my friends, spent a lot of time crying in the washroom and eventually hurting myself. It was a dark place for a couple years.

> I've been bullied for being Chinese. I frequently hear people use "Asian" as an insult, in the context of, "That's so Asian of you" or "You're pretty for an Asian."

> I'm bullied with common stereotypes regarding being East Asian. Many white or non–East Asian people in my school seem to share the sentiment that there are "too many of [you]." I also regularly encounter Asian kids who pride themselves on being "white-washed" and join in the mocking of other students they consider "fobby."

> I was bullied in high school because I could only afford two pairs of pants. People thought it was disgusting. I was the only one in my

leadership class who couldn't afford to go on the leadership weekend kayaking trip, and others were just mean about it.

I have had people make fun of me many times about the fact that I'm bisexual. Even gay people, whom you would expect to be understanding, put me down. Coming out in high school was moderately easy, or as easy as it could be when I came out as gay, but when I came out as bi it was a really big struggle.

I have a reading disability as well as a problem with the muscles in my legs. Both have been commented on by teachers, friends, peers, etc.

I've been teased and bullied about being bisexual before. I don't freak out; I kinda let it slide because a lot of the time people don't actually understand what being bisexual means. It hurts, and why wouldn't it?

I've experienced bullying over being a girl. I was really into cars when I attended high school, and people made fun of me for being a girl taking automotive as an elective. They said I was only doing it to "get to" the guys, and even some of my former friends would say that I only did it to flirt with men, because I "couldn't possibly be interested in cars."

I have been bullied for being bisexual as well as for being skinny. Most of the time I would simply be left out and had no friends. Other times I would be called names or talked about.

In high school I experienced bullying from a teacher because I identify as a lesbian. He would not allow me within five feet of any other girl in the school, not even teachers. If he would see me close to a girl, he would physically move me.

Since the third grade people have been bullying me about how my hair is so nappy and how my skin is so dark.

These stories reflect both how wide-ranging bullying is and how profoundly it is influenced by broader power dynamics and structural discrimination. Bullying is defined as: "The use of force, threat, or coercion to abuse, intimidate, or aggressively impose domination over others. The behaviour is often repeated and habitual. One essential prerequisite is the perception, by the bully or by others, of an imbalance of social or physical power. Justifications and rationalisations for such behaviour sometimes include differences of class, race, religion, gender, sexuality, appearance, behaviour, body language, personality, reputation, lineage, strength, size or ability."[3]

As we learned in chapter 6, it's important to name each form of aggression for what it is and not throw everything indiscriminately into the bullying broom closet. Bullying is much larger than the complications of children's relationships; it is based in largely held societal beliefs and attitudes, and their incumbent structures. So, revenge porn needs to be recognized and named as sexual harassment and racial slurs need to be recognized and named as racism. These are not just "bullying."

While anti-bullying programmes abound, a serious gap exists in both curriculum and strategies to make them effective. Zero-tolerance policies and a one-size-fits-all approach do not work. Bullying expert Dr. Shelley Hymel says that bullying is about the learning of power. According to her studies, many bullies take their behaviour into later relationships in the forms of workplace violence, dating violence and partner and child abuse. She notes that when authority figures intervene with lessons instead of punitive measures, we can provide kids with alternatives to bullying. For example, we can re-channel bullying behaviours like gossiping, exclusion, mocking and name-calling toward socially appropriate leadership skills, instead. Dr. Hymel promotes social and emotional learning (SEL) which supports positive relationships, ethics and good decision-making through emotional literacy, co-operative learning and social problem-solving training.[4] After twenty years of research and development, this promising practice for bullying prevention is just now gaining momentum in schools across North America.

Specifically naming the structural forms of discrimination at play in each case builds awareness around them. And devising education and strategies based on this more targeted perspective helps break down the sweeping issue of bullying and makes it easier for us to more effectively address it in its many guises. Some kids understand this and are doing it already in movements like student-led Gay-Straight Alliances (GSAs) that work to improve the school climate for all students, regardless of sexual orientation or gender identity and expression. These kinds of initiatives specifically address homophobia and the power issues inherent in this form of discrimination.

We brought this topic up with Dr. Amy Adele Hasinoff, whom we met in chapter 3. Dr. Hasinoff said that meanness is a learned behaviour. When we told her that there seems to be an assumption that girls being mean to each other is part of who girls are, she disagreed. "Society dismisses this form of subverted aggression as a strange kind of normal," she said. "The idea that 'there is something wrong with girls' is not a productive way to look at it." We have a tendency, she explained, to treat teenagers as if they are somehow separate from society. But they aren't—they are part of it, and when we stop and remember this, it explains a lot about their behaviour. "If they have these problems, we need to look at why," Dr. Hasinoff explained. "Where do they get homophobic bullying from? They get it from society. Where do they get slut-shaming from? They get it from their environment. Girls didn't invent being mean to each other; they got that from us. Look at the way society dealt with Miley Cyrus: 'Oh look at Miley. She is being such a slut. She is too sexual. It's so inappropriate.' Girls hear adults saying that. Biases and judgments come from adults, from our culture."

How can we expect kids to solve the bullying problem when we, as adults, set such a poor example? When countries bully other countries into war? Or when cultures of dominance and discrimination perpetuate fear of the "other" and of difference? Maybe one way we can truly support kids while they deal with social power dynamics is to frame the issue, and its solution, within this broader context.

With this in mind, we set out to see how girls are navigating power in their social lives, in their intimate relationships and as individuals acting inside this bigger, more global setting. We wanted to hear from them about how they deal with anger and aggression and where they feel they may be beginning to take on outdated power structures to create new spaces of empowerment and change.

DEMYSTIFYING THE MEAN GIRL: CHANNELLING GIRL ANGER

Many of the power issues we heard about in our discussions with girls were centred on boys. This surprised us a little. While we have come a long way in empowering women and achieving political and social equity, there still seems to be a lingering belief that girls access power by "getting the guy." Girls told us that they believe boys have power, which means that girls' social lives are organized around gaining access to that power through public approval from boys and, through boys, approval from other girls.

At the skate park in Los Angeles, 16-year-old Cassie, told us about dealing with what she called the "girlie world." "I was friends with these guys," she said, "and the girls around them would try to butt me out. I was like, 'I'm not coming in on your territory.' Girls are brutal to one another; girls are really mean.

"It's a girlie-girl world," she continued. "It's hard to make girlfriends that are not catty and talking behind your back. It's really sad. They feel like this behaviour makes them cool to someone else, so they use drama to find their niche and ways to seek approval."

In Whitehorse, Siobhan, 14, shared her experience with this dynamic. "There are a lot of misunderstandings and insecurities between girls over boys. Even with best friends there is sabotage, rumours, mood swings and talking bad about people, so that friends are not friends anymore. Like my friend Jane—we were best friends. She liked this guy and he became her new boyfriend. When they got together they started saying bad things about me and now my best friend won't talk to me anymore. Girls can change when they get together with a guy."

Other girls in Whitehorse also had lots to say on the subject. Aware that it's hard to protect your reputation in a small town, where private matters become everybody's business and can be amplified a hundred times on social media, they were reluctant at first to bring it up. They were careful to tell us, like the girls in other cities did, that they were not, in fact, having sex, but that several of them had been called a slut, and were suffering stigmatization as a result. We pointed out that this is how slut-shaming allows girls to control each other; it is designed to make girls fear their own bodies, fear what they do with their bodies and fear how they dress and talk and behave, in case it is read the wrong way and their reputation is ruined. That got them talking.

"Girls are so insecure that they think there is no way that the guy they like will like them," offered Sisley, 16. "All girls hope that guys like them. If a guy does like you, then you have to boost it up to make sure he still likes you. It's so dumb. Why do you have to change if he already likes you?"

"I find that the people who call other people sluts are either jealous of what people have done or how they look," said Mallory, 15.

"Girls that have boyfriends are the complete package," 14-year-old Eva told us. "The girls who don't are missing something. So they get mad and call each other sluts. You are not supposed to want relationships—it's looked down upon—but the reality is that every girl wants to be in a relationship. So there is competition going on all the time."

In a context in which girls think they have to jockey for popularity to gain a degree of social power, fighting is inevitable. One way these emotions manifest is through covert actions like backstabbing, rumour spreading, anonymous hating on digital platforms and forcing the exclusion of others via guerrilla-style combat. So many of the girls we talked to said how much they wished that they could punch each other out, and that the drama could end there.

We asked the girls we met in New Haven if they felt they were able to deal with conflict, and how they coped with the girl dramas in their lives. Anamaria, 15, told us, "I'm scared to say something. I keep my comments to myself." Louisa, 16, said, "Some people take it the wrong way and come at me sideways, which is scary. Girl fights are brutal, and fist fighting doesn't even fix the psychological fighting. It makes it worse and makes it last longer."

Talking to girls about the way that girls shame each other brought us right back to power: Are girls acting out of anger over the fact that they are disempowered? Are they lashing out at each other to claim some power, even if it hurts their closest friends? Clearly, girls need support to find more constructive ways to negotiate their way through the social minefield of girlhood and adolescence, and to transcend the limits of defining their worth and power through external validation and negative power dynamics.

With few tools to analyze these issues, girls struggle to understand why they feel trapped in uncomfortable roles, why they treat each other harshly and how to resolve their relationships to each other, to boys and to themselves. How can girls be supported to cope with things like aggressions, frustrations and anger, which are more typically attributed to boys, and break free of the catfight cliché?

One important way we can help girls in this is by encouraging them to recast this narrative. On our tour, we've heard girls say really inspiring things about themselves—things that rework this script. They've told us that being a girl means being brave, bossy, powerful, smart, hard-working, loyal, strong, forgiving, self-conscious, open and expressive, caring, loud, competitive, ambitious, wise, patient and able to withstand high pressures and a lot of rejections. They've also said it's about being able to give birth, "which is the most brutal and most heroic thing to do on earth!" Girls use their power in many constructive and healthy ways. They help and protect each other in their friendships, they use their smarts to excel in school, they play sports, they rebel and they use their power to influence their peers and their communities.

Several girls have also told us that while boys hide the bad stuff about themselves, girls hide the good stuff: their leadership qualities, like strong self-assertion, taking the initiative, speaking out—the very things we want girls to nourish. If the good stuff includes conviction and passions, how can we help girls channel ferocity in a positive way?

As Dr. Hymel pointed out earlier, when adults intervene with lessons instead of punitive measures, these qualities can be transformed into good leadership skills. When girls are encouraged to turn their frustrations and anger toward speaking out against injustice or pursuing activities still thought to be male, such as martial arts, kick-boxing and team sports, they are natural-born leaders. Many of the changemakers we've met in this book are great examples of how girls are channelling their anger and using their power to take on the issues and structural obstacles that disempower them.

But girls who do use their power to test and rebel against oppressive social norms are often labelled "bad girls" and degraded and shamed. These girls use aggression and their sexuality to access power outside the gender box; they can scream no, hit back and join the boys. This play can be fun and attractive—people want to be around it. The trouble is, these girls are at risk if the whole thing falls apart. If a "bad girl" binge drinks, what are the consequences? If she has sex with multiple guys, what is the fallout?

In some contexts, female aggression is a matter of survival. It can also be considered a form of self-esteem and status, and is accepted and condoned in certain circumstances. For example, girls coming from an economically marginalized context may be encouraged and even expected to win physical fights. When girls are exposed to and subjected to physical violence as part of their home and community lives while growing up, they may use violence to protect and express themselves.

But in the North American schools we visited, we heard how girls' aggression is too often miscoded as disorderly conduct. Girls are still measured against middle-class, "good-girl" cultural norms, and non-compliance is met with school disciplinary policies, "behaviour problem" labels, and/or criminalization. Many girls feel it's impossible for them to deal with anger. They feel they need to conceal their negative feelings and express them through meanness.

Some experts on this issue argue that the difference between the way girls and boys fight is rooted in the way mainstream culture has socialized boys to be masculine and girls to be feminine in very particular ways.

In *Odd Girl Out*, Rachel Simmons writes that the stereotypical femininity that girls have to embrace is an underlying cause of their aggression, and the way they are taught to wield it. She quotes Peggy Orenstein, who says, "The perfect girl never has bad thoughts or feelings . . . speaks quietly, calmly, is always nice and kind, never mean or bossy." Simms herself adds, "Girls must be abnegating, and demure; girls must be nice and always put others before themselves; girls get power by who likes them, who approves, who they know, but not by their own hand. They silence themselves rather than speak their true feelings."

But this cultural norm is not true for all girls. African-American girls, for example, are socialized to have flexible gender roles; possessing a mix of both "masculine" characteristics (typically seen as assertiveness, self confidence, independence, taking responsibility and individuality) and "feminine" characteristics (typically seen as nurturance, emotional expressiveness, dependence and empathy).[5] In fact, research shows that African-American children have higher self-confidence than Caucasian children and that a key factor that influences this outcome and positive self-concept *is* flexible gender roles as well as positive body image and academic achievement. African-American girls are also found to more often accept their appearance in a positive way and to reject the mainstream media and marketing's standard messages of beauty.[6] As adults, we can recognize and validate these positive factors and use them as ways to nurture girls' self-awareness and understanding of their own power and how they can use it.

Another example of how prevalent ideas about gender are being challenged is in the queer and transgender community. People who identify as gender fluid, genderqueer or non-binary (a category for gender identities that are not exclusively masculine or feminine) don't see themselves as either male or female.[7] Their expression of their gender identity fluctuates on a spectrum between the two polarities of masculine and feminine, so a less rigid approach to gender is at play. In Indigenous communities and many other cultures, this non-binary approach to gender is celebrated and even revered. As these issues become mainstream through youth activism, media and fashion personalities like Hari Nef and Andreja Pejić and pop culture figures like Laverne Cox and Caitlyn Jenner who have undergone sex-reassignment therapy and surgery, they create groundbreaking opportunities to rethink gender codes and recast culture norms, freeing them from traditional limits. However, in fighting on the front lines of this cause with their bodies and their lives, the courageous trailblazers in this movement pay a high price for nonconformity. Transgender youth face elevated rates of violence, alienation, mental health issues (including depression and suicide), poverty and criminalization. Despite this, they are a growing force, fearlessly pioneering transformation.

The roller derby girls gave us examples of how they challenge gender scripts and encourage girls to find pathways to accessing power, "We practise building strength as a way to feel physically what power is and what alternative narratives might be like," said Mel. "We take space and teach the other girls how to take space, too."

"One thing that we coach and practise," said Sami, "is that it doesn't matter what size your frame is, or what your body shape is like. You can take space on a track or in a room. If you believe 'I can move somebody' you can, with your body and your intent." This self-assertion is what helps their team win, they explained—and we noted that it's also what all leaders do effectively to be magnanimous power players.

"In fact," added Alex, "we're into redefining what a hot girl looks like based on strength. In derby we are rewarded for being physically strong, because what you want is to take up space on the track. It's a badge of honour if your pants rip because your quads are exploding because you've been working out at the gym. It's attractive because it is powerful."

"When we see a girl playing on Team USA," agreed Mel, "we're like, 'Oh my God, she is so strong.' We're like, 'Wow, that's power! We want those big muscular thighs.'"

When we gathered some of the moms in our neighbourhood to talk about navigating power and girl relationships, Jenny, mother to nine-year-old Ruby, had this thoughtful piece of advice to share: "Girls need help with self-love, non-competitive appreciation of the beauty of others, learning to ignore the hierarchization effect of the male gaze and battling interpersonal jealousy that undermines friendship. They need help practicing self-love, above all. Media literacy and critiques of representation are fine, of course, but I'd rather see them as an opening point to other, deeper conversations." Jenny said that she tries to do this with her daughter in several ways, by commenting frequently on what she finds beautiful about people with non-normative bodies; by never saying anything negative about her own appearance and body; by talking about Ruby's beauty very casually, as something that is a matter of luck rather than of value—and always following it up with "more important, you are strong, smart and funny." Jenny also tries to lightly make fun of prevailing beauty standards, while conveying to Ruby that it's normal to be influenced by them.

DEMYSTIFYING VIOLENT GIRLS:
OVERPOLICED AND UNDERPROTECTED

If we travel a little further along the continuum of power and aggression, we land on the next sensationalized and highly troubling narrative about violent girls. The mainstream seems to presume that the more equal women become, the more depraved and violent they become, too. It is here that we come up against some of the most disturbing realities of how things like the criminal justice system, the welfare system, the health system, homelessness and poverty—and racist, classist attitudes and judgments—limit girls' ability to exercise power.

While media headlines would have us believe that girl violence is on the rise, the reality is that girls have very low rates of serious and violent crime. In the US, arrest laws and changes in law enforcement policy appear to have had more of an impact on arrest rates than have changes in girls' behaviour.[8] According to the American Bar Association, supposed increases in girls' violent behaviour in the US might be explained by "the re-labeling of girls' family conflicts as violent offenses, the changes in police practices regarding domestic violence and aggressive behaviour, the gender bias in the processing of misdemeanor cases, and, perhaps, a fundamental systemic failure to understand the unique developmental issues facing girls."[9] In fact, it is understood that when girls fall into the criminal justice system and become criminalized, it is often as a direct result of trauma; having been victimized and abused as children, in situations that are largely linked to structural racism and growing up in poverty.[10]

When we were on the West Coast, we met women from Justice for Girls, a Vancouver activist organization that works to address social justice and promote the health and well-being of teenage girls living in poverty. They had commissioned a research report on how girls are criminalized, and the results were hard-hitting. In *Locking Them Up to Keep Them "Safe": Criminalized Girls in British Columbia*, author Amber Richelle Dean uncovered—by speaking directly to girls between the ages of 15 and 19—that, "the notion of today's 'violent girl' is more myth than reality. In instances when young women do use violence, they often employ it in self-defence or as a last-ditch attempt at resistance against the systemic, symbolic, or personal violence perpetrated against them."[11] When these girls are labelled "at risk" and then treated as deviant, their stories gets skewed into sensational media coverage that hides the truth and promotes ideas of girls gone violent and wild.

According to Amber Dean, girls are overpoliced by authorities and, at the same time, underprotected from violence and harm. "The tendency to incarcerate young women . . . is related both to our society's lower tolerance for 'disobedient' females and our strong desire to control or limit the behaviour or freedom of young women 'for their own good' or for their protection," she reported in *Locking Them Up*. The criminal justice system justifies locking up "disobedient girls" in the name of keeping them safe from pimps, abusive relationships and drug dealers, all the while controlling girls instead of addressing the violence in their lives. For example, girls are at a high risk for non-compliance offences or 'status offenses'—like consumption of alcohol, truancy or running away. Dean adds, "Violence against girls tends to serve two functions: it is used to pre-emptively teach young women subservience and acceptance of our male-dominated culture, and it is used to punish girls who resist subservience or conformity to traditional female gender roles.

In these ways, violence functions as a form of 'policing' of young women's behaviour as well."[12] So, while girls police each other through slut-shaming, public shaming and being mean, societal structures reinforce conformity to these social codes on a whole other level, through state violence and criminalization.

But this isn't the case for all girls. Annabel Webb, co-founder of Justice for Girls and a graduate in international human rights law, told us that the kind of surveillance, male violence and abuse of state power that Amber is talking about is very specific to a girl's position in society. In Canada, girls who are poor, girls who are in state care and girls who are Indigenous are much more targeted. Specifically, she told us, "It is the intersection of gender, race, class, disability, sexual identity and histories of colonization that determines the way in which girls will be penalized for breaching patriarchal norms." In some cases, girls are criminalized for behaviours that are technically illegal but in most cases would be overlooked or dismissed with a warning if the case concerned a white middle-class girl or a boy.

"Often, when homeless or Indigenous girls attempt to get protection from male violence, their calls result in them being criminalized rather than being treated as victims of violence," said Annabel. She told us about a mom who called 9-1-1 to protect her daughter, an Indigenous girl of 15, from her violent adult boyfriend. The police showed up, separated the two—and brutalized the girl, who had to have surgery the next day to reconstruct an arm that was broken in several places. Instead of protecting her from sexual abuse, the police viciously assaulted her, while her abuser got off without even a warning.[13] "This is a tragic example of the way sexism and racism define Indigenous girls' experiences with the police and can only be understood as the continued legacy of colonization," said Annabel.

We learned that the criminal justice system plays a role in perpetuating violence against girls through racist and unaccountable systems, and that physical and sexual abuse are experienced by girls at the hands of the very authorities who are meant to protect them. While incarceration rates are trending downward for sentenced girls, pretrial detention, which has remained consistent, is rife with abuses. Annabel went on: "Pretrial detention can mean being in a lock-up in an RCMP detachment in a small community, where a couple of male officers are doing illegal strip searches in extremely humiliating conditions. Human rights abuses including this sort of sexual violence and harassment happen all the time in pretrial custody, but there is virtually no credible or effective mechanism of independent police oversight. Girls are left with no accountability or recourse for the abuses they endure. Sadly, over time, girls resign themselves to these abuses as an expected part of a life that is already devastated by sexual abuse, poverty, addiction and, for some, an intergenerational legacy of colonial violence."

Surveillance takes on a whole other reality for girls who are homeless. "Girls who are on the street are subjected to very high levels of surveillance by violent boyfriends, pimps or dealers, and by the police, mental health workers, social workers, medical officials, prison guards, outreach workers, alcohol and drug workers. Everything these girls do is monitored and/or documented. While it is critically important to keep records, often records are used within the criminal justice system as a justification for limiting and restricting a girl's freedom instead of responding to male violence," Annabel added.

That kind of state power, policing and surveillance is extreme for Indigenous girls, who make up approximately 50 percent of incarcerated girls and women in British Columbia, Canada.[14] When young women engage in serious violence, it is usually because they themselves have been victimized and brutalized. Their expression of rage is deeply rooted in powerlessness and is often an acting out of internalized—and intergenerational—sexism, racism and poverty.

This is not a good-news story but it's one that needs to be told. When headlines sensationalize the myth of violent girls, society condones violence and abuse, and turns away from girls who need care, healing and support. The roots of poverty and violence are overwhelming in this reality. How, in wealthy countries like Canada and the US, do we not feed, clothe, house and educate every child? How, in "progressive" societies, do we justify the blaming, shaming and punishment of girls for the state of poverty?

Thankfully, there are leaders—often young women—who are taking on these issues so that we can all move forward. Justice for Girls, for example, is at the cutting edge of change here. Through smart and savvy criminal justice monitoring, advocacy and public education, they are shining light on the gaps between international human rights law, domestic protections and the reality of young women's lived experiences of inequality and discrimination. They are also supporting girls to transform their experiences and become changemakers themselves.

GIRL POWER WITH DEPTH AND MEANING

Back at the taco bar with the roller derby girls, we wrapped up our interview feeling moved by the potential and untapped power that all girls and women have to offer the world. If what was once politicized girl power has been hollowed out by commercialization and commodification, girl power today is emerging with new-found depth, connection and possibility. This phenomenon is bigger than anything any glossy ad campaign or marketing scheme can seize, package or sell. As we have seen, there are many ways we can help girls understand how to use their power, but there is still work to do. This path of discovery, where we continue to learn to tap into and execute our powers, is one we need to walk together.

Alex, Mel and Sami had a final insight to offer us as we put our coats on to head out into the wintry evening. They stressed the importance of working with strategy *and* intuition as individual girls and as team players. Mel explained how when they play derby, they don't have a playbook. "After fifteen seconds into the game, you have to go with your intuition, so instinct is something you train for. Communication is huge, both verbal and non-verbal. And you don't always have to be the hero. 'Where am I right now and where does my team need me to be?' is the question. We need to understand, in every scenario, where the team needs us to be."

Now that we're well into the digital age, the idea of building positive and powerful community is a tangible, potent reality. Hearing how the derby girls connect intuition and wisdom to their power on the track made us think back to San Francisco, where we talked with Christine Grumm about the amazing innate strength and wisdom that girls have. This is a very real force that requires attention, nurturing and love. Christine had said: "Educating girls isn't enough. Part of making change is listening to girls. If you don't listen, you have no idea what girls are saying. Girls have a hard time finding their wise voice. They can find their bitch voice, even their bully voice. Their wise voice is never allowed to find its space. We need to find that space and give girls the megaphone."

SURVIVAL KIT

INVITE GIRLS into deeper conversations about the power dynamics and social dynamics they are living. Have conversations about the gender and cultural expectations placed on girls. Talking about these issues provides an important political literacy that opens up new and empowering ways of seeing and acting in the world. It also offers more options for coping and making choices.

FOR GIRLS' RIGHTS and advocacy resources related to gender violence and criminalization, visit www.justiceforgirls.org and the Canadian Association of Elizabeth Fry Societies and The Center for Gender and Justice in the US.

TEACH GIRLS that collaboration *and* competition are good. Give girls opportunities to practise being competitive and bring awareness to the experience by supporting them and having conversations about what they are learning and how they are coping with the challenges of what they're learning. Talk about how it feels to win and to lose. Give girls the opportunity to be collaborative and to work as a team. These are skills and tools that apply to all areas of life for its duration!

HELP GIRLS DISCOVER their gifts and passions. Ask, "What is going to challenge you and make you happy? What are your goals?" Instead of looking to the outside, and waiting for others to tell her what her qualities are, encourage her to look within herself to find her skills, passions and gifts, and to go for it!

CELEBRATE beauty in others. Talk to girls about what it means to love ourselves and to celebrate the gifts and beauty of other girls and women at the same time.

GIVE GIRLS the experience of community, belonging and support. Be curious about what girls are up to. Let them know you're there to listen or just hang out. Become familiar with what they are up to so you can foster the togetherness that harnesses sisterhood.

BULLYING doesn't happen in a vacuum and girl bullying isn't new. Many grown women carry scars and stories from bullying experiences in childhood. We also often find that they struggle with similar poisonous cultures in their workplaces and relationships as adults.

INNOVATIVE AND EFFECTIVE ANTI-BULLYING PROGRAMMES like social and emotional learning and restorative justice are examples of approaches to violence prevention that are gaining traction and results. Advocate for these new models in your schools and communities so that we can work toward transforming our educational systems. For restorative approaches check out Restitution Self-Discipline, and its chief educator, Diane Gossen, here: www.realrestitution.com. For SEL approaches check here: peacegrantmakers.ca/symposium.

HELP GIRLS find healthy ways to express anger and aggression. Let them be angry at home if they need to be; hold that space for them to keep them safe, and find long-term activities that nurture a more natural interaction with their strong feelings. Sports, martial arts, theatre, writing, music, self-defence classes and creative self-expression are amazing ways for girls to discover and express their power.

ENCOURAGE GIRLS and boys to trust their intuition, their "wise voice." Validate and bring awareness to this expression by encouraging them to look within and listen to themselves more. Practise this by asking them to answer questions with their intuition and their personal wisdom.

LET GIRLS BE STRONG, outspoken, assertive and empowered. They have a lot to give the world as thinkers and leaders.

YOU DON'T HAVE TO BE A
SUPERHERO

10

WHAT ABOUT THE BOYS?

ON A CHILLY EARLY WINTER MORNING, we drove to a college in Ottawa to meet with a coed pop culture and gender class. As we wove our way through the snowy streets, we talked about how, in the hype surrounding the empowerment of girls, a counter-movement claiming that schools are failing boys has emerged. A couple of days earlier, we had interviewed Michael Kaufman, co-founder (with former Canadian politician Jack Layton and college professor Ron Sluser) of the White Ribbon campaign, an international network that positively challenges the harmful "manhood" stereotypes that lead to violence against women. Michael has written and spoken extensively on the topic of men and masculinity, and is a world-leading expert on the state of boys today. He told us that boys still face many of the same pressures regarding masculinity that they have faced for years.

"The ideas and ideals of manhood that we have developed are impossible to live up to," Kaufman said. "We are always supposed to be strong, powerful, have answers, show no fear, be in control, have no feelings. This is what sets up boys for failure. If you don't live up to all that, you're not a real man, and if you're not a real man there's something wrong with you and you will be physically and emotionally vulnerable to attack. This has been true for some time; it is also cross-culturally true. The relationship and contrast between socially constructed and individually experienced manhood, combined with enormous pain in the lives of men themselves as men, means that fear, isolation, disquiet and pain are the hidden secrets in the lives of boys and men. This fear lives deep in the hearts of teenage boys."

Kaufman believes that the power and privilege men have created for themselves comes with a tangible cost; it's a paradox central to the lives of boys. "We make enormous promises to boys," he elaborated. "We tell them, 'You will have power and you will be in control.' Even if a boy isn't directly told this, it's part of our collective imagination; they are surrounded by images of who is 'the boss.' If he practises and works enough, then he believes he will have that power, too. As he goes through puberty, he sees other boys, compares himself unfavourably and starts to believe that he must be the only one who doesn't live up to these expectations." Boys have coping mechanisms, Kaufman told us. "Boys distance themselves from other boys and they shut down. You don't want to show too much caregiving [as a boy], or be discovered as not being a real man. For some boys there is a use of violence as a frustrated way of upholding dominance. With this limited script, we set boys up for failure."

And while all of this is going on, something new has been added to the mix. These days, girls are competing with boys in areas where boys used to win by default. Girls are excelling and achieving on many levels: academically, in the arts, in business and in engineering. In the past, boys were assumed to be society's convincing talkers and natural leaders. Today, they see that this isn't the case—or at least it's not exclusively the case. This changing landscape can leave boys confused and embattled, haunted by impossible ideals and expectations and confused about where they stand.

"What do they do?" Kaufman asked rhetorically. "They fight, engage in risk-taking behaviour, drug and alcohol abuse, violence that includes verbal violence and violence against girls. There often isn't an hour in the lives of teenage boys where they don't receive, hear or commit verbal abuse. The need to prove their manhood is ramped up." In what is almost a caricature of this ideal, there's even an increasing emphasis on body image, and pressure for boys to display the sculpted muscular bodies of superheroes, action figures, video game heroes, movie stars and sports stars. "But bulked up supersized masculinity is indicative of enormous insecurity," says Kaufman, "[and] we see the extreme impacts over time and accumulated life experience. Statistically, men are more likely [than women] to be addicted to alcohol and drugs, to commit suicide, to be in prison and to die younger."

SECRETS OF BOYHOOD

With these sober thoughts in mind, we pulled into the college parking lot and headed to our friend Kara Knight's class. As the students filed in, Kara lit up the overhead screen while greeting each one of them by name. Today it was Nathan and Dimitri's turn to present their music video critique—one in a line of presentations that Kara's students, in small groups, would complete over the course of the upcoming month. Each group had been given the task of choosing a music video to discuss with the class in terms of cultural influence and message.

It is Kara's routine to talk to her students about ideas that are rooted in everyday pop culture, like friend-zoning, social-media "likes" and what's trending on Twitter; it's an invitation for them to feel open with her in exchange. It's an approach that seems to work in this class of thirty-five 17-to-21-year-olds of diverse ethnicities spanning a global spectrum ranging from the Mediterranean to the Middle East and much of the Caribbean. They're learning to chime in with their own experiences of the culture they live in, which makes the world feel somehow a little more supple in their young hands—something we saw when we got to hear from them about their world views, where an openness and confidence is evident.

Nathan, 18, and Dimitri, 17, strutted in their Adidas two-piece track suits and Nike pump shoes to the front of the class. They had chosen Nelly's "Tip Drill" for their presentation. As soon as everyone was seated, the room came to life with the raunchy video featuring half-naked women twerking their way across the screen in a variety of indoor and outdoor domestic settings while the singer and his friends wave money at them. Nathan and Dimitri suggested that the video objectified women. "It was made in 2003," they told the class, "so this video set a precedent for the videos we see today that border constantly on pornography and make girls feel that guys will only like them if they dress 'inappropriately,' and [that] condition guys to seek girls who are 'overly sexualized.'"

When Nathan veered into comments about how these women were only valued for their bodies and the sex they could provide, Kara offered a second possible interpretation. "Hang on," she said. "You may be 100 percent right. It's impossible to know for sure, but there are other ways we can look at this that may be more empowering to women in the sex trade [or women performing sexy roles in music videos]. Remember what we said last week about the strip club, Nathan? These women are at work. It's a different thing to say that women are objectified no matter what they do, particularly when it works against them. But here these women are objectifying themselves for money, right? Who is empowered in this situation? Is it the man? If he's walking out of the club with an empty wallet and an erection, and she's walking out with a bag full of cash to perhaps join her loving boyfriend who has cooked dinner for her, who is the powerful one?"

Questions like these, which turn assumptions inside out, have revolutionized the thinking of both the girls and the boys in the classroom. When Nathan and Dimitri finished their presentation, Kara moved on to the next part of the day's lecture—showing Sinead O'Connor's appearance on *Saturday Night Live* in 1992, the night she sang about sexual corruption in the Catholic Church and ripped up an image of the pope on national television. This sparked a lively in-class debate about political protest in art before and after the Internet, the new "like" culture and how needing to be "liked" polices and may prevent dissidence, and whether Miley Cyrus, who compares herself to Sinead O'Connor (a comparison O'Connor is not excited about), is political or not. Some of the boys suggested that Cyrus might be trying to say that it's okay to be sexual; some of the girls responded that perhaps she might be trying to show that it's okay to go from being a "good girl" to being a "bad girl." All agreed, though, that her message was unclear and diluted and contained nothing like the power of O'Connor's. "I'm all for showing that there's a path to take if you want to go from good to bad—we don't all have to be Taylor Swift," quipped Kara, now pacing at the front of the class, "but I can't stand behind a star who slaps black girls on the ass." Kara was referring to Cyrus's now-infamous performance at MTV's 2013 Video Music Awards ceremony, for which she was highly criticized for appropriating black hip-hop culture in a way that objectified and denigrated black women's bodies.[1]

The class's total engagement in this dialogue demonstrated the safe kind of thrill that young people feel under the tutelage of a strong-minded and candid adult, the kind that allows alternative views to be carried around with confidence. We also got the sense that Kara has given her students a new way to think about life and relationships—one that liberates them from the stereotypes gathered via family, cultural traditions, mainstream society and masculinity peer pressure. As we moved through our day with these teenagers, and saw the kinds of people they were—and the ideas and feelings they're having—it reinforced the value of and need for this kind of education, including in primary and secondary school years.

From Kara's point of view, open discussions about gendered expressions in pop culture—especially ones that delve into the experiences of teenage lust and relationships—are vital. For boys in particular, this kind of straight talk can improve their success at the thing many of them care about most at this age: scoring with girls. In the end, this alone makes the topic a key portal to addressing how gender, power and masculinity play out in the lives of heterosexual young men. Over coffee a few days earlier, Kara told us that "the boys who stray from the masculine stereotypes, especially at this age, risk rejection by their families, by their friends, too, and may be vulnerable to bullying. I think the one area where they can really connect with ideas about masculinity and vulnerability is relationships."

So many of the girls we met told us that the expectations for boys to play a masculine stereotype is frustrating. Guys are celebrated for their sexual conquests and, as a result, the guys they know fall into two categories: hook-up heroes who display no emotion at all, or, at the other extreme, the emotionally needy. The boys from Kara's class confirmed this assessment when we hung with them in the hallway after class. "There's just no place to be emotional; it's totally uncool to show any feelings," Terrell, a suavely dressed boy of twenty told us. "We are emotionally isolated." Peter, an arty-looking guy of 17, with red curls and baggy jeans, agreed. "After our moms, the only other people we can tell our feelings to is our girlfriends. So that's why some girls feel like their boyfriends are emotionally needy—it's our only place to unload."

This was not what we expected to hear. And yet, we know how pressured girls are by stereotypes, so why wouldn't the same be true for boys? Boys are supposed to be strong, cool, capable, talented, aggressive, assertive and skilful providers. They are *not* supposed to cry or show emotions and vulnerability. They should never feel hurt, and if they do, they should never show it. They should take charge and know how to lead in every situation. They should be dominant among their male peers and a stud among their female peers. They should feel and act privileged, and oppose or neglect whatever interferes with this. If sometimes this doesn't work out according to the script, then they should feel angry and express it.

We saw how acutely aware the boys in Kara's class were of these struggles in their own lives, and how eager they were to talk about them. Nathan said, "In class we analyzed a Lil Wayne video like the Nelly video. Now [after really looking closely at pop culture with Kara], I think more critically and deconstruct the messages around gender norms. We know that life doesn't have to be that way. The videos portray the masculine ideal: 'bitches' are 'only good for sex'; you're supposed to be rich and have lots of cars and lots of girls at lots of pool parties. It's not really like that in real life."

They said those pressures impact boys more when they are younger teens, but that with time and life experience, kids mature. "We understand what we want to be like and we learn that we don't have to follow those roles," said Dimitri. Seventeen-year-old Roberto, a sweet-faced boy wearing his baseball cap backwards, agreed. "In real life, we sort of know that soon we will find love. We will settle down and have kids."

"But we still want to 'go to the club, buy bottles and get girls,'" said Peter. "Obviously not big mansions and cars, but still . . ."

"It's confusing, you are supposed to be where they are [the pop role models], you aren't there, and there is a feeling of *why* are you not there?" reflected Nathan.

We asked if they see any changes in the representation of boys in the media.

"A bit," Dimitri said. "But there is still a limited representation. There needs to be more . . . change."

"Singers like Drake try to introduce the idea that it's okay to be emotional, but in this cool way where there are still some pool parties and girls. He never makes eye contact with the audience in his videos, though, which makes him feel inauthentic to me and probably to a lot of other guys," said Terrell. "Lack of eye contact means he is not confident in the message he is sending."

Knowing that it's a challenge for boys to find spaces to express themselves emotionally, we asked them where they think they can do this. They said not really anywhere. They agreed that boys need to talk about their feelings, but told us that this is seen as weak and boys are bullied when they don't conform to the idea of being "strong."

In just the first few minutes of our discussion, these boys had identified the contradictions they are living with on a daily basis—the expectation to perform a narrow definition of masculinity, reinforced by messages from mainstream culture, set against a changing world with changing beliefs and values around gender norms. But like the girls we met in chapter 2, the boys showed that they are able to identify and examine the stereotypes that trap them. "If you just focus on what the media tells you, then it doesn't work," said Nathan. "Instead, we need to ask, 'What can I take from the media that is useful and [how can I] merge it with real life?'" All of them said that Kara's class has helped change their perspective, and has had an impact on the language they use. One told us how he even challenges other guys in his peer group when they use sexist language.

Kara told us that students new to her class often say things like, "I can't believe we haven't learned this earlier, and why is that? We have to study Shakespeare, but we don't get the media, gender and culture content that is actually relevant for us today. I wish I had learned this sooner." It's encouraging to hear from boys that they want to enter this dialogue. As we saw in just one afternoon, this type of discussion can help boys make new choices and feel confident about them.

The boys discussed how society works hard to create distinct gender roles—to separate boys' and girls' experiences. "That's human nature. We like to be able to label people; it's how we make sense of things," said Martin, 18. "So, if we can say, 'Those people are gay,' 'Those people are trans,' we can be less scared of difference. We like to put people into boxes. We like forcing conformity on people."

"We keep trying to separate men and women," added Peter. "We focus on how different we are instead of how similar. When we focus more on our similarities, and have conversations about sexuality—what we want out of our relationships and things like that—then we find common ground. The more we focus on the things we have in common, the healthier we can be in relationships. That's why guys need to be part of the conversation about violence against women. How can you effect change without getting guys on board?"

"We need to include boys *and* girls in all this because we need to continue to bridge the gap," said Dante, 17. "There is no 'other.' We are all just individuals."

We brought up the Rehtaeh Parsons case we described in detail in chapter 7, involving the 17-year-old girl from Nova Scotia, Canada, who took her own life in 2013 when the bullying she experienced after a video of her gang rape went viral became unlivable. We mentioned the fact that the main boy involved admitted to committing rape, but didn't know it was rape. We then asked if guys are willing to talk openly about rape culture.

"Some are willing and some are not," answered Marco, 18. "Outside of our [gender and media] class, we don't talk about rape."

"We don't talk about it amongst ourselves," said Nathan after a long silence. "It's hard to say anything about it. We talk about it in our media class. I don't know why we don't talk about it with our friends."

We asked them what they thought the barrier to this conversation was. Dimitri said, "Nobody wants to think they are 'that guy,' and guys don't want to see themselves as the rapist. There is a risk involved when all guys are being thrown in the same basket—where all guys are seen as misogynist and violent. It shuts down any talking about it because we don't relate."

"It's like, yeah, we are going to get drunk," added Justin, 19. "We are going to get with some girls but we don't think we are going to rape; that's just wrong."

Marco, who comes from an Italian family, said, "If you have parents who are really identified with traditional cultural values, then they tend to believe that girls should be passive and boys should be dominant. These kinds of ideas get worse as we get older. Some parents are really identified with their son's masculinity. So when these two people come together and a girl who has learned to be passive meets a boy who is supermasculine, it doesn't quite add up to a healthy relationship."

"The only way to find a solution is to talk about it, I guess," said, Peter. "And everyone needs to be involved, including teachers and even younger kids."

Dimitri agreed. "There is always going to be someone who understands and sympathizes. We need to give people the chance to talk about stuff."

We asked if awareness campaigns could help more boys to open up. "There isn't one campaign that will capture everyone," said Peter. "Grassroots stuff is good, it's got feeling. With the Internet we have a good venue that didn't exist before. Social-media campaigns can get a lot of people talking and you can say things anonymously if you want to, which is sometimes easier."

Horus, 19, who joined us late and had been just listening, brought up the importance of teachers like Kara. "If you have teachers who are awesome and cool and open the door to talking about important stuff, you can really change things in schools."

PORN AND PLEASURE

As our conversation continued, Kara's students brought up the two default "educators" through which macho values are reinforced and consumed: pornography and video games. These popular entertainments, which are widely accessible, can influence how boys experience life. If they're alone in their bedrooms, or with friends, consuming the fantasy of hard-core, violent sex, there is no insight offered. There is no lens through which boys can see how what they're experiencing relates to reality, or conforms to the stereotype of how a man is expected to perform a virile, dominant and in-control sexual role. In a typical porn scene, the man's desires are pandered to above his partner's and he is cast as the Casanova who makes all the right moves—and succeeds in making the girls scream with pleasure at supposed (multiple) orgasm. Physically, there is hardly a pubic hair to be seen, and emotionally, there are nearly no signs of real-life sexual connection, like curiosity and mutual admiration, vulnerability and shyness, feelings or passion-fuelled sexual generosity.

Dimitri and the others recognized the gulf between porn fantasy and reality. "Porn is false," said Horus, slumping a little against one of the lockers. "I haven't tried anything you see in porn. I know the girl isn't going to be down with it."

"I think pornography ruins your mind," said Peter. "It isn't reality. Somewhere along the line you need more than what you see. You need to feel it. And you try certain things to get it. You are supposed to be finding your own experience. If you watch it instead of doing it, you never get to experience real things."

"It gives you this whole idea of you that's wrong," Marco chimed in. "It's so disappointing when you try it for real. I think we should be taught about how the images on the Internet can ruin your viewpoint toward sex. Schools should be teaching about porn and warning us away from it."

"It's important to be able to tell the difference between porn and real life," said Ryan, 18. "You need to understand it's fake, and real sex is different. Porn is just for pleasure. It's entertainment made for you. And the people doing it get paid a lot of money."

"It's there, all over the Internet," remarked Justin, "and it's not going away. In porn, a girl's sexuality is the value. I'm sure girls watch it, too."

Kara takes on media literacy in her class, so we weren't surprised to see how these young men were able to understand and find their way through porn culture. Wouldn't it be great if all boys accessed this critical awareness earlier? As we found out in chapter 3, sex ed rarely includes learning that most pornography is a script based on male fantasies, or what consent is, or how to create healthy sexual relationships and positive experiences for everyone involved. This awareness could empower teenagers not just by speaking directly to what they're going through and opening doors to more forthright conversations, but by helping them untangle the jungle of information they receive through porn sites, chat rooms and hearsay.

The girls we spoke to about pornography believe that it heightens their male partners' expectations. We told the boys this and asked them how they learned about pleasure for their female partners, how they approach it and how porn influences this.

"We want to give girls pleasure," Dimitri began. "All the guys in porn make the girls scream [with pleasure]. If you're with a girl and she's not enjoying it, it makes you feel shitty. You want to please your partner."

"If you are going to please the girl, it's going to make it so much better," said Terrell. "If she is not having a good time, it's not going to be fun."

"If you pay attention when you are having sex you figure out what works," Nathan said confidently. "I want the girls I'm with to have a good time."

"You don't want to ask the girl [how to make it good for her]; you will look like a loser. So you ask friends," said Martin.

"You can't talk about real stuff like that, no way," Marco disagreed. "We don't talk about technique."

"There are a lot of guys who believe that it's part of their role to be performing," said Terrell. "There is a pressure. But I think that the issue is that sex should be more of an exchange [with partners]."

"I don't think technique comes into the equation," said Dante. "It's more about a score. It's more about, 'She was hot, and I scored.' I don't remember ever having had a conversation related to technique. Not all girls can cum vaginally. If you know this, it's more useful to talk to the girl to find out what she likes."

"The pressure is more about, 'How can I get the girls?'" added Horus. "Some people can't get the girls—so I'm asking, 'How did he get the girl?' We think things like, 'He was muscular, so that's what he did to get the girls.' I know a lot of guys who go to the gym to be bigger for that reason."

"It's not a secret. If you can actually think for yourself, instead of relying on what the media tells you, then you quickly figure out that feeling good isn't only about you," concluded Peter.

This sounded promising, although we also recognized that the boys probably felt like they needed to impress us with their "girls' pleasure" awareness. We didn't ask for details about how they're putting theory into practise. After we spoke to some of their female classmates, we wished we had.

Katie, a flamboyant 19-year-old Vietnamese young woman told us, "Lots of guys won't go down on girls but it's a deal breaker if we don't give blow jobs."

"They say it smells like fish and we pee from there," added Stacy, who is white and 18.

"Guys pee from there, too," added Mireille, 17, a Pakistani-Canadian girl.

Farrah, 19, from Kuwait, asked, "If they know this why won't they do it more?"

It's uplifting to hear that some teen boys have intentions and experiences of discovering how to please a girl, and also that male-centric pornography doesn't translate in all cases to male-centric sex practices. Still, given the he said/she said nature of the stories we heard, it's clear that there are bridges to build in the sexuality and relationships department.

Coed group discussions on this topic might be really groundbreaking. We remembered an interview we'd had with an 18-year-old breakdancer from Texas called Jerome. He was very open about the boyhood pressures to perform masculinity and how dance helped him to express emotion and vulnerability. He told us that he grew up on porn and was so freaked out when he saw a real vagina with hair on it that it grossed him out—but that he was over that now. When we talked to his girlfriend a little later, though, she told us that he asks her to wax her pubic hair. This revealed the subtle and not-so-subtle ways that porn-influenced expectations can seep into intimate relationships.

EMOTIONS AND VIDEO GAMES

While leaning against their lockers talking about sex, Kara's male students also mentioned video games. Although gaming manufacturers gross twice as much as Hollywood and four times as much as the art world, it's still considered a culturally "underground" activity, cared about only by kids and gaming geeks. But with so many consumers—and so many *young* ones—games are, in fact, a serious influence on developing minds. Most video games are filled with gratuitous violence and specifically, violence against women. If boys are engaging in an activity that, with the click of a controller, gives them the ability to manipulate and master their environment by shooting and killing at whim to emerge as the uncontested hero, is this not another form of media that reinforces masculine stereotypes and, in some cases, glorifies their dominance and violence? Kara's male students, like many of our interviewees, told us they enjoy playing video games because it is a fun pastime and a way to relieve stress.

"People are saying that gun violence is related to video games but I don't think that's true," Horus said. "They're fun and part of social life; it's reality versus fiction. Video games are like porn; you know that it's fake."

"I disagree," said Terrell. "There are studies that show that the way you spend your time does affect the way you behave and express yourself and take out your frustrations."

"Girls play video games, too, but it's guys that get blamed for aggression. We're put in this box," Dante said. "The way society talks about aggression and guys isolates us."

+++

Just as we were wondering why such a strong cultural influence is so rarely discussed on public forums, the #Gamergate scandal broke—shining a light on the traditionally male-dominated industry's struggle to maintain this status quo and its resistance to adapt to a shift in consumption demographics. Fifty percent of gamers are now female, and these users are after more complex games with stronger female characters.[2]

The scandal originated when gaming members alleged biased journalism about a new game, *Depression Quest*, created by gaming developer Zoë Quinn about her real-life depression.[3] *Depression Quest* is narrative and emotional, and it lacks the traditional action and externalized violence of old-style games. Zoë's boyfriend posted a blog falsely accusing her of entering into a relationship with a journalist in exchange for positive coverage of her game. The controversy escalated when it turned into a targeted harassment campaign against Quinn which included violent sexual harassment and death threats. The campaign, coordinated under the hashtag #Gamergate, exposed the inherent sexism in the male-dominated video game culture.

Anita Sarkeesian, a feminist media critic—outspoken about the need for better female representation in video games—has also been a target of #Gamergate and has been forced to move homes and cancel public talks because of death threats. Her work focuses on deconstructing stereotypes around women in pop culture as well as highlighting issues surrounding the targeted harassment of women in online and gaming spaces.

+++

As we sat around the lockers discussing the incident, Dante characterized #Gamergate as a case of "personal issues" between Quinn and her ex-boyfriends, demonstrating that even Kara's politicized students can't always see beyond the popular discourse that pits sexist forces against well-intentioned boys.

We spoke to a high school teacher, Joshua Gibson, about this issue. In his Vancouver, BC, classroom, he makes it a priority to bring a "gendered lens" to his lessons. "#Gamergate is not unique," he told us. "It is the same argument you see anytime a conversation around equality starts. The privileged class always speaks up against it and attempts to hold on to what they think they are entitled to. At the same time, any 'privileged male' looks at the 'you're privileged' claim and perceives that as an attack. Really, we are just failing to talk boys and men through the nuances of the conversation so that they can play a violent video game and know that it does not make them a misogynist just because the game itself has misogynistic elements." Teaching boys how to critique the games they are enjoying raises awareness about the ideas of gender and violence that are re-enforced in certain video games as well as in broader culture. Rather than put boys on the defensive, this approach invites them to be constructive participants who are part of the solution.

Despite all of this, video games *are* evolving. Serious gaming now includes educational gaming, rehabilitation gaming, independent creative gaming and other sub-genres that are emerging from some of the work done by girl game developers to make video games a cultural power with more visible social and economic traction. Progressive gamers understand that girls are not a threat here but an asset.[4] And we have an opportunity to encourage this change in a way that empowers both boys and girls. What #Gamergate amplifies is the negative and violent backlash against women taking place in a non-traditional arena.

#Gamergate can be seen in another way, too: as a microcosm of society at large. Thought about this way, it allows us to glean an understanding of how boys are treading water in a world where masculinity norms are still enshrined, imposed and rewarded even as that world is evolving to include a more complex and diversified sharing of power. Gibson elaborated on this: "The majority of boys probably don't see themselves as having power, which means that today's boys hear claims of 'privileged male' but that doesn't always align with their perceived reality. So this puts them in the position of feeling attacked for having something they don't think they have. It isn't that boys sit there and think, 'I have the power and I am not sharing.' What happens is that we tell them they have something and they think, 'WTF are you talking about? I'm 17, I have never had a girlfriend, these games are an escape from a world where I get picked on. I'd love to go to college but my family can't afford tuition, and you're trying to tell me that I have privilege and power and that this activity that I love is bad? Fuck off!'"

Now that girls are taking their place in the world, boys have to figure out how to adapt to rapid social change and how to be allies with girls in the many spaces they share. Often, they have to figure this out all on their own. The confusion boys feel in this, combined with the ongoing societal pressure to stay strong and avoid vulnerability, can be a breeding ground for misguided, angry, sexist reactions that harm boys as well as girls.

BOYS AND CONSENT

The news blared from the radio as we swerved into the driveway of our friend Melanie's suburban home in a small town in Ontario, another stop on our voyage to meet and talk to boys. The sex-assault and choking allegations against Jian Ghomeshi filled the car, along with allegations of Bill Cosby's multiple and repeated rapes, Charles Manson's new 26-year-old fiancée and the revisiting within these stories of Woody Allen's and Roman Polanski's sex scandals. It was all there, and it got us thinking: How can we talk about sex and violence and girls and not talk to boys?

"I'm going to order pizza, vegetarian for you and the boys love all-dressed, are you in?" Melanie asked, opening the door to her cozy home, where her son and his two friends were waiting for us on the plush sofa. They were sitting one beside the other, looking like nervous soldiers, and they smiled timidly when we introduced ourselves. When the pizza arrived, they relaxed and started to tell us about some of their pastimes.

"I play *Call of Duty*," said Tommy, 15. "I play football, too, but video games are different; you can talk to your friends online and it's a different way to get out your aggression. Like you can compete with your friends. It gives you a rush, it gives you adrenalin, it's kind of emotional."

"We get full contact out on the rink," said Kevin and Zack, both 14 and both hockey players. While they ate their pizza and emptied cans of soda, they recounted the fist fights that often break out during games—how the gloves come off and everybody cheers.

When the last crust was tossed into the pizza box, the boys got more daring and shifted the discussion from video games to sexting. "One of my best friends received a picture from this girl he went to school with," said Kevin. "She was kind of naked. He sold it to his friend for five bucks and a bag of chips. The guy's dad went on his phone and saw it. The dad called the school and my friend got suspended."

"I don't go to that school and I didn't talk to that girl, so I don't know if she had any repercussions," said Tommy, "but I don't think the girl's status goes down because of sending sexy selfies. Reactions depend on the girl and on the picture. Underwear is different than fully naked."

"It doesn't make a difference," Zack said. "If he has the photo, he has the power. It doesn't matter if it's headless."

"I only ever got one," Tommy said, with a boyish grin. "I don't do it; I don't find it that exciting. I used to when I was younger; it was awesome."

"When you get more introduced to real-life sex, you lose interest in the picture. It's not like I'm doing something with the picture," said Zack, making clear his preference for interacting with a real girl and not her photo.

"Guys do show their friends. You shouldn't send those kinds of photos," cautioned Kevin. "If you're a girl you shouldn't send a sexy selfie to someone who says you're pretty. For our age group it's a way to be cool and get your rep up. It's like, 'I can get as many girls as I want, I can get girls to do anything I want.' You can't prove that, so photos are proof."

"It's about status. It's a trophy. Some people think it's funny," said Zack.

"If a girl does it, they don't get judged. It's very open. It's accepted. I think it depends on where you live," added Tommy.

"People want to see it," said Kevin.

"Yeah. They want people to send them the photo; they want to receive it. It *is* like a trophy when you get to show it around. It's hard to explain," said Tommy. "Some people I know are like that, they expect everything to be like porn."

"My mom talks to me about porn," said Zack.

"At school, in health class, they are talking about porn. They say, 'It's just acting, and has nothing to do with real life.' Porn is scripted and they get paid to do it," said Tommy.

"My health class just talks about puberty," said Kevin.

"It depends on the teachers you have and the school you're in, if people are open and will talk to you about this. Some of my friends expect a lot from girls because no one is telling them that porn is acting and not real," said Tommy. "It's the only way that they see sexual things happen, they only have this one source. It's a way to be educated. But people aren't going to go up to adults to ask them if it's real."

"Some guys expect girls to do unrealistic stuff," said Zack.

"Some guys have this idea to go to parties and get drunk, and when the girls get drunk it gives them an opportunity to live out that fantasy that they see in porn," said Kevin. "Your brain or body is saying you want to do this, she isn't going to remember, that's what some people think. I don't approve of it, it's disgusting."

"My teacher, he takes his time to tell us about consent," said Tommy. "Because we are teenage boys. It actually helps a lot. He is a really good teacher. The other boys just get puberty ed."

"If parents and authorities weren't so uptight about sex and porn we would all know more. They leave you to figure it out by yourself," said Kevin.

"I haven't heard of porn sites for girls," said Tommy.

"Creepy, because if they watch it, they think that's how guys act," said Kevin.

Their conversation moved into performance anxiety and the embarrassment of girls thinking that boys should be like porn stars, and we got a sense of how this is a real issue for boys, and affects their confidence. But we were still stuck on the idea that some boys think consciously about going to parties to have sex with girls who are drunk.

Kevin, Zack and Tommy have mothers who talk to them about consent and pornography and provide good sex education, but the majority of boys don't have access to the kind of information that can help them take clear, strong and conscious actions that collaborate with girls and women to end violence, and to create a reality where healthier, happier relationships benefit everyone. When we asked them what they thought of the Rehtaeh Parsons case, they said they understood that it was rape and that, "Society is uptight. A lot of people don't talk about the weird and scary things between each other and we really need to."

CHANGE

In a recent rush of end-of-school-year concertgoing, I attended a choir concert in an elementary school auditorium where Stromae's "Papaoutai" [a pop-rap song that reached number one in both Belgium and France in 2013 and has more than 300 million views on YouTube] was sung, with visible passion, by an ensemble of preteen boys. This was the second time in a week that I'd seen "Papaoutai" sung by a kids' choir. Stromae, who is a Belgian national of Flemish-Rwandan descent—and whose father was emotionally unavailable when he was a boy, and then killed in the Rwandan genocide—sings (in French), *Where are you father, where are you?* and warns that emotional absence is inherited; that it breeds endless and unspoken sadness in boys. *Everyone knows how to make babies*, the song concludes, *but no one knows how to make fathers.* Hearing little boys sing this song onstage with all their hearts afire moved the entire audience at both concerts I attended. When I looked around I saw that many people were crying. I was inspired to see how an enlightened music teacher had taken on a song about what boys feel when dealing with the emotional absence of their fathers, especially alongside a larger cultural movement where fashion, music, art and literature are beginning to show signs of change in their representation of boys and men.

~Caia

Pop culture has recently been introducing a fresh face of masculinity. Youth culture figures like Jaden Smith, emerging designers like Devon Halfnight LeFlufy, Hood by Air (HBA) and Stromae himself, whose line features a hybrid of African motifs and British schoolboy preppiness, are making male fashion more playful, eccentric and feminine. Rap and hip hop have been transforming, too, in the hands of young musicians like Yung Lean, ecco2k, Thaiboy Digital, Lauren Auder and Spooky Black—teens at the helm of a DIY "sad boys" musical movement that's gone viral. Boys who make music in their bedrooms about sadness have millions of followers. These initiatives use emotion and inspiring diasporic and street influences to open new doors of self-expression that are ambidextrous, androgynous and full of twenty-first-century spirit. On the more mainstream side of the spectrum is Justin Bieber. With his fifty-million-plus Instagram followers, he ranks as one of most "liked" people on earth. He earned his social-media visibility in a sea of hugely popular girls like Beyoncé, Ariana Grande and Selena Gomez by being "a sensitive guy"—a fact that proves it's possible for guys to maintain their swagger while being emotionally expressive and proudly owning what in the past might have been labelled "feminine traits."

The thing about a trend is that once its time has come, it's truly everywhere. In a cultural atmosphere where Kanye West has been singing about feelings, Drake has initiated meditations on loneliness, Frank Ocean has started discussions about hip hop, sexual orientation and feminism, and a whole new generation of Internet rap stars has invented a musical form that reappropriates the macho masculine leitmotif, we are hopeful that boys are finding a voice for their unnamed struggle, and that the struggle itself is transforming. Is it possible that we are reaching a place where we finally understand that emotional expression and freedom is a breakthrough for boys and, by association, a breakthrough for girls?

Educating boys so they, too, can express themselves and be part of the solutions for addressing emotional isolation and gender-based violence is a vital process. Michael Kaufman's White Ribbon campaign addresses these issues in practical workshops with boys. Sessions explore realities for women and girls, as well as pressures on men and boys and ways that they can become allies in the movement toward gender equality. Kaufman says that he is seeing a shift in social codes around boyhood. "We see that more and more young men are able to hug each other, that there is more space for physical expression, and that there is less explicit homophobia."

But the most important shift Kaufman is seeing—and the one with the greatest potential impact when it comes to rewriting the social order—is changes in fatherhood. "Fathers are becoming equal parents and there is now a generation of boys who have been brought up by men who are caregivers and nurturers. This means that boys are internalizing images of masculinity that are more traditionally associated with women. That's a big contrast from distant fathers. Those dads who aren't feeding, changing, playing with and looking after their children develop a fantasy presence in young boys' minds. Because boys are now incorporating a new image of caregiving fathers, a healthier masculinity is emerging. Among other things, research suggests that such boys are less capable of committing violence. The reason is this: the main quality you need to be a good caregiver is empathy—to feel what your baby or young child feels. Boys who witness caregiving by their fathers or other adult men internalize empathy as part of their self-definition. And if they have more empathy, they are less likely to use violence in their lives because they can imagine and undertand the pain it will cause. This is one of many reasons why the big shifts toward gender equality are very positive for boys and men."

People like Michael Kaufman and Joshua Gibson and Kara Knight are all playing instrumental roles in this changing of the guard. Through classes and seminars and informal discussions, they are offering knowledge to teen boys and young men in the hopes that they will find intimacy and self-expression in their relationships, and that this will launch a social change both behind closed doors and in public spaces.

Whatever we can do as parents, friends, teachers, coaches, siblings and relatives to speak to kids about masculinity, healthy sexuality and consent can contribute to this much-needed work. *This* is what will allow today's boys to become a new breed of men—men who are strong, yes, but stronger still for being emotionally intelligent, expressive collaborators in the creation of a much more safe, equitable and less violent future.

SURVIVAL KIT

CONFRONT FEARS OF TABOO SUBJECTS AND OPEN UP IMPORTANT DIALOGUES with kids. If we keep silent about sex, pornography, emotional isolation and violence, boys are left to work these secrets out on their own.

WATCH THE MUSIC VIDEOS AND VIDEO GAMES your kids are playing and talk to them about these. How do they feel when they're engaging in them? What do the characters say and do? Even if they are fantasy, do they conform to a healthy or an unhealthy model of gender roles and gender collaboration? Talk to boys about violence against girls and women in games and videos.

EXPECT BOYS TO DO DOMESTIC CHORES AS MUCH AS GIRLS. Also, invite them to nurture their younger siblings or the newborn babies that friends bring over. Reward them for showing empathy and care for others.

DEMAND GOOD SEX EDUCATION IN SCHOOLS. Good sex ed covers topics that include consent, healthy relationships, sexual diversity and gender stereotypes. Deep knowledge of these topics is a gaping hole in most teenage lives. In the wake of too many tragedies and scandals, there is a growing movement to include consent in sex-ed curriculum in North America. Teaching consent demystifies the blurry lines kids are grappling with and the culture we live in that perpetuates violence.

ENGAGE BOYS IN CONVERSATIONS ABOUT THEIR VULNERABILITIES AND UNCERTAINTIES. Ask questions and encourage them to answer honestly with their feelings. How are they feeling about their love interests? How are they feeling about their bodies? Are they nervous about sex? What would they like to know?

SUPPORT BOYS TO DEVELOP EMOTIONAL INTELLIGENCE and the capacity to express a wide range of feelings and emotions. Check out *The Mask You Live In* by Jennifer Siebel Newsom. This film helps students from kindergarten through university develop social and emotional learning (SEL) and critical consideration of gender roles. See more at: therepresentationproject.org/film/the-mask-you-live-in/school-screening -curriculum/#sthash.BfqcJjsk.dpuf

ENCOURAGE MEDIA LITERACY IN VIDEO GAMES. For ideas, check out Feminist Frequency, a video web series that explores representations of women in pop culture with a focus on video games (http://feministfrequency.com) and the work of activist artist Angela Washko, who is the founder of the Council on Gender Sensitivity and Behavioral Awareness in the *World of Warcraft*; she creates performances inside *World of Warcraft*, the online video game, to initiate discussions about feminism and sexual consent within the game play: angelawashko.com/home.html

RESOURCES FOR BOYS AND MEN

- Man Talk. Speaks to guys about healthy relationships, consent and communication: www.michaelkaufman.com/mantalk
- Promundo. Promotes gender justice and the prevention of violence by engaging men and boys in partnership with women and girls: promundoglobal.org
- White Ribbon. A global movement of men and boys working to end violence against women and girls, and to promote gender equity, healthy relationships and a new vision of masculinity: www.whiteribbon.ca
- Moose Hide Campaign. A movement of men taking action against violence toward Aboriginal women and children: moosehidecampaign.ca
- HeForShe. A solidarity movement for gender equality: www.heforshe.org
- Priya's Shakti. A comic book project about a mortal woman and the goddess Parvati who fight against gender-based sexual violence, misogyny and indifference in India, through love, creativity and solidarity: www.priyashakti.com/about
- Jackson Katz. An anti-sexist male activist, educator and writer: www.jacksonkatz.com/wmcd.html

MICHAEL KAUFMAN'S RULES FOR CONSENT

Rule 1: When it comes to sex, only yes means yes.

Rule 2: As a male, it's your responsibility to know if you have consent.

Rule 3: Nothing you've already done gives you permission to do the next thing.

Rule 4: If you're intoxicated, you can't give or get consent.

From Michael Kaufman's pamphlet *Man Talk*

PORN LITERACY 101

- Porn is not real.
- Sex in porn is not the norm; it is cinema, like stunts.
- Porn is scripted; this means pleasure is a performance.
- Bodies in pornography are not the norm (size, shape, body hair, sex positions).
- Twenty-minute porn vignettes are staged and filmed over several hours.
- Most of the women acting in porn are being paid a lot of money. The more she engages with sexual extremes, the more she is paid. The guys are paid a lot less.
- Don't buy it that kids are having hard-core sex and that "everyone is doing it." The truth is, they aren't.
- Experimenting and trying new things can be exciting and a healthy part of a partnership. It's important, though, to keep the following in mind:
- Understand consent, what it means and how to attain it.
- Don't assume that your partner will find pleasure in porn-inspired sex.
- Don't expect porn-star behaviour from real-life partners and hook-ups.
- Be realistic when negotiating sexual experimentation with your partner.
- Remember that porn actors perform for money. How does your partner's pleasure and desire factor into your request? How is this an exchange?

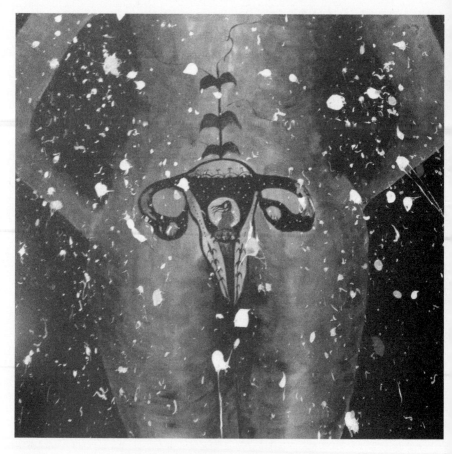

"Land as Body" by Megan Kanerahtenha:wi Whyte.
The land often mentors and mirrors the way we
build relationships with our own bodies; we are creation.

11

CRACKS THROUGH THE CRACKS:
GIRLS IN THE FAR NORTH

WE ARRIVED IN WEMINDJI by propeller plane, the kind that is balanced by body weight, contains only a handful of seats and soars like a bird over vast expanses. Our soundless landing in the sweeping white landscape brought us to a remote reservation hugging the James Bay at the mouth of the Maquatua River in the far north of Quebec.

We were greeted on the snowy tarmac by Mickey DeCarlo, an Ojibwa, mother of four, grandmother and health care professional from Ontario who for the past fifteen years has been living and working part-time in Wemindji as a counsellor, trainer and mental health worker. As she drove us through town, she told us how she fell in love with this Cree community the first time she visited, and pointed out the wellness centre—her working headquarters—adjacent to the one grocery store and café on the reserve. We drove past the youth centre, the sports arena and the surrounding neighbourhoods.

Mickey told us how hunting and trapping for food and the continuation of cultural tradition is very important among the community, but also that Wemindji has changed a lot over the past ten years now that mining is one of the main sources of income and there are roads into what was only recently a fly-in community. The sports arena is brand new, as are many of the houses.

Not long after our arrival, the special Friday-evening pizza party began to gather downstairs at our accommodations in the local church. A handful of girls arrived, took off their boots and changed into the moccasins provided at the entrance. Mickey's eldest daughter, Michaela, a mother of two herself, was already preparing pizzas in the kitchen. The girls ran in to make their own alongside her. Trinity, a 13-year-old with large brown eyes and a riotous laugh, invited us to join in, too.

We asked the girls how they spent their time, what music they were into and what life was like generally for Cree girls living in Wemindji. Floating seamlessly between Cree, English and a hybrid tween lingo, the girls talked excitedly about Facebook, Vine and Twitter; listed their favourite pop music performers, which included Demi Lovato, Bruno Mars and One Direction; and shared gossip about who is doing what with whom, and why. After dinner and a craft-making workshop, more kids arrived, the music was turned up and a spontaneous dance party broke out. A boy demonstrated his skill at the K-pop Shuffle, and showed us how to do it, too.

Like girls we met everywhere on our girl tour, we saw how girls growing up in Wemindji are immersed in pop culture and explore and experiment with their identities and self-expression. They like to hang with their friends and on social media; they navigate social pressure and bullying; and they deal with sexuality and all that comes along with adolescence. They also live in a remote community. So social media connects them in new and important ways to their friends and relatives in neighbouring towns, and to the larger world. But at the intersection of gender and First Nations identity, girls in Wemindji contend with the legacy and impacts of colonization and residential schools—as do Indigenous girls across North America—in very specific ways. Over the course of our stay, the girls we met told us their stories of struggle and insight, and we learned how they're reclaiming their culture and traditions to forge leadership and visions for the future.

A NIGHT AT THE YOUTH CENTRE

We were invited to stop in at the youth centre after our pizza/dance party to say hello to some other local girls. The centre has long hours and as such is one of the community's liveliest meeting spots for kids. When we arrived, we saw six 12-year-old girls intently engaged while

Manny, an elder, demonstrated how to clean and prepare a caribou. He talked as he worked, telling us that he often mentors his grandchildren and other young people in the community, teaching the traditional ways to clean and prepare the animals they hunt. The work took hours, and the girls participated patiently while they moved between video games and helping to prepare packages of caribou meat to share with local families. Nina and Moray ran upstairs to the kitchen and returned half an hour later with a plate full of meat, quickly fried with salt and pepper, to share with the four other girls.

As the night went on and the work continued we learned about this gang of six, who call themselves "The Key of Awesome." Nina, Moray, Tamson, Kanti, Minerva and Mila have known each other all of their lives. The girls spend a lot of time together and have developed a unique style. Moray has long, thick hair that she's dyed strawberry blond and rinsed with violet—it looks '80s rock 'n' roll. Minerva is tall and muscular; she wears boys' clothes with great flair. Mila, Tamson and Nina are petite and share a style that somehow crosses Taylor Swift with the band Van Halen. "We are not ordinary girls," they told us, "that's why we call ourselves 'The Key of Awesome.'"

We asked what "ordinary" girls are like. The group looked at one another and laughed. Tamson said, "'Cool girls.' But we don't think they are cool. They think they are cool because they smoke and get high."

"They are mean," said Mila. "They talk negatively about people."

"I used to be friends with them," Minerva said, "but they started to gossip about my friends. I stopped hanging out when they got mean."

"We are weird," added Moray proudly. "We understand each other. We do stuff that other people don't do. We're into learning our traditions and listening to diverse music, not necessarily the top-ten hits. We love lots of different kinds of music. We don't smoke or get high. We don't care about what other people think. Most of the high schoolers do drugs. We don't want to because our families won't be proud of us. I decided to be myself, and make the right kind of friends. The other kids do drugs to be cool. That's not important. Family and friends are important, so we decided to be different from the other girls."

THE YOUTH CENTRE'S BACKSTORY

Like Mickey DeCarlo, her two adult daughters, Sarah and Michaela, are First Nation Ojibwa. They also spent time in their early adult years in Wemindji, a small Cree community of 1,240 people. Sarah and Michaela come back regularly to conduct workshops—Sarah as a video artist and musician, and Michaela as a social worker. Sarah, the younger daughter, has been leading media arts projects and making films at the youth centre for the past fifteen years.

One of the girls who worked on those early films is Skyler, who now has a job at the youth centre. She is 18 and following her passion to make films—as an artist, and with the local youth. She works with the younger girls and encourages them to express their ideas and feelings through filmmaking. She told us that she is fundraising for more equipment, but in the meantime, they work with whatever they have.

As the media arts coordinator, Skyler takes this on as a mission. "I grew up in Wemindji, the baby of the family. I started working with Sarah when I was 12. We made creative and fun films with her but also films about issues that our community struggles with: teen pregnancy, suicide, bullying, violence—teen issues. She was very helpful. Whenever I wasn't up for filming she would talk to me and motivate me and remind me it's something I love to do."

As "The Key of Awesome" moved from caribou-meat feasting to video games, Skyler invited us to sit around her desk and began to tell us about her life. "I come from a family that are alcoholics and drug addicts. I did these at a young age, too. I started drinking at 12, marijuana at 16, but I quit drugs when I was 17. When you quit in this place, you are alone because most of your friends are still consuming alcohol and you get left out. It's really hard. My co-worker is who I hang out with. We are in the same boat, we don't drink as much as we used to. It takes a lot of strength and there is a lot of boredom. For me, my bedroom is my safe haven, and my videos. In my bedroom on the Internet, a few hours before I go to bed, I think of ideas for films. I watch YouTube and I listen to music. That's when my ideas start rolling in.

"I'm saving up money to buy my film equipment so I don't have to depend on anyone else. It makes me feel strong that I know what I'm doing, that I have a passion and a plan for my future. Our traditional teaching is also a support, I love it that these girls are into it, too. Like a lot of us, I used to be in the bush for a few months every year with my grandparents, uncles and aunts, learning the traditions. Hunting, cleaning and skinning animals, making clothes."

Like many of the young people we met in Wemindji, Skyler feels both a pull to leave the community to go to college and a desire to stay. "I want to apply for film school. My parents want me to get a job first and to learn what it is like to work. I am determined to go to college but if I go away, I will come back. I don't want to leave these kids. It's amazing how much I love these kids."

By then, it was getting late. "The Key of Awesome" had moved on to Facebook chats with friends in faraway places and they didn't overhear this adoration from Skyler. When the centre closed down for the night half an hour later, we headed out into the cold wilderness. "Watch out for the wolves!" they warned as we walked into the starlit darkness.

VALENTINE'S DAY

The next day (having survived the wolves) we attended another party, this time in the community centre. Red roses and heart-shaped chocolates were laid out on the long trestle tables set up for the occasion, and a caribou stew was boiling on a portable stove. Sixty community members gathered to celebrate Valentine's Day. They invited us to join them and gave us each a rose. As we sat with our plates of stew among the many adult couples, some talked to us about the environment and band politics in Wemindji. We learned that a lot of families still have traplines and go into the bush as much as they can. They can be on the land for six months, drawing on their knowledge and traditions, something that they tell us sustains food, health and happiness. While their partnership with the Goldcorp mining company means economic success for the community, there are downsides, too: some of the long-standing trap-lines have been flooded for hydroelectricity and large regions of fishing are cut off due to mercury contamination. A big map of the region on the wall behind us signals safe and unsafe areas to fish. A lot of people from Wemindji work at the nearby mine and leave their home and kids for weeks at a time. Many are still figuring out how to handle this.

We heard more about life in Wemindji when we met after lunch with 21-year-old Diana, a programme assistant at the wellness centre. She told us how the economy is strong here and that employment rates are high. There are protected lands to ensure the continuity of traplines. She said the fish aren't good anymore on her family's line, which reinforced what we'd heard over lunch. She also told us that if the store runs out of milk in Wemindji, it's a big problem: it's a five-hour return trip to the next town with a grocery store that sells milk. The local grocery store features a dearth of fresh produce and aisles of expensive processed food, but, Diana qualified, "Our freezers are filled with bear, moose and geese, and fresh blueberries, blackberries and gooseberries."

Diana grew up in Wemindji but left twice and returned, feeling that it was important to come back to the reservation to support its youth and to contribute to the healing of the community. She plans to get her master's and doctorate degrees in social work. "I am mostly a counsellor," she said about her work at the wellness centre, "listening to the stories that the girls need to tell, and giving them practical advice about how to come out of negative situations to follow their dreams." She wants to do this because of her own experiences, and how much better she feels since working through them. Diana experienced racism and exclusion when she lived off-reserve, and struggled with peer pressure to drink and use drugs when she returned. She confided that she was sexually abused by her friend's brother when she was 14. Her friends discouraged her from getting help, and she was shunned when she tried to speak out about it. Thankfully, her mom was a strong role model and taught her about her rights, and was there to talk to and offer guidance. But even so, her experiences led to depression and a suicide attempt.

"In our culture, almost everyone is reserved. They don't speak because those who do speak are considered loudmouths and will be shamed." Diana believes that the tendency to stay quiet is a legacy from colonization and the residential school experience, where children who spoke were beaten. "Before colonization it wasn't shameful to speak out, but you had to be respectful of all living things. I say to the girls, 'You were born with a mouth, are you using it?' I'm seeing a change. Girls are finding their voices and standing up for themselves."

The idea of finding a voice is linked to another change Diana is seeing in Wemindji girls—one that we saw, too. "Girls here are really returning to the Cree roots and using this knowledge to empower their sense of self, and ability to claim their identity. I know how to clean a beaver, a goose, and other birds. I will learn to clean a bear once my boyfriend kills one for me. There are lots of us like that now."

This theme of reclaiming tradition and culture was repeated in our talk with Veronica, whom we met after Diana. Veronica is a creative and strong 17-year-old. Her experiences of being bullied, losing a sibling and surviving physical violence and substance abuse drove her to write about her life in a blog series that was published online and garnered a large following. "When you're young you think you can only have more friends if you drink and smoke," Veronica said. "As a young teenager I was pressured into smoking, then I thought I could solve my problems with alcohol. I started sneaking around getting alcohol. I thought I had all these friends. We got busted by the police for underage drinking. My mom told me when I was 16, 'You can drink but you have to know when enough is enough,' so I quit and I lost my friends. That's when I started writing." She recounted how her uncle and grandfather encouraged her to express herself, and pointed out how girls need their fathers, too, and how important it is that the men in the community show and teach girls things. "Some girls hardly speak up, so when they hear other girls speak, it inspires them. I think my stories have inspired some people," said Veronica.

Despite her moment of indie-literary fame and her plans to study to be a journalist, Veronica is clear about how she sees her future—like

Diana and Mary and so many of the Indigenous girls living on-reserve who go away and then choose to return, she wants to do what she can to contribute to the healing and thriving of her community. "My boyfriend is also Cree, I want to be[come] fluent in Cree. I want to learn to make moccasins and gloves. Last year, my uncle took me to camp and I finally got to go hunting at goose breaks [a centuries-old Cree tradition where, in the spring, the community hunt the geese that are flying north]. My uncle took me to his camp and I plucked a goose and caught a fish and learned to cook traditional dishes. I want to visit and learn from other communities. Where my boyfriend is from, they do stuff like whale hunting. I want to stay in Wemindji and continue our traditions because the Crees are starting to lose their ways." Veronica is worried about the loss of native land and the environmental degrada tion that's followed in the wake of the mining projects. She also knows a lot of families that are dealing with the disruption of parents having to leave to work at the mine. "Fathers need to be here to teach their kids hunting and trapping skills. If I become a journalist I can do a radio show from here or write stories about life here. There is a lot to say and it's entertaining. I want to live in Wemindji and do that work."

LEGACY AND OPPORTUNITY

Valentine's Day continued when Mickey invited us to her place for dinner. Her husband, Randy, had cooked a big chili with their daughter Michaela, and a handful of neighbouring kids had made poutine with homemade gravy. The kids sat around the living room, very much at home making jokes with their hosts. We could see the sense of family they feel with Mickey, and the ways in which the idiom about how in tight communities everyone is everyone else's child hold true here.

When they had eaten and helped with the dishes, the kids settled around the table with a board game, and we sat with Mickey on the couch to hear her thoughts about the state of girls in the community. Mickey began by giving us some context—how she has lived here for fourteen years and learns new things all the time. "This is a very harsh environment, and people living in Wemindji can survive on the land for months. Modelling the survival traditions is how they are passed on to the younger generations."

Mickey believes this way of teaching was interrupted by residential schools and the ongoing trauma that First Nations communities experience due to colonization. "Generations of children were removed from their parents and homes in the residential school era. When they went to residential school, they were institutionalized. Children were psychologically, physically and sexually abused. They were taken to foreign places with foreign language and customs, deprived of their ancestral language and culture. They weren't parented, so they didn't learn parenting skills; their nurturing and development was interrupted," she said.

In Canada, the residential school system was enforced through the Indian Act of 1876 and implemented until the last school was closed in 1996. This policy, which was put into place to lawfully remove children from the influence of their parents and cultures, has been recently declared an act of genocide by the chairman of the Truth and Reconciliation Commission of Canada, Justice Murray Sinclair. In total, about 150,000 First Nations children passed through the residential school system, and at least six thousand of them died while attending school.[1]

Indigenous lives and identities have been legislated through policies and laws, including the Indian Act and the disruption of traditional economic base, which continue to impose state-level harm on their communities and weaken the roots and the connection to their ancestral knowledge. In Canada, we see this harm through high rates of missing and murdered Indigenous women and girls, high rates of Indigenous children in the foster care system, increasing rates of Indigenous women in the criminal justice system and the removal of children or their caregivers from their homes.

These experiences have left intergenerational marks, and play out in girls' lives in quite specific ways. For girls in Wemindji, the residential school legacy of trauma, silence and shame keeps girls isolated, Mickey explained. This has an impact on their self-confidence and on their ability to break out of cycles of oppression and violence. As in many northern and First Nations communities, domestic and sexual violence are big problems, and girls are often afraid to go to the police when they experience rape or physical abuse. "When we call social services, nothing is really done," Mickey said. "Often the girls aren't believed and action isn't taken. We can't remove girls from their home, so we teach them how to stay safe if they are in a risky situation. We also educate girls about their rights and we use harm-reduction approaches. For example, we tell girls, 'If you drink at a party, make sure you have a friend with you who doesn't leave you alone.'

"Wemindji is also beginning to establish traditional healing practices to deal with violence and abuse. Traditional sentencing circles, for example, which bring everyone affected into a circle to look right into each other's eyes. Those who have done harm own up to their wrongs and are accountable to their victim and that victim's family. It's a very powerful exercise. Addressing things this way often results in reckoning and reconciliation, so the abuse doesn't happen again."

Mickey told us that she used to think she would like to change the world. But now she sees that if you always look at things as a problem, then these things can never be fixed. If instead we focus on the strengths and assets that exist in people and communities, we find creative ways forward. This approach has changed the way she talks to people, and the way she listens. "Change happens in the small, everyday actions we take. I think this generation of Wemindji teens is going to break the cycle."

We recalled a recent collaboration that convened fifty girls ages 13 to 18 from across the North, including Wemindji, for leadership training. When we explored questions around how girls are coping with the extraordinary high incidences of sexual violence and suicide, we found that they are tired of their lives being painted as impoverished and violent. The girls wanted to talk about what they love in their communities, the strengths that enable them to cope with their situations and the gifts they possess to make change. They told us about how they are celebrating their traditions and connections to nature, their close-knit circles and the richness they experience in their relationships, their culture and the eccentricity of the people they know.

Girls in Wemindji are not alone in their efforts to strengthen their communities. They are part of a larger movement led by girls and young women with intergenerational support from uncles, grandparents, elders and mothers, that is pointing to alternative ways forward that are politically astute and focused on the connection between women's bodies and reproduction, the land and environment and their cultural traditions. As we finished our tea and sank deeper into Mickey's cloud-like couch, we felt optimistic: this distinctive thinking and approach is the innovative leadership necessary to address the environmental and social crises of our time.

LUNCH WITH MEGAN

There is an emerging political and environmental movement, led by Indigenous youth, which combines the resurgence of cultural tradition with social media, art and social justice. To learn more about how this movement is mobilizing changes across North America, we had lunch with Megan Kanerahtenhawi Whyte, a 25-year-old First Nations Mohawk artist, young mother and art therapist who sits on the National Indigenous Young Women's Council.

Megan was introspective when she told us about the work she has done in her community, revealing how her involvement has affected her own life. "Growing up as an Indigenous girl in today's society is like living between two worlds—my culture and the rest of the world. As a result, I am always driven to make sense of my identity. One of the biggest challenges we face as young people is the media, which often reduces Indigenous people to one-dimensional characters or stereotypes. Because of this, we have to both define ourselves and redefine ourselves for others. I think that by reclaiming our cultural history and our own teachings, we can better understand and strengthen our Indigenous identities," she said. She raised the questions she's been asking in her creative interventions within her community. "What is traditional identity and what is contemporary identity? Can they coexist? How does the media inform these identities and how do I integrate core values from my traditional culture with mainstream society?"

Megan discussed how mainstream pop culture, fashion, movies and sports all appropriate Indigenous culture. "This misuse and non-consensual use of images colours Indigenous people and our relationship to the world," she told us. "This misappropriation teaches the world that the Indigenous presence is unimportant and reinforces non-consensual relationships that can extend into discussions around missing and murdered Indigenous women. With this continuous bombardment and seemingly uphill battle, how do we become comfortable with our own identity as Indigenous people, reclaim it and break the stereotypes to act as ourselves?"

Recalling her own experiences on this front, Megan said, "I think back to the high school I attended off-reserve, in which students asked me if I lived in a teepee, which demonstrates the level of education around Indigenous people in elementary schools and families. Even at the university level, people said to me, 'Are you sure you're Indigenous? You are so light-skinned.' There is a whole society moving through life completely oblivious to the fact that Indigenous people exist and to the systemic struggles we face. We are romanticized through sensual images like Pocahontas. I think these one-dimensional assumptions are what reinforce the racism that creates difficult situations, and these assumptions start right from childhood. I went to teach in a Montreal elementary school about my own culture not long ago and this boy told me that he was surprised that I was not wearing leather, later telling me that he was a skilled hunter. While wearing leather and hunting are still prevalent parts of my culture, what needed to be explored was the context in which they occur. By building the context, we reduce appropriation and harm. These stereotypes reinforce negative ideas and still, sometimes we feel we have to become these stereotypes to understand ourselves. It's like we are trying to prove to the mainstream North American culture, and to ourselves, that we are Native . . . without fully understanding what it is to be Native."

Leading up to the past Halloween, Megan launched a sticker campaign to combat cultural appropriation of Indigenous cultural clothing. The message of her campaign was, "It's not just a Halloween costume." The stickers she created were stuck onto surfaces in public spaces like wash-rooms and pinboards and then reproduced in photos on social media.

"Romanticizing and sexualizing Indigenous girls through stereotypes is what I believe to be one of the causes of the high numbers of our missing and murdered and the ignorance surrounding it. The stereo-types dehumanize our young women, and can make us into objects in constant need of 'saving' who do not 'require consent.' In some cases, we have learned to internalize this outlook. This phenomenon extends outside of Halloween and into other outlets like TV and fashion. When Disney princesses are prim and proper and then Pocahontas is this fero-cious sexual being, for instance, what does that say to young girls and, perhaps more concerning, to young boys? It's a stereotype that depicts Indigenous women as sexually available, in the sex trade, asking for it— like this is the whole of their life, like this is what they do, like they're only this. And even if our women are in the sex trade, no one stops to think about the realities that put them there. In some communities, there is no access to health care or education and, most often, these women do not have any other choice of income to support their families. Our women should not be punished or dehumanized for the realities that systemic violence, legislation and stereotypes have created in our communities. Those kinds of ideas contribute to the statistics around rape and murder of Indigenous women." With these kinds of accessible and provocative campaigns, Megan is creating a platform for discussion and transformation.

Using the Internet to raise awareness and propel messages like Megan's "It's not just a Halloween costume" campaign, may help to bring about change. Ideologies are malleable in places like Instagram. "It's exciting that with social media, the world gets smaller, and more connected conversations happen between Native and non-Native peo-ple," Megan was happy to tell us. "Things are changing. We are a gen-eration who can now recognize the harm inherited from generations of colonial trauma and residential schools, and that awareness helps to fuel new ways of being. Young Indigenous people want to know more about who we were in Indigenous history and what we are now. We are more involved in political discussions because that is part of redefining who we are. On the shoulders of our ancestors, we are reclaiming our identities in loud ways."

One of the ways Megan has been applying this idea is by restoring rites of passage. A rite of passage occurs at key points throughout a person's lifespan—losing a tooth, for example, or having a child—and is honoured through ceremonial practices. Megan's community is restoring the ceremony that recognizes puberty, where young people are celebrated and prepared for adulthood. The teens are recognized for who they are and their gifts for the community are valued. "People who aren't Indigenous have this clichéd notion of our connection to the land," Megan told us. "They see it as, 'Yeah, they talk to animals.' But our connection to the land is much broader, deeper and ancestral than that. We understand the interconnection between the earth, people, animals, nature and our ancestors, all of which have teachings for each other. It is the lessons in how the land changes over seasons and over time that mentor us in how to balance and model healthy relationships, and how the balance of these creates healthy relationships between all living things."

With the rites of passage, Indigenous leaders are adapting traditional knowledge to explore experiences teenagers are facing today, like addictions, sexuality and coping with media and its influence on their identity. Their intention is to equip youth with tools for thinking critically and respecting themselves and one another.

To illustrate this, Megan told us about using rite-of-passage ceremonies to address consent as a fluid agreement that implies integrity—whether approaching the land, sex or platonic relationships. "In our rites of passage, young boys, for instance, learn how to relate to touching a woman through the metaphor of consent and the land. We tell young men, 'The work and emotion we put into preparing a garden is how you should treat your partner, the person you love. If you want an abundant garden treat it well, water it, till it, give good thoughts to the soil, care for the animals who provide that manure, honour and respect your garden and she will flourish and nurture you back.'"

Megan sees the reconnections that First Nations young people are making to their roots as not only transformative and regenerative for themselves, but also as fostering positive connections with non-Native communities. She explained that her own Mohawk culture is a traditionally matrilineal society where women are recognized as powerful sacred spiritual beings, respected and valued as life-givers and reflections of the earth. Women built the community through their roles in the political clan systems and through the knowledge they passed on as mothers and grandmothers. This can be inspiring even to girls who aren't coming from Indigenous cultures. "It's like, 'Hey, I'm a woman, too, I give life, too.' I give life—that's powerful for girls everywhere to see. Other cultures can benefit from our teachings just as we can benefit from theirs," Megan said.

"We see the human struggle reflected in the land struggle—that spiritually, we, human beings, and the earth, share the same energy, and that the balance of the planet depends on how we nurture this connection," said Megan. It's a belief that is pivotal in her art, the art therapy she practises for healing in the Indigenous community and the unique activism young Indigenous girls are trailblazing. "A lot of my art looks at comparisons between women's bodies and the earth, and makes links between violence done to the land through resource extraction and violence done to women's bodies. I use my art as conversation starters. If we think we can do whatever we want with the earth, take what we want, use what we want however we want, this is a problem. The earth is our first mother, our first model of a woman, so we can't talk about fracking and high statistics of missing and murdered girls and women separately—they have to be talked about together. Environmental damage through extractive industries also has a direct impact on the health of our children, our food ecosystems and our reproductive health."

Like Skyler in Wemindji, Megan understands that artistic expression is an important medium for creating social transformation. "I was a really shy person as a kid. I didn't want to share my thoughts," she remembered. "But art and theatre opened me up in ways that I would probably never have otherwise. Art is my voice. The grassroots work I've been doing has taught me that other young people have thoughts and a voice, too, and that they don't always know how to use it. With the arts kids can see, 'I can make a song and I can dance and I can draw.' Art, social media and creative activism give motivation to young people. It makes them excited to connect to their own roots and their own identity—and to start a conversation with the world."

Megan, an inspired leader who began this work as a teen herself, is in turn inspired by the way the Indigenous girls and young women who are leading at the local grassroots level are gaining momentum and visibility, and are influencing decision-makers.

Megan is part of a growing movement of global Indigenous youth leadership creating community-based responses to violence. Young Indigenous women are also a force for change at national and international levels. This movement has been actively involved in UN negotiations on the rights of Indigenous peoples. Through international human rights mechanisms, they advise on a variety of issues, including the child welfare system, reproductive rights, HIV/AIDS and environmental concerns and policy.

First Nations girls are at the forefront, tackling some of the most pressing challenges we all face: spiritually, socially and environmentally. We are seeing waves of this dynamic new vision surfacing in local, meaningful ways in Wemindji as well as globally. And, in chapter 12, we will meet one young Indigenous woman in particular who is taking on global problems alongside the United Nations, using an activism all her own.

SURVIVAL KIT

ADVOCATE for school-based education that offers Indigenous histories, as well as the history of colonization and how white settlement and colonial violence gave way to a broad spectrum of intergenerational harm, including residential schools, the Indian Act, the removal of land rights, the disruption of a traditional economic base leading to poverty, the removal of kids from their homes and the overrepresentation of Indigenous children in the foster care system.

DECONSTRUCT stereotypes in kids' media and games. Practice critical thinking around stereotypes of Indigenous culture. For example, discuss Halloween costumes that overly sexualize or romanticize portrayals of Indigenous women, and point out that games of "Cowboys and Indians" perpetuate entrenched racist notions that have harmful effects.

CALL OUT discrimination that sexualizes or promotes violence against Indigenous girls and women.

FOR INFORMATION ON INDIGENOUS YOUTH-LED ACTIVISM on reproductive and environmental justice, and supporting Indigenous young women's leadership, visit the Native Youth Sexual Health Network: http://girlsactionfoundation.ca/en/indigenous-young-women-lead-our-stories -our-strengths-our-truths-edited-by-the-native-youth-sexual-health-network

FOR RESOURCES ABOUT FIRST NATIONS YOUTH AND FAMILY ADVOCACY and campaigns that promote rights to health and education visit First Nations Child & Family Caring Society of Canada: www.fncaringsociety. com/what-we-do

FOLLOW INSPIRING INDIGENOUS YOUNG WOMEN

- Check out the new Cree teen-girl superhero Equinox, a comic art heroine created by Jeff Lemire as part of the DC Comics Justice League United: dc.wikia.com/wiki/Miiyahbin_Marten_(Prime_Earth)
- *Mohawk Girls* is a dramatic comedy about four young women figuring out how to be Mohawk, find their place and find love in the twenty-first century. It airs on the Aboriginal Peoples Television Network (APTN).
- Megan Kanerahtenhawi Whyte is an artist and art educator from the Mohawk Nation of the Haudenosaunee Confederacy. Her website showcases multimedia visual art and exploratory media to address issues of Indigenous rights, cultural traditions and hybrid identities for local Native and non-Native communities. megankanerahtenhawlwhyte.com/tag/native-art
- Tanya Tagaq is an Inuit throat singer practising a tradition she learned in her native Nunavut. Her voice is so moving—a fact attested by her four Juno awards and international performances alongside the likes of Björk. Her recordings give everyone an opportunity to participate in her rich Inuit tradition. Go listen: tanyatagaq.com
- Skawennati makes art that addresses history, the future and change from an Indigenous point of view. Her pioneering new-media projects draw on the psychological survival skills unique to Indigenous people and include the online gallery/chat space and mixed-reality event, CyberPowWow (1997–2004); a paper doll/time-travel journal, *Imagining Indians in the 25th Century* (2001); and TimeTraveller™ (2008–2013), a multi-platform project featuring nine machinima episodes.
- Edmonton-born Enoch Cree Ashley Callingbull Burnham was 2015's Mrs. Universe, the first Indigenous woman to win the title. Ashley has used this platform to advocate for missing and murdered Indigenous girls and women, and to bring awareness to Indigenous poverty, the need for political visibility, healing and empowerment. To watch this inspiring woman speak out, and to learn more and spread the word about Indigenous issues, follow her on Twitter: twitter.com/ashcallingbull

+++

GIRLS AS CHANGEMAKERS:
GOING LOCAL AND GLOBAL

LATE IN OCTOBER 2014, we arrived in Toronto for Strong Girls, Strong World, a conference that brought together girls and influential Canadians to explore the important issues girls face in Canada and globally. The conference was held at Central Technical School in the city centre, in honour of the International Day of the Girl. Malala Yousafzai was due to speak that day about the Nobel Peace Prize she had won a few weeks earlier. At 17, she was the youngest ever recipient of the prize, which was awarded for her work advocating for girls' right to education in Pakistan. Her participation in the conference was a highlight for the five hundred girls in attendance.

Malala was also going to receive an honorary Canadian citizenship from then prime minister Stephen Harper. Unfortunately, a rare shooting in Ottawa forced Malala and the prime minister to abandon the journey. Although the girls were deeply disappointed, they went ahead with the rest of the conference with perhaps even more commitment, faced as they were with an all-too-vivid reminder of the fragility of life and the necessity to push onward with efforts for positive change.

As we made our rounds, meeting both participants and leaders, we were impressed by the range of work going on, much of it at the grassroots level and beneath the surface. There were dozens of inspiring local and global projects, all dreamed up and executed by teenage girls.

We met Andrea, 17, one of the co-founders of Project Slut (see chapter 4), who was participating in Tatiana's workshop on entrepreneurship, social innovation and how to practise self-care. After the workshop, we met Serena and Tatum, two 16-year-old best friends from Toronto. In our brief encounter, the two underlined how strongly they feel about racial injustice and the discrimination they encounter as queer girls. Serena told us she plans to build a social enterprise; she is designing makeup palettes to manufacture and sell so she can donate some of her revenue to helping the family of Michael Brown (the African-American man who was shot by a white police officer in Ferguson, Missouri, in 2014, an incident that ignited the Black Lives Matter movement). Tatum, who is of Mexican descent, plans to study law so that she can fight the criminalization of marginalized communities. It's an issue to which she feels personally connected as many of her family members have been through the criminal justice system. Serena and Tatum talked about how they see transgender kids, especially, being hyper-criminalized and told us they are committed to making change on this front. We talked about Isa Noyola, the Indigenous transgender Latina queer two-spirit activist who is also working on the political front lines in the US to eliminate oppressive systems that criminalize trans and queer immigrant communities of colour.

Another workshop leader, Anjali Katta, stopped to chat. Anjali is a charismatic 18-year-old from Vancouver, British Columbia. She has been volunteering in the slums of Mumbai since the age of 12, and has initiated projects there that have been transforming the lives of girls. She founded GirlsCo. in Vancouver, a youth-run non-profit organization that seeks to educate and inform youth about the issues that women and girls face, locally and globally. She hosts workshops and summits on gender equality in Vancouver high schools while simultaneously raising money for school-age girls living in India. She had recently spoken at the UN for International Day of the Girl Child and was in Toronto for a workshop called "I Lead Change," about how to be a girl leader in a changing world.

Anjali sauntered up wearing long French braids that fell the length of her back. We were curious to hear how her various projects were progressing, including her recent selection by the government of Canada to advise them on their new Girls and Young Women's Advisory Council.

She had some time between workshops, so we got to hear more about her personal story and how it led to her being so proactive, at her age, in the political and philanthropic spheres.

We sat on school desks in an airy classroom as girls flowed past, some of them stopping to listen. "One of my first memories is from about age five, serving food at a soup kitchen alongside my mother," Anjali told us. "My family are from India and they came from poverty. They have always been aware of giving to others and raised me that way. My aunt lives in Mumbai and whenever we would go there we would drive past this massive area of slums. When I was 12, I really noticed it and I said, 'OMG, the most expensive house in the world is one kilometre away from these slums!' This realization really shocked me. When we got to my aunt's, my dad and I did some research on the Internet and found an organization based in Canada called One! International Poverty Relief that founded two schools for boys and girls who live in these slums. So I went there and I met Amina on my first day. She was 14 and I was 12. She said she was at school because she had nowhere else to go— she had been raped and got pregnant, and was disowned by her family. She didn't even know that abortion was possible. Just hearing that and thinking to myself, 'Oh God, in two years I will be her age,' made me want to do something. I met other girls with similar stories and realized that sexual violence and the abandonment of the victims is actually very entrenched in India. A lot of girls affected by rape don't speak about it. I started a petition when I got back to Vancouver to raise awareness about this and got two hundred signatures. Then I did a radio show about it and things snowballed into me founding GirlsCo.

"GirlsCo. raises funds for the school where I met Amina," Anjali continued. "A lot of girls live far away from school and one of the biggest things that stops them from coming to school is having their periods and not being able to afford pads. It's like, 'Do we buy milk or do we buy pads?' Which is a no-brainer, especially because there is still a huge stigma around menstruation in India; they opt to buy milk. We are now investing in having pads for all girls so they don't miss school. This initiative is having a positive impact. The smallest things can make the biggest difference. One of the girls in the school got really good marks because she stopped missing class during her period and she will be the first girl to pass grade ten at this school. She wants to be a nurse. Isn't that cool? We are going to begin investing in pad machines so girls can make their own pads, it will be a business for them while also providing pads and more freedom for them in their lives."

Anjali also conducts workshops in North American schools. Her last workshop was with a group of grade-six girls who asked, "Why do girls have to shave their legs?" "I Googled it right away—I use a lot of Internet in my workshops," Anjali told us, "and we discovered together that in the 1940s a shaving company started an ad campaign for leg shaving so that girls would look prepubescent and virginal. The girls were like, 'Eww that's weird, I don't want to do that.' If you get to the root of notions it's eye-opening. Girls begin to see: 'I'm in charge of myself in the face of these messages around me and I can control how I respond to them.' With younger kids we just hang out. If they think you're just a little more experienced in life than them but not a lot, they feel comfortable, not afraid to ask what they might think are dumb questions and be judged for not knowing things. So being only a couple of years older is the best in this situation. It's what really works for me right now."

Being a leader and knowing how to be successful; having the confidence to get signatures and raise funds and lead workshops; speaking to adults and to younger people; creating business plans that are executed on the other side of the world—these are all things that Anjali has been doing since the age of 12. There is a great need for the kind of peer learning Anjali is providing. It's rewarding work and it's lots of fun, but it requires developing a thicker skin than many kids have normally developed by this age. Anjali is often dismissed by adults, who tend to think that what she is doing is "cute" or "well-intentioned, but not that important." She comes up regularly against teachers and peers who assume she lacks credibility and try to shut her down. "A lot of my friends are into the work I am doing, but I'd say that 50 percent of my grade doesn't care," Anjali explained, describing the apathy and, sometimes, opposition she meets along the way. "We gave a violence-in-dating seminar not long ago and half my grade was so unwilling to see women as disadvantaged. They were like, 'Where did you get your stats from?' as if I had made them up. When I go to schools and speak, a lot of people get up and leave. Some people don't care, but a few always stay behind to really listen and get into it. The media has picked up on a lot of the issues I like to talk about and it's becoming trendier to be an activist interested in gender equality. Now, more and more people stay around to hear me speak. It's important that I keep doing this even if some people are against me. A lot of people feel threatened that a girl is able to be smart and come up with good ideas. It's like those kinds of people think there's a set amount of power in this world and if a girl takes some they feel they have to reassert their prowess. I am female and I have long hair; I wear makeup and nice clothes. But guess what? I'm fierce."

Anjali's experience and abilities echo some of the qualities that we see in other examples of girl leadership. She has strength and perseverance, and finds ways to push through challenges or a lack of support. She is resourceful and trailblazing. She also looks beyond strictly girls' or women's issues. Like many of today's girls who are acting for change, she is taking on local and global concerns and connecting her empowerment to issues such as poverty and systems of discrimination. Anjali is one of many bright young girls who are stepping up to be powerful players in shaping a new world. Girls are seeding transformations in everything from media production to environment and climate change. They are critical leaders in creating a planet that is just, sustainable and healthy.

THE DINNER PARTY

The Strong Girls, Strong World conference got us thinking. Clearly, *many* girls are having an impact. Why, then, does the mainstream rarely hear their stories? What we get when we skim the daily papers or tune into the news are features on one or two high-profile activists-turned-celebrities. These activists can, of course, be extremely powerful. But in shining the spotlight on them, we are missing a huge part of the picture: all the girls who are effecting change "under the radar," at the grassroots level.

As we saw at the conference, social innovation and entrepreneurship are one way that girls can lead change at any level. We made plans to have dinner with a few more girl leaders—most of whom have been part of the Girls Action Foundation and leadership training in different parts of Canada—to find out more about what they've been up to.

We made our way to a Thai restaurant in downtown Toronto, where we met Natasha Burford, who spoke to us in chapter 5, and the rest of our party, all willing and more than able to talk about what girls need in order to unleash their creativity and lead change. Natasha brought Enoruwa, 21, a student, writer, gamer and activist, and Schanelle, an 18-year-old law student and organizer. Both are leaders of WORC It Inc. (Women of Race Climbing It Together), the organization Natasha founded in 2005 as a summer camp project for girls from a tough Toronto neighbourhood. Enoruwa and Schanelle both started as campers and worked their way up to leadership roles.

We also invited Khadra Ali, 30, and her sister Muna, 31, the co-founders of Gashanti Unity, a group that empowers young Somali girls through media-arts leadership development and business training. Our dinner guests were mostly a little older than the girls we'd been speaking to on our tour, and we were curious to hear about what their "in the field" experiences as activists and social entrepreneurs had taught them. How do they define (or redefine) traditional forms of leadership? What do they see for the future?

We started, though, with some different questions. "What is the secret recipe that moves a girl into action?" we asked. "How does she know she can create a different world?" Over plates of appetizers, we set up the recorder and launched into a lively, four-hour dinner party and discussion. Each one of these five leaders had an unforgettable presence: Schanelle with her incredible energy; Khadra and Muna with their strength and articulation, Enoruwa with her caring, reflective nature and Natasha, who's the most spirited woman. Their stories inspired so much hope, and made us feel so much love for them and the important work they are doing.

Natasha started by telling us about why she founded WORC It. "My community, Jane and Finch, is known as a 'priority needs' neighbourhood. I grew up seeing some of my friends murdered, seeing government-built townhouses burn down because they didn't have fire alarms, and the families literally dying. I just got tired of watching the news and seeing my community overshadowed by violence. I finally realized I could not wait for someone else to do something."

A pivotal experience helped Natasha see that she had to take action to transform her community herself and, more important, that she had the power to do it. This experience was mentorship. Through Natasha's relationship with her mentor, she learned about her strengths. "Growing up, I didn't have any mentors. My sister got me in trouble more than she helped me. I remember going to a national leadership training at Girls Action Foundation, where I met Tatiana. I was invited to participate as part of a project I was involved in with a Toronto youth organization. I saw all these amazing women in this one room—I had never been around so many diverse women: leaders, organizers and activists making a difference in the world. We discussed the issues our communities were facing and ways to mobilize resources, build partnerships and networks of support, and how to build capacity for leadership. It sparked something in me. It gave me a plan. I decided that I wanted to work with young women and I wanted to give girls what I didn't have. If I had had a plan, or guidance when I was their age, it would have saved me from stuff I went through."

As the main course dishes began to arrive and the discussion got livelier, each of the guests at the table shared a similar experience. Schanelle, who has been mentored by Natasha and is one of the WORC It Aspiring Leaders (the young women's division of WORC It), remembered how she used to be shy and nervous. This was before she joined the leadership camp six years ago. "That summer, I learned to socialize more. We learned how to give workshops, and to facilitate them." She also gained personal organizational skills and credits WORC It for her success at school. "It encouraged me to get involved in many things at school.

We met the mayor of Toronto at the time and I was recognized for my contributions. Eventually, I became a chair of Aspiring Leaders. I learned to write grants, run an organization and manage a lot of paperwork." At 18, she's already helming it like a CEO twice her age. When we commented on this, Schanelle said, "My mom is a single mom. I think I have grown up a lot faster because of the early maturity I got from helping my mom. Mentally, I am so ahead of the game." Schanelle wants to study law so she can be a powerful legal support in areas where there is injustice and struggle.

Enoruwa was also shy, and had been bullied before she started at WORC It. "I struggled with a lot of things. I was socially awkward and not very friendly. I didn't want to go to the summer camp because I was afraid of the other girls—and at first I didn't like it. Over time, I realized that these were not the girls who bullied me. One of the older girls talked to me about confidence. She told me, 'There is so much potential in you. You don't see yourself as others see you. You have to see yourself in a different light.' That was very motivating and powerful. It was sincere, I could feel that she saw something in me, and that I should be able to see myself in a beautiful light. I stepped out of my shell after that. It was a significant moment. I wouldn't be who I am if it wasn't for Natasha and WORC It."

Enoruwa spoke about her leadership and life experience at a recent event. She talked about her struggle with depression, self-harm and hospitalization. After her talk, some girls from the audience stayed to chat with her. "They had so much to say," recalled Enoruwa. "Everyone has a story to tell. When you are going through something and you think you are alone, and then another girl comes up to you and says, 'I've gone through that. I understand what you are saying,' that is powerful. Just knowing that someone you can relate to is going through something you are going through, too, is really significant. You don't feel as lonely. It's important to be able to have experiences like that."

Throughout our tour, we've seen how powerful it is for girls to be given a safe space, a place where trust and honesty are nurtured and where they can be themselves and connect with other girls over shared or common experiences. We thought about how important that moment was for us in our own experiences, and how it helped to set our problems within larger social and political contexts. The move away from experiencing fear or shame can be a catalyst to accessing our own power, and to realizing that we have the ability to influence change. Girls need more opportunities like this to discover that power for themselves.

Khadra and Muna said they, too, could relate to feeling isolated and alone. "We are challenging the traditional norm of a young Somali woman, like the image of women staying at home," Khadra explained. "We needed the support and the mentorship from our girlfriends to talk about the struggles with identity. My sister and I started by creating a space with our friends. Then we wanted to expand and create something for everyone else, so we founded Gashanti Unity."

Ghashanti Unity is a group of young Somali women in Toronto whose mission is to provide mostly Somali but also other immigrant girls and young women with a safe atmosphere in which to develop their gifts, abilities and positive relationships. "There are a lot of issues girls have to deal with that they are afraid to talk about," Khadra continued. "Gashanti uses art as a platform to have that conversation and then we support girls to learn the leadership ropes and gain the confidence to go out and do what they want. It's really inspiring."

"We have always been entrepreneurial," Muna added. "We were invited to a wedding and we weren't all going to go because there was going to be a male DJ and a male photographer and some of us wouldn't be able to take our hijab off. I was like, there is an opportunity here." The experience gave these sisters the idea of founding a social enterprise to offer female DJ and photography services for all of the community's women-only events, and to use this as a way to create economic opportunity for Gashanti members. They made a business plan and developed the skills they needed, like advertising and management, and they provided part-time employment for other young Somali women who wanted to work with only women. As Gashanti Unity has grown, they've been able to offer cultural competency, film and photo workshops to girls at large. "We know what it's like to struggle. We want girls to walk out of

Gashanti Unity with skills for employment, and while we're doing that we get to see girls turn their hardships into positivity," said Khadra.

Everyone at the table agreed that this is an emerging social and political trend, that girls are making the connection between personal experiences and systemic issues like poverty, violence and climate change. Girls are on the front lines of the harm caused by social and environmental injustice, and they are on the front lines leading the changes that need to happen. Enoruwa put it succinctly when she said, "I feel girls were previously seen as unable to occupy leadership positions because they apparently didn't have the toughness or the wits to do so, or they were too soft, which is totally inaccurate—the toughest and most intelligent people I know are women. So now that women are in those spaces we can bring in new ideas and perspectives [to a space] that used to be very limited to whatever the traditional leadership thought of as right. We are bringing in new ways to lead, new ways to plan, new ways to look at the world. I think because this leadership is very social justice driven, that aspect of bringing to light injustices and unequal power dynamics is driving things forward and is allowing for large-scale mobilization." Enoruwa added that the Internet really helps. "Now we have all sorts of girls who previously wouldn't speak up raising their hands online to say, 'Hey, this is important to me—hear me out.'"

When we asked about how emerging leadership can be supported by adults, Muna told us about her recent experience on a task force aimed at supporting young people in the Somali education system. The boys have been struggling with high dropout rates, but the girls are doing well. In the task force created to address boys' dropout rates, only five of the twenty-five participants were young women. "We need young women's perspective on change," Muna said. "Too many times our perspective is missing, and we are the people who understand the links to family dynamics and to the encompassing structures. Young women have vision and need to be part of the conversations and the solutions."

By this time we were into dessert and the restaurant was getting quieter. Natasha said that she wanted to see more girls have the opportunity to take up leadership but confessed that it's hard to get financial investment. Girls want to take action and see a project through from beginning to end. "It's such a beautiful thing to watch them in action," agreed Muna. "To see girls dream and make their dreams happen." With a desire to give these dreams traction on an international level, Gashanti Unity is working to connect with the Somali community across North America, and to build bridges from the West to Somalia.

CONNECTING THE LOCAL TO THE GLOBAL

These days, the "girl issue" is a hot topic on the global stage, as is investing in girls as agents for change. The World Bank has determined that investment in a girl's education means she will, in turn, invest in her family, community and economy. Others, such as international governments and non-governmental organizations, are also positioning girls to be a key resource for global change. Young women like Muna and Khadra, who have on-the-ground experience as activists and advocates for girl issues, believe this is a simplistic approach to a complex phenomenon.

On the one hand, it is empowering to think that just one girl can impact change. On the other, it is essential to understand the underlying context and deeply entrenched systemic inequalities girls are up against. What happens, for example, when sexism within a family or community keeps girls at home—cooking, cleaning, bringing home water and raising their siblings—rather than heading out to school?

Muna and Khadra have witnessed how young Somali women are transforming these types of challenges into opportunities. Technology is an important platform for spreading the word on local stories and the kinds of solutions small communities, often led by girl activism, are finding to complex problems. Many girls are writing blogs about their day-to-day lives—their friendships, their community, the things they believe in, their challenges and how they are imagining ways forward. But, Muna told us, "You wouldn't hear that story in the mainstream media. When you think of Somalia, you think of female genital mutilation. You think of Somali sea pirates and of Sharia law. You never hear about the young woman who is actually fighting the system, helping victims of sexual assault and rape. Those are the stories I wish I heard more about."

Khadra agreed, "We don't hear the stories where we, as Somali girls, are empowered and *we* are educating our community and *we* are helping ourselves. How do we feel about Western NGOs providing us with a solution? Have we come to a decision about what we need before the world has created a campaign to solve our problems?" She told us about a media project she did with Somali youth. "You know the 'Happy' video, by Pharrell Williams? Well, we did one and we made it with all the young locals interested in the arts. They are interested in the same stuff as us. They just don't have access to the tools to make art, which are such valuable resources." Muna and Khadra want to see non-traditional forms of education for girls in Somalia, too, education that can support girls to be entrepreneurs and creative agents in their economies.

The Arab Spring provided a vivid example of how technology can unleash the power and courage of grassroots girl-led activism. Twenty-six-year-old Asmaa Mahfouz posted a video on YouTube asking all of Egypt to "Come down with us and demand your rights, my rights, your family's rights." That video went viral, and helped ignite a fire that would take down the regime in Egypt and lead to widespread revolution in the Arab world. Through the blogosphere and high-traffic social-media sites like Facebook, Twitter, Tumblr, YouTube and Instagram, local change can be globalized.

Now that we are deep inside the digital age, the idea of building positive, powerful, borderless community is a very formidable reality. Girls like Myanmar's Thinzar Shunlei Yi—a 23-year-old peace builder, youth government ambassador and the coordinator of her country's National Youth Congress—uses social media to mobilize youth behind every issue on her political agenda. In doing so, she is successfully pressuring her government to acknowledge girls' voices and change non-progressive policy. Zeitun Tifow, a 24-year-old activist from Kenya, uses digital platforms to create conversations between her community and the world. She told #YouthTalks, "Social media has freed us from old ideas. It has allowed us not to feel alone in terms of where we would like to be, and shown us what other people around the world experience, as young people with ambitions—who they are and what they're like. It's good to be exposed to people outside our own kind. This has given us a voice and a support network. If our elders are finding it hard to understand us, we can turn to each other. We can connect with others who believe in our struggle or are going through the same thing."[1]

In the West, too, girls are using technology to advocate for consent, call out slut-shaming, create culture, mobilize Indigenous sovereignty, force brands to represent girls positively and encourage decision-makers and the public to take note of everything from the date rape epidemic to #Blacklivesmatter protests. Girl activists are changing their communities, yes, but by combining their strong voices with the tools that technology provides, they are also changing the world.

ZOE

Inspired by our dinner companions' stories of power, influence and social, cultural, political and economic change, we kept the conversation going the following morning, with a Skype call to dynamic changemaker Zoe Craig. We were in our pajamas in our East Coast hotel room; she was in her pajamas on the West Coast, sitting up in bed in her dorm at Pearson United World College (an international postsecondary school for emerging leaders and changemakers) before a long day of classes and political meetings. With her hair piled on top of her head and her earphones on, Zoe looked like the quintessential 17-year-old high school girl.

Zoe is half Musqueam First Nations. She grew up on a reserve in Vancouver with her mother (her dad died when she was young). She received a scholarship to attend an off-reserve elementary school, one of the most prestigious private schools in the city. The disparity between the economic reality of her home life and the affluence of her school life left a lasting impression and inspired her interest in activism. "I would get up to go to school every morning and go through the reserve, where houses were falling apart, broken glass and garbage were everywhere, to the other side of town to this pristine school. Seeing the wealth inequalities was hard; it's hard to come from people who have nothing to a school where people have everything," Zoe recalled.

When she was 13, Zoe had an opportunity to work at Justice for Girls, a trailblazing organization advocating for Indigenous girls living on the streets and getting caught in the criminal justice system (see chapter 9). The experience has had a tremendous impact. "Seeing something so wrong made me open my eyes and understand that the problems I thought I knew were way bigger than my point of view, that they go so much wider, and that we stand up for so many people when we do this kind of work," Zoe told us.

At 15, Zoe did an internship through Justice for Girls working on the issues of children's rights and the environment. "We knew there was a link between girls' health and the environment but we had to prove it." She researched and blogged about the Rio+20 world summit; talked with renowned ecologists David R. Boyd and Severn Cullis-Suzuki to understand as much as she could about climate change; memorized the constitution and the articles of human rights; and learned how to draft a UN resolution. "There was never a gendered lens that set out how girls are affected by climate issues," she said, explaining that women and girls experience the worst impacts of climate change, by far. The damaging impact that environmental issues have on women's health and mortality rates, and its effects on the breakdown of labour and the spikes in violence against women and girls, all exacerbate the inequalities that already exist for them. "For example," Zoe told us, "when girls eat toxic fish that are poisoned as a result of runoffs and tar sands, this can lead to infertility in reproductive systems that are still developing. Girls' reproductive systems are really dangerously affected by air and water pollution and pesticides. Breastfeeding mothers who are exposed to these environmental pollutants get poisoned milk, and this severely affects their health and the health of their babies."

When Zoe and her friend the American Rekha Dhillon-Richardson (also 15), went to Geneva to present their work to the United Nations Committee on the Rights of the Child, they linked Canada's failed record on climate change to children's human rights. Zoe argued,

"My inherent right to life, and my right to culture as an Indigenous person are being jeopardized not only by climate change but by my country's lack of environmental standards and policies. Canada must give children a say in environmental policy." She told us, "We don't think it's fair that kids' voices aren't respected in court and that we are not consulted regarding the future. It's our future. We want to defend ourselves."

Now in her final year at college, with classmates from around the world and extracurricular activities that include learning to develop policy, advocacy skills and business strategy, Zoe has high ambitions and several options for her future. Along with activism, she has also taken hosting roles on TV—on *U=US*, for example, a teen television series that airs on the Aboriginal Peoples Television Network—that have inspired a desire to work in entertainment, where she can broadcast her ideas in a different venue.

It's refreshing to hear Zoe talk about this kind of visibility and commitment to change-making as if it's the most natural thing in the world. "My peers are all changemakers," she told us. "They are all invested in education and the future. We don't care about traditional politics. To us it's not political parties that matter. The *issue* is what matters—and people's visions for an issue. Like, what are you going to do about climate change? Oil sands? What are you going to do about the mayor who doesn't care about your ideas? We care so much, but it's different than our parents' generation. We understand that agency is really about what *you* are going to do about an issue that you care about. Our elders have a wise saying: 'We don't inherit the world from our ancestors; we borrow it from our children.'[4] This is something I truly believe in, and like many of my peers, I don't trust adults to safeguard our future. We are pragmatic about this. For example, we are interested in finding some way to lower emissions sensibly. We can do this by shifting from unsustainable to sustainable resources, building more solar power, and slowly weaning off "dirty" resources. It's the slow steps and the commitment that makes it possible to create a sustainable future."

Zoe is currently working with Justice for Girls on putting together a girls' summit for climate change. "We can't just say that we want decision-makers in power to listen, and not have a plan," Zoe explained. "Our thought is if we could just shift the focus from the negative to celebrate the good, we could get a lot done. Society is also more willing to listen to girls; they are excited to hear what young girls have to say. We see this and we want to put these problems to bed."

While GirlsCo. founder Anjali has been outgoing about her agenda and bold in devising awareness campaigns (she often includes boys, asking them to re-post and re-tweet, which they sometimes refuse to do), Zoe has taken a different approach. She's very quiet about her work. "I've kind of lived a double life," she says. "I've been very private about what I do when I'm not at school. One of my teachers found out about the UN presentation, though, and she made a thing about it at school. Some people saw me hosting *U=US*. For sure, it inspired people. They had no idea. I think it showed them that anything can happen if you work hard enough."

What an inspiring end to the last leg of our North American tour. All we could think of when we hung up from speaking to Zoe, with all the commentary from all the other girls in this chapter and in this book swimming in our minds, was that if there was ever a doubt that girls are incisive thinkers, pragmatic solution-finders and fearless warriors on the many crucial paths along the quest for brighter tomorrows—we now have proof that girls are our world's best allies.

SURVIVAL KIT

FOSTER GIRLS' PASSIONS AND STRENGTHS. Girls have purpose and paths. More women are needed in positions of power, making decisions and leading visions for our future world. We start this with girls.

SHINE LIGHT ON, AND CELEBRATE, THE STRENGTHS AND ASSETS GIRLS BRING TO THE WORLD. Point them out, nurture them, resource them.

SUPPORT PEER LEARNING AND PEER MENTORSHIP OPPORTUNITIES FOR GIRLS. It means so much to younger girls to receive the attention and earned knowledge of an older girl, and can make a real difference in their future choices.

NURTURE POSITIVE GIRL RELATIONSHIPS that build solidarity and community between women and girls. Be a role model of this for your daughters or nieces or students. Project a world view where girls are champions of and support for one another, where girls lift one another up, not push one another down.

ENCOURAGE GIRLS NOT TO BE SWAYED BY THE OPINIONS OF OTHERS. Tell them that being bold, being confident, and even being *over*confident are good.

LISTEN TO GIRLS' LIVED EXPERIENCES and ask how they would approach the challenges they see and experience. Be careful not to think you have the solution or answer to someone else's struggles. Cultural contexts need to be considered when supporting cross-cultural change efforts.

CHALLENGE GIRLS TO PUSH BACK AGAINST STANDARD NARRATIVES and girls' cultures that reinforce feelings of insecurity. Help girls to get comfortable with being big in their self-image and energy, taking up space, challenging the status quo. Find ways to demonstrate strength, assertiveness, confidence and integrity. We can be both vulnerable and strong; it's not an either/or proposition.

> *Encourage girls to own their opinion and their voice. Teach girls that dissent from the mainstream is okay, and that it's also okay to put your hand up even if you don't think you have the right answer.*
> Anjali Katta, founder of GirlsCo.

REFRAME LIFE EXPERIENCE. Help kids see the bigger picture and locate negative and positive experiences within broader systems and structures. Understanding how systems and structures interact in society creates opportunities for inspiration and vision for solutions.

DEMONSTRATE THAT MISTAKES AND FAILURES ARE OPPORTUNITIES to learn and grow. Ask, "What did you learn from this? What does this experience show you for the future?" Share your own failures and the lessons you've learned from those.

RECOGNIZE LEADERSHIP IN ITS MANY FORMS. Today, everyone is required to co-create change. Encourage girls and boys and adult supporters to see and recognize the diverse forms that leadership and change may take. You don't need to be a high achiever to be a creator of change.

RESEARCH GIRL ACTIVISM AND ACTIVISTS and talk about them at the dinner table.

+++

HOTEL THOUGHTS

AFTER WE HUNG UP WITH ZOE, we made coffee and lay in our beds talking about her, and Anjali, and all the girls we'd met at the conference and at dinner. These conversations helped to crystallize so much of what writing this book was about—hearing from girls about their challenges, their hopes and dreams, their strengths and new ways of seeing things, and what they need to succeed and play fully realized roles in the world. We thought back to all the incredible girls that we've met during our Girl Tour, and what in their thoughts, projects, insights and passions, they're doing to collectively shape our world.

It's really hopeful to imagine a world where these girls are leaders. We talked about the growing call for women to take positions of power in corporate North America, as well as on political, cultural and economic fronts. In the corporate sector, mentoring programmes offer a pipeline for executive leadership to support the advancement of women to executive levels. In politics, similar movements are monitoring women's involvement and are mandated to encourage and support women to enter the field. But it would be a mistake to think that just because Hillary Clinton, Arianna Huffington and Sheryl Sandberg are at the top, we have achieved our mission.

We need to imagine a future in which women are not just leading but also transforming outdated systems and co-creating the world. We need to harness women-led entrepreneurship to tackle our greatest social and environmental challenges. It's not that women bring something "different" to the table; it's that their experiences and vision, which are often anchored within the struggles of their communities, need to be front and centre as we make systemic changes. When women take their place at the table in this critical work, society is better equipped to synthesize and respond to the fast-paced adaptations we must collectively make to meet the great challenges of our era. It makes sense for us to nurture leadership, strength and self-advocacy in girls.

Girls are redefining and inventing new ways to be leaders. We are amazed by how skilfully girls rise to leadership when they are given a chance and some support. Leadership is everywhere. But it shows itself in a variety of ways, and it doesn't always look like the traditional leadership models to which we've become accustomed, with a charismatic hero leading the way. It can be demonstrated in small gestures or big actions, in political domains and at the grassroots level, and in media, culture, arts and political activism. By digging deep into the roots of culture, these girls bring meaning and transformation to outdated approaches and old, rusty systems. They see intersections between disciplines as part of their world view. They are truly innovating.

Whether in the personal sphere, like Safia, Maude, Tasha and Lili, or in schools and in communities, like Project Slut in Toronto, Mission Girls in San Francisco or influencing policy at the UN, like Zoe and Anjali—we have seen how girls are a force for change. Knowing how powerful and promising many young women already are in so many contexts and how they are growing more so each day, it's incongruous to see how the picture all too often painted in popular culture, in newspapers and in our imaginations hangs on to the "girls are dangerous or in danger" narratives—as if girls are in trouble and not in control of themselves, their sexuality, their schooling and their futures. Mainstream media often frames today's kids as apathetic and disengaged, hedonistic, individualistic and self-serving. Adults often lament about youth culture, believing that the emerging generations are not upholding the traditions of political engagement or activism started by previous generations.

And yet, when we stop and really look around, an entirely different picture emerges. Girls are not "problems" waiting to be solved. Often, in

304 + GIRL POSITIVE +

fact, girls represent solutions. They are taking control of their own lives, rewriting the story that has for too long defined what it means to be a girl and taking leadership roles on key issues at local and global levels. Are we too busy worrying about girls and focusing on the mainstream to see what's going on at the grassroots level, just outside of the spotlight? Are we even capable of recognizing what we see when we see it, or are we still stuck on old ways of understanding and doing? Teen activist Zoe Craig explained it well when she said that kids no longer trust adults to take on important issues with the necessary intensity, passion and urgency. Instead, they are tackling problems themselves, in their own ways. The power of girl leadership resides in the knowledge that sometimes problems need to be confronted in new ways—and in the willingness to do just that.

During our extended road trip, we saw this in action many times over. Girls from LA to Montreal and from Whitehorse to Detroit are organizing themselves and communicating in ways that bypass traditional politics. This emerging DIY approach not only deals with target problems more efficiently and effectively than has been possible before, it also introduces a new political model, one that merges much more seamlessly with digital society and the new economy.

So much of what inspires girls to act grows out of issues that have affected them personally. Girls feel supported when they break the isolation of their experiences and find a space where they can make sense of what is happening to them, and locate their experiences within a broader socio-political context. When they are able to do this, they can begin to focus on developing their insights and passions, and eventually transform some of these into action. If policy-makers see youth only as *objects* of public policy, rather than as *subjects* who shape its formation, they are failing to get in on one of the world's best-kept secrets: that girls are citizens-in-the-making with an enormous amount to contribute—through ideas, mobilization of power and social-media visibility—to the growth of society and culture.

Supporting girls and young women as agents of change requires more than brand messaging that bills girls as "empowered." It demands more than commodifying girl power as if it is linked to a product, and more than a glossy international campaign that makes it seem as if it's a *fait accompli*. Real empowerment comes when we reframe girls' challenges: from focusing on the individual girl to tackling the dynamics of the social, political and economic context she lives in. Real empowerment comes through recognizing and encouraging the girls who are devoted to making changes, big and small, and supporting their work financially and socially.

As we poured another coffee and prepared to pack our bags, we reflected on how privileged we feel to know these smart, driven visionaries. We are also absolutely sure that—from every perspective—girls are an excellent investment.

NOTES

Introduction: Why Girls?

1   A selfie is a photographic self-portrait, usually taken with a smart phone and shared on social media.

2   #YesAllWomen is a counter narrative social media movement against misogyny and classism that ignited after Elliot Rodger, a 22-year-old man, went on a shooting spree on Isla Vista, near the University of California Santa Barbara, killing six people before committing suicide.

Chapter 1: Unfinished Business

1   The World Bank, *The World Development Report: Gender Equality and Development*, Washington, DC: The International Bank for Reconstruction and Development / The World Bank, 2012, http://siteresources.worldbank.org/INTWDR2012/Resources /7778105-1299699968583/7786210-1315936222006/Complete-Report.pdf.

2   Shauna Pomerantz, Rebecca Raby and Andrea Stefanik, "Girls Run the World? Caught Between Sexism and Postfeminism in School," *Gender & Society*, 27, no. 2 (April 2013): 191, doi: 10.1177/0891243212473199.

3   Maria Shriver and the Center for American Progress, *The Shriver Report: A Woman's Nation Pushes Back from the Brink*, New York: RosettaBooks, 2014. As cited in Charlotte Alter, "11 Surprising Facts About Women and Poverty From the Shriver Report," *TIME*, January 13, 2014, http://time.com/2026/11-surprising-facts-about -women-and-poverty-from-the-shriver-report/.

4   The United Nations Entity for Gender Equality and the Empowerment of Women, "Facts and Figures: Economic Empowerment Benefits of Economic Empowerment," last modified April, 2015, accessed February 22, 2016, http://www.unwomen.org /en/what-we-do/economic-empowerment/facts-and-figures#sthash.9YNkCW48 .oyhqFIKz.dpuf.

5   The Conference Board of Canada, "Gender Income Gap," accessed February 22, 2016, http://www.conferenceboard.ca/hcp/details/society/gender-income-gap.aspx.

6 Catalyst, "No News Is Good News, Women's Leadership Still Stalled in America" (press release), 2011, last accessed February 23, 2016, http://www.catalyst.org /media/no-news-bad-news-womens-leadership-still-stalled-corporate-america.

7 As cited in The Representation Project, "Cause and Effect" (infographic), last accessed April 22, 2016, http://therepresentationproject.org/educator-school/#free-resources.

8 Pomerantz et al., "Girls Run the World?," 185–207.

9 Girls Action Foundation, Juniper Glass and Lee Tunstall, *Beyond Appearances: Brief on the Man Issues Facing Girls in Canada*, Montréal: Girls Action Foundation, 2013, 8–30. See also The Girl Scout Research Institute, *The State of Girls: Unfinished Business, Executive Summary*, New York: The Girl Scout Research Institute, 2013, 5–12, http://www.girlscouts.org/content/dam/girlscouts-gsusa/forms-and-documents /about-girl-scouts/research/sog_exec_summary.pdf.

10 Kevin J. Vagi, Emily O'Malley Olsen, Kathleen C. Basile and Alana M. Vivolo-Kantor, "Teen Dating Violence (Physical and Sexual) Among US High School Students: Findings from the 2013 National Youth Risk Behavior Survey," *JAMA Pediatrics*, 169, no. 5 (2015): 474–482, doi:10.1001/jamapediatrics.2014.3577. Cited in Liz Szabo, "Study: 1 in 5 Girls Victim of Teen Dating Violence," *USA Today*, March 2, 2015, http://www.usatoday.com/story/news/2015/03/02 /teen-dating-violence-study/24127121/.

11 Girls Action Foundation, "Girls Action Foundation on Violence Prevention" (infographic), accessed February 22, 2016, http://girlsactionfoundation.ca/en /infographics/girls-action-on-violence-preventions.

Chapter 2: Disempowered and Duped?

1 American Psychological Association, *Report of the APA Task Force on the Sexualization of Girls: Executive Summary*, Washington, DC: American Psychological Association, 2007, http://www.apa.org/pi/women/programs/girls/report-summary.pdf.

2 "Othering" is a process "by which the dominant group creates a division between themselves and non-normative 'others,'" such as racial minorities, people with disabilities, elderly people, trans people and more.

3 For a full history of this phenomenon, see Dawn H. Currie, Deirdre M. Kelly, Shauna Pomerantz, *Girl Power: Girls Reinventing Girlhood* (New York: Peter Lang, 2009).

4 Being "liked" via the "like button" on a social-media platform such as Facebook or Instagram.

5 *Wikipedia*, s.v. "ASKfm," last modified on February 28, 2016, https://en.wikipedia.org/wiki/ASKfm.

6 To read more about the economy of visibility, consult Sarah Banet-Weiser, "Keynote Address: Media, Markets, Gender: Economies of Visibility in a Neoliberal Moment," *The Communication Review*, 18, no. 1 (2015): 53–70, doi: 10.1080/10714421.2015.996398. See also Sarah Banet-Weiser, *Authentic™: The Politics of Ambivalence in a Brand Culture* (New York: NYU Press, 2012).

7 For more on this topic, see chapter 3.

8 "Ho" is a slang word derived from the word "whore" popularized in the rap and hip-hop video culture of the 1990s.

9 Jaclyn Friedman, "Women of Color Seen as Always Sexually Available," *Women's News*, October 29, 2011, http://womensenews.org/story/cultural-trendspopular-culture /111029/women-color-seen-always-sexually-available.

10 According to *Wikipedia*, the politics of respectability are the "attempts by marginalized groups to police their own members and show their social values as being continuous and compatible with mainstream values rather than challenging the mainstream for its failure to accept difference." *Wikipedia*, s.v. "Respectability politics," last modified December 7, 2015, https://en.wikipedia.org/wiki/Respectability_politics.

11 Maya Dusenbery, "Feminism is Totally Cool with Beyoncé Posing in Her Underwear," *Feministing*, January 18, 2013, accessed February 17, 2016, http://feministing.com /2013/01/18/we-are-totally-cool-with-beyonce-posing-in-her-underwear/

12 Ibid.

13 Caroline Caron, *Vue, mais non entendues. Les adolescentes québécoises et l'hyper-sexualisation* [Seen, but Unheard. Teenage Girls Speak up about Hypersexualization in Quebec] (Québec: Presses de l'Université Laval, 2014).

14 We will hear more from Tasha in chapter 4.

15 We will hear more from Anna in chapter 10.

16 For more on Molly's work, see her recent autobiography, Molly Crabapple, *Drawing Blood* (New York: Harper, 2015).

17 Girls Who Code, "About," accessed February 18, 2016, http://girlswhocode.com/.

18 "Twine is an open-source tool for telling interactive, nonlinear stories. You don't need to write any code to create a simple story with Twine, but you can extend your stories with variables, conditional logic, images, CSS, and JavaScript. . . . Twine publishes directly to HTML, so you can post your work nearly anywhere. Anything

you create with it is completely free to use any way you like, including for commercial purposes." For more see https://twinery.org/.

19 Meghan Holohan, "Why This Tampon-Themed Video Game Is What the World Needs Now," *TODAY Health & Wellness*, September 15, 2014, accessed February 18, 2016, http://www.today.com/health/tampon-run-period-themed-video-game -you-didnt-know-you-1D80148651.

20 The Representation Project, "How Mothers are Redefining Girly," YouTube video of an interview with author Melissa Wardy, May 9, 2014, http://www.youtube.com /watch?annotation_id=channel%3A52f581fe-0-2e7e-9955-20cf301cc1b6&feature =iv&src_vid=NswJ4kO9uHc&v=nG_e_T1qUsU

21 Pink for girls and blue for boys is not even a particularly old stereotype. It was developed well into the twentieth century—before that, red was for boys and blue was for girls. See Margaret Hartmann, "The History Of Pink For Girls, Blue For Boys," *Jezebel*, April 10, 2011, last accessed April 22, 2016, http://jezebel.com /5790638/the-history-of-pink-for-girls-blue-for-boys, and Jeanne Maglaty, "When Did Girls Start Wearing Pink?," *Smithsonian*, April 7, 2011, last accessed April 22, 2016, http://www.smithsonianmag.com/arts-culture/when-did-girls-start-wearing -pink-1370097/?no-ist.

22 Imogen Russell Williams, "Picture Books That Draw the line Against Pink Stereotypes of Girls," *The Guardian*, July 30, 2015, http://www.theguardian.com /books/booksblog/2015/jul/30/picture-books-that-draw-the-line-against-pink -stereotypes-of-girls?CMP=share_btn_fb.

Chapter 3: I'm Sexy and I Know It

1 Sexting refers to the sending of sexually explicit images or text messages via cell phones and social media. Learn more about sexting here: https://amyhasinoff .wordpress.com/book/.

2 We will learn more about these girls in chapter 6.

3 Sharon Lamb, "Feminist Ideals for a Healthy Female Adolescent Sexuality: A Critique," *Sex Roles*, 62, no. 5 (2010): 298, doi: 10.1007/s11199-009-9698-1.

4 Michelle Fine, "Sexuality, Schooling and Adolescent Females: The Missing Discourse of Desire," *Harvard Educational Review*, 58, no. 1 (1988): 29–53.

5 Lara Karaian, "'Sextploitation': Rethinking the Relationship between Sexualisation, 'Sexting' in Law and Order Times" (paper presented at the symposium "Girlhood

Studies and the Politics of Place: New Paradigms of Research," Cardiff University, Wales, October 10, 2012), https://www.academia.edu/8218505/2015_-_What _is_Self-exploitation_Rethinking_the_Relationship_between_Sexualisation_and _Sexting_in_Law-and-Order_Times

6   Amy Adele Hasinoff, "Blaming Sexualization for Sexting," *Girlhood Studies*, 7, no. 1 (2014): 102–120 and Amy Adele Hasinoff, *Sexting Panic: Rethinking Criminalization, Privacy, and Consent* (Chicago, Illinois University Press, 2015).

7   Lara Karaian, "Lolita Speaks: 'Sexting,' Teenage Girls and the Law," *Crime Media Culture*, 8, no. 1 (2012): 65.

8   Lucie O'Sullivan, "Tweeting, Texting, Teens & Chat: The Internet and Sex in the Lives of Youth," YouTube video from the Ideas That Matter Speaker Series, University of New Brunswick, April 6, 2011, last accessed February 22, 2016, http://www.unb.ca/initiatives/ideas/topics-speakers/lucia-o-sulllvan.html.

9   Kelly Wallace, "Is Your Teen Using Apps to Keep Secrets," CNN, March 16, 2015, accessed February 22, 2016, http://www.cnn.com/2015/03/16/tech/teen-sexting -apps-hide-messages/.

10 Lara Karaian, "'Sextploitation,'" ibid.

11 Airial Clark, "What is Sex-Positive Parenting?," *The Sex-Positive Parent* (blog) accessed February 22, 2016, http://thesexpositiveparent.com/about/what-is -sex-positive-parenting/.

12 "Pornography Statistics: Annual Report 2015," Covenant Eyes, accessed March 25, 2016, www.covenanteyes.com/pornstats/.

13 Globally, the porn industry is a $97 billion a year industry, with $10–$12 billion of that coming from the United States. See Chris Morris, "Things Are Looking Up in America's Porn Industry," NBC News, January 20, 2015, last accessed February 23, 2016.

14 Labia size, shape and colour has become a porn-spawned fetish.

15 "Lesbian-Gay-Bisexual-Transgender Youth FAG," Youth Suicide Prevention Program, accessed March 29, 2016, http://www.yspp.org/about_suicide/gay _lesbian_FAQs.htm. We recognize gender identity expands beyond LGBT to include LGBTTQAI*.

16 Hailey Trimmier, "Vlogger Laci Green Controversy & Death Threats Explained," *Femisphere* (blog), April 30, 2013, last accessed February 22, 2016, http: //sociallyresponsibleit.blogspot.ca/2013/04/feminspire-vlogger-laci-green.html.

17 "State Policies on Sex Education in Schools," National Conference on State
    Legislature, last accessed February 22, 2016, http://www.ncsl.org/research/health
    /state-policies-on-sex-education-in-schools.aspx.

18 "Safer Sexting Tips," *Amy Hasinoff* (blog), last accessed April 22, 2016, https:
    //amyhasinoff.wordpress.com/sexting-tips/.

Chapter 4: Inside the Hypersexuality Hype

1 This gang rape and killing of two teenage girls happened in Uttar Pradesh, India,
   in 2014, when two girl cousins went to the field they used as a toilet, at night. See
   Wikipedia, s.v. "2014 Badaun gang rape allegations," for the full story, last modified
   April 15, 2016, https://en.wikipedia.org/wiki/2014_Badaun_gang_rape_allegations.
   See also Charlie Campbell, "Photos: Indian Village Shocked By Brutal Rape and
   Murder Case," *TIME*, June 2, 2014, accessed February 20, 2016, http://time.com
   /2811636/india-rape-hanging-photos/?iid=sr-link4.

2 See Rebecca Klein, "High School Student Accuses School of 'Shaming Girls
   For Their Bodies' With Dress Code," *The Huffington Post*, July 2, 2014, accessed
   February 18, 2016, http://www.huffingtonpost.com/2014/06/02/lindsey-stocker
   -dress-code_n_5432687.html.

3 Cecilia D'Anastasio and StudentNation, "Girls Speak Out Against School Dress
   Codes," *The Nation*, August 27, 2014, accessed February 18, 2016, http://www.
   thenation.com/blog/181375/girls-speak-out-against-sexist-school-dress-codes.

4 See http://girlsrockmontreal.com/ and http://girlsrockcampalliance.org/about-2
   /about/.

5 American Psychological Association, *Report of the APA Task Force*, ibid.

6 Self-objectification is defined by the America Psychology Association as the
   process by which "girls internalize an observer's perspective on their physical selves
   and learn to treat themselves as objects to be looked at and evaluated for their
   appearance."

7 American Psychological Association, *Report of the APA Task Force*, 2–3.

8 Ibid., 4.

9 Vincent Ng, "How Disney Princesses Became a Multi Billion Dollar Brand"
   MCNG Marketing, March 18, 2013, accessed February 18, 2016, http://www
   .mcngmarketing.com/how-disney-princesses-became-a-multi-billion-dollar-brand
   /#.VseQSLkrKgQ.

10 Examples of pop culture texts include M. Gigi Durham's *The Lolita Effect* (New
    York: The Overlook Press, 2008), Maggie Hamilton's *What's Happening to Our
    Girls* (Sydney: Penguin, 2007) and Diane Levin and Jean Kilbourne's *So Sexy So
    Soon* (New York: Ballantine Books, 2008). As cited in Sue Jackson and Tina Vares,
    "Media 'Sluts': 'Tween' Girls' Negotiations of Postfeminist Sexual Subjectivities in
    Popular Culture," and Jessica Ringrose, "Are you Sexy, Flirty, or A Slut? Exploring
    Sexualization and How Teen Girls Perform/Negotiate Digital Sexual Identity
    on Social Networking Sites," both in Rosalind Gill and Christina Scharff, eds.,
    New Feminities: Postfeminism, Neoliberalism and Subjectivity (London: Palgrave
    MacMillan, 2011).

11 Ibid., 134–135

12 Girls Action Foundation et al., *Beyond Appearances*, 20.

13 Abigail Jones, "Sex and the Single Tween," *Newsweek*, January 22, 2014, accessed
    February 18, 2016, http://www.newsweek.com/sex-and-single-tween-245090.

14 A very good definition of "rape culture" by West Virginia's Marshall University
    Women's Center is: "an environment in which rape is prevalent and in which
    sexual violence against women is normalized and excused in the media and popular
    culture…. Examples of rape culture include: blaming the victim; trivializing sexual
    assault; tolerance of sexual harassment; publicly scrutinizing a victim's dress, mental
    state, motives, and history; assuming only promiscuous women get raped. . . ."
    https://www.marshall.edu/wcenter/sexual-assault/rape-culture/.

15 For more on this issue, see chapter 9.

16 We'll hear more from these girls in chapter 7.

17 Caroline Caron, "Getting Girls and Teens into the Vocabularies of Citizenship,"
    Girlhood Studies, 4, no. 2 (2011): 70–91. See also Caroline Caron, *Vue, mais non
    entendues. Les adolescentes québécoises et l'hypersexualisation* [Seen, but Unheard.
    Teenage Girls Speak Up about Hypersexualization in Quebec] (Québec: Presses de
    l'Université Laval, 2014).

18 Ibid., *Vue, mais non entendues*. For more of Caroline's work in this area, see her
    chapter "Social Media and Youth Civic Engagement: A Developing Field of Inquiry,"
    in Aiden Buckland and Caroline Caron, eds., *TEM 2014: Proceedings of the Technology
    & Emerging Media Track –Annual Conference of the Canadian Communication
    Association* (Saint Catharines, May 28–30, 2014) http://www.tem.fl.ulaval.ca
    /webroot/wp-content/PDF/Saint-Catharines_2014/CARON-TEM2014.pdf.

19 Slut-shaming is the act of criticizing and shaming a woman for her real or presumed
    sexual activity, or for behaving in ways that someone believes are associated with her
    real or presumed sexual activity. It is a form of social stigma applied to women and
    girls, who are perceived to violate traditional expectations for sexual behaviour.

20 Jessica Valenti, "Pledging Virginity To Dad: A New Doc Explores the World of
    Purity Balls," University of Southern California's *Religious Dispatches* (blog), July 11,
    2012, accessed February 18, 2016, religiondispatches.org/pledging-virginity
    -to-dad-a-new-doc-explores-the-world-of-purity-balls/.

21 Advocates for Youth, "Comprehensive Sex Education: Research and Results,"
    September 2009, accessed February 2016, http://www.advocatesforyouth.org
    /publications/1487.

22 Kate Harper, Yasmina Katsulis, Vera Lopez and Georganne Scheiner Gillis, eds.,
    Girls' Sexualities and the Media: The Power of the Media (New York: Peter Lang,
    2013), 4.

23 Kari Lerum and Shari L. Dworkin, "'Bad Girls Rule': An Interdisciplinary Feminist
    Commentary on the Report of the APA Task Force on the Sexualization of Girls,"
    Journal of Sex Research, 46, no. 4 (2009): 256, accessed February 18, 2016, http:
    //faculty.washington.edu/lerum/Bad%20Girls%20Rule.pdf.

24 Brett Relander, "How to Market to Gen Z, the Kids That Already Have $44 Billion
    to Spend," *Entrepreneur*, November 4, 2014, accessed February 18, 2016, http:
    //www.entrepreneur.com/article/238998.

25 The sums will be even higher now but the original source was "Kids Getting Older
    Younger," *Modern Buyer Behaviour* (blog), December 1, 2013, accessed April 1,
    2016, https://modernbuyerbehaviour.wordpress.com/2013/12/01/kids-getting
    -older-younger/.

26 Sarah Banet-Weiser, "Branding the Post Feminist Self: Girls' Video Production and
    YouTube," *Mediated Girlhoods: New Explorations of Girls' Media Culture*,
    Mary Celeste Kearney, ed. (New York: Peter Lang, 2011).

27 See the comment section "A Time Capsule of 1970s Sexism," *The Age*, April 6,
    2014, accessed February 22, 2016, http://www.theage.com.au/comment/the-age
    -letters/a-time-capsule-of-1970s-sexism-20140405-365yt.html.

28 Layla Sayeed, "Stand up To Unilever's Hypocrisy Over Skin-Lightening," *The
    Guardian*, July 16, 2010, accessed February 18, 2016, http://www.theguardian
    .com/commentisfree/2010/jul/16/unilever-hypocritical-promoting-skin-lightening.

29 Rachel Browne, "Teachers Would Make Students Feel Ashamed for Their Choices," *Flare*, December 1, 2014, accessed February 18, 2016, http://www.flare.com/culture /project-97-project-slut-toronto-interview/.

Chapter 5: Who Gets to "Lean In"

1   The Girls Scout Research Institute, *The State of Girls*, 39

2   Josh Mitchell, "About Half of Kids With Single Moms Live In Poverty," *The Wall Street Journal*, November, 25, 2013, last accessed February 2, 2016, http://blogs.wsj .com/economics/2013/11/25/about-half-of-kids-with-single-moms-live-in-poverty/.

3   Girls Action Foundation et al., "Beyond Appearances," 25.

4   Sheryl Sandberg and Nell Scovell, *Lean In: Women, Work, and the Will to Lead*, (New York: Knopf, 2013).

5   Ratchet is a black, working-class term that has been popularized in in rap and hip hop culture meaning "I'm real. I'm ghetto. I am what I am." Some black women have embraced ratchet "as an attempt to de-pathologize it and to celebrate both its edginess and its roots in the southern working class." Some view it as a derogatory stereotype and part of a larger problem with how black women are portrayed in media such as *The Real Housewives of Atlanta*, *Basketball Wives* and *Bad Girls Club*. For more visit: http://nymag.com/thecut/2013/04/ratchet-the-rap-insult-that -became-a-compliment.html

6   Othering is a process by which the dominant group creates a division between themselves and non-normative "others," for example racial minorities, people with disabilities, elderly people, trans people, and more.

7   Meredith Bennett-Smith, "*Sports Illustrated* Called Racist For Using 'Exotic' People In Swimsuit Issue," *The Huffington Post*, February, 15, 2013, http://www .huffingtonpost.com/2013/02/15/sports-illustrated-racist-exotic-swimsuit _n_2696162.html.

8   Deepa Lakshmin, "Read This Before You Call Someone 'Exotic,'" MTV, October 15, 2014, last accessed February 22, 2016, http://www.mtv.com/news/1964574 /read-before-calling-someone-exotic/.

9   The MTV Look Different campaign—a media initiative trying to erase racial, gender and sexual orientation biases—is educating and raising awareness of racial micro-aggressions, which they define as "brief and commonplace statements or actions that can be intentional or unintentional. They communicate slights and

insults, and can have a harmful or unpleasant impact on the person experiencing them." Individually, microaggressions are minor events but when they are repeated, they have a cumulative effect on a person's everyday life and dignity.

10 Yoonj Kim, "#NotYourAsianSidekick Is a Civil Rights Movement for Asian-American Women," *The Guardian*, December 17, 2013, accessed March 5, 2016, http://www .theguardian.com/commentisfree/2013/dec/17/not-your-asian-sidekick-asian-women -feminism. See also Suey Park, "The Viral Success of #NotYourAsianSidekick Wasn't About Me, But All of Us," *xoJane*, January 21, 2014, accessed March 5, 2016, http: //www.xojane.com/issues/suey-park-notyourasiansidekick.

11 Aaron Kuriloff and Timothy W. Martin, "Connecticut, America's Richest State, Has a Huge Pension Problem," *The Wall Street Journal*, updated October 5, 2015, last accessed February 23, 2016.

12 Kimberlé Williams Crenshaw, Priscilla Ocen and Jyoti Nanda, *Black Girls Matter: Pushed Out, Overpoliced and Underprotected*, New York: African American Policy Forum and The Center for Intersectionality and Social Policy Studies, 2015, 16. http://www.atlanticphilanthropies.org/sites/default/files/uploads/BlackGirlsMatter _Report.pdf.

13 The school-to-prison pipeline refers to the policies and practices that push students out of classrooms and into the juvenile and adult criminal justice systems. This pathway is the result of inadequate resources in public schools, zero-tolerance policies and other severe disciplinary measures such as the use of police in schools, disciplinary alternative schools and the involvement of legal courts and detentions for school children. To see more on this consult the American Civil Liberties Union here: aclu.org/fact-sheet/what-school-prison-pipeline, accessed March 28, 2016.

14 Crenshaw et al., *Black Girls Matter*, 16. http://www.atlanticphilanthropies.org /sites/default/files/uploads/BlackGirlsMatter_Report.pdf.

15 Monique W. Morris, *Race, Gender and the School-to-Prison Pipeline: Expanding Our Discussion to Include Black Girls*, New York: African American Policy Forum, 2012, 9, http://www.otlcampaign.org/sites/default/files/resources/Morris-Race-Gender -and-the-School-to-Prison-Pipeline.pdf.

16 Ibid., 9.

17 Antoinette Campbell, "Police Handcuff 6-Year-Old Student in Georgia," CNN, April 17, 2012, http://www.cnn.com/2012/04/17/justice/georgia-student -handcuffed/.

18 Morris, *Race, Gender and the School-to-Prison Pipeline*, 11.

19 Crenshaw et al., *Black Girls Matter*, 7.

20 This is a very fast growing movement in the U.S. For more information visit http://www.papertigersmovie.com and www.traumainformedschools.org.

21 Restorative justice is an approach to justice that emphasizes the need to repair the harm done by crime with a focus on accountability and reconciliation with victims and the community at large. According to thought leader John Braithwaite, it is "a process where all stakeholders affected by an injustice have an opportunity to discuss how they have been affected by the injustice and to decide what should be done to repair the harm." Dr. Carolyn Boyes-Watson considers restorative justice to be a "growing social movement to institutionalize peaceful approaches to harm, problem-solving and violations of legal and human rights." See John Braithwaite, "Restorative Justice and De-Professionalization," *The Good Society*, 13, no. 1:, (2004): 28–31 and Carolyn Boyes-Watson at Suffolk University, College of Arts & Sciences, Center for Restorative Justice (2014).

22 The Girl Scout Institute, *The Resilience Factor: A Key to Leadership In African American and Hispanic Girls*, New York: The Girl Scout Institute, 2011, 2, http://www.girlscouts.org/content/dam/girlscouts-gsusa/forms-and-documents/about-girl-scouts/research/resilience_factor.pdf.

23 Julie Gerstein, "This Girl's Gorgeous Handmade Prom Dress Just Broke the Internet," *Buzzfeed*, June 9, 2015, last accessed February 23, 2016.

Chapter 6: Twerking in Detroit

1 John Newsome, "Lawsuits Say Fraternity Fostered Culture of Misogyny," CNN, November 1, 2014, accessed February 18, 2016, http://www.cnn.com/2014/10/31/justice/lawsuit-phi-kappa-tau-fraternity/.

2 John Foubert, "Rapebait e-mail Reveals Dark Side of Frat Culture," CNN, October 13, 2013, accessed February 18, 2016, http://www.cnn.com/2013/10/09/opinion/foubert-fraternities-rape/index.html.

3 As cited at Futures Without Violence, "Get the Facts," accessed February 22, 2016, http://www.futureswithoutviolence.org/resources-events/get-the-facts/.

4 Catherine Hill and Holly Kearl, *Crossing The Line: Sexual Harassment at School. American Association of University Women*, Washington DC: AAUW, 2011, 11. http://www.aauw.org/files/2013/02/Crossing-the-Line-Sexual-Harassment-at-School.pdf.

5   As cited on Girls Action Foundation, "Violence Prevention" (infographic), accessed February 22, 2016, http://girlsactionfoundation.ca/en/infographics/girls-action-on-violence-preventions.

6   "How A Young Community Of Entrepreneurs is Rebuilding Detroit," *Fast Company*, April 15, 2013, accessed February 19, 2016, http://www.fastcompany.com/3007840/creative-conversations/how-young-community-entrepreneurs-rebuilding-detroit.

7   Chimamanda Ngozi Adichie, "The Danger of a Single Story," TED Talk, July 2009, accessed February 19, 2016, http://www.ted.com/talks/chimamanda_adichie_the_danger_of_a_single_story.

8   Snapchat is a mobile app that allows users to send and receive photos and videos that erase after viewing, which encourages its young users to send images they normally wouldn't send.

9   Vine is a new form of social networking involving the posting of a short video, usually five to ten seconds long of compiled clips depicting random personal experiences that are normally funny. These are posted to places like Twitter, Facebook and YouTube for public viewing and commenting.

10 Girls Action Foundation et al., *Beyond Appearances*, 8.

Chapter 7: Blurred Lines and Grey Zones

1   Murray D. Segal, "Independent Review of the Police and Prosecution Response to the Rehtaeh Parsons Case," October 8, 2015, http://novascotia.ca/segalreport/Parsons-Independent-Review.pdf, p. iii, 11, 17, 38, 55, 56.

2   "Hospital denies Rehtaeh Parsons was strip-searched," CBC News, June 8, 2013, accessed June 20, 2016, http://www.cbc.ca/news/canada/nova-scotia/hospital-denies-rehtaeh-parsons-was-strip-searched-1.1303368.

3   Murray D. Segal, "Independent Review of the Police and Prosecution Response to the Rehtaeh Parsons Case," October 8, 2015, http://novascotia.ca/segalreport/Parsons-Independent-Review.pdf and Elizabeth McMillan, "Rehtaeh Parsons case review finds system 'failed,'" CBC News Nova Scotia, accessed June 20, 2016, http://www.cbc.ca/news/canada/nova-scotia/rehtaeh-parsons-case-review-1.3262111.

4   Jana Davidson and Connie Coniglio, "Child and Adolescent Mental Health and Addiction Services in the Halifax Regional Municipality," Nova Scotia, 2013, http://novascotia.ca/dhw/mental-health/reports/Child-and-Adolescent-Mental-Health-Review.pdf.

5 Glen Canning, "Rehtaeh Parsons Was My Daughter," April 10, 2013, accessed February 27, 2016, http://glencanning.com/2013/04/rehtaeh-parsons-was-my -daughter/.

6 Glen Canning, "The Rape of Rehtaeh Parsons," August 9, 2013, http://glencanning. com/2013/08/the-rape-of-rehtaeh-parsons/.

7 Child porn charges against 2 teens in Rehtaeh Parsons case," CBC News, August 8, 2013, www.cbc.ca/news/canada/nova-scotia/child-porn-charges-against-2-teens-in -rehtaeh-parsons-case-1.1320438.

8 Jessica West, "Cyber Violence Against Women," Vancouver: Battered Women's Services, 2014, http://www.bwss.org/wp-content/uploads/2014/05 /CyberVAWReportJessicaWest.pdf.

9 "Fact Sheet: Violence Against Women," Canada Research Institute for Advancement of Women, 2013, 8, http://www.criaw-icref.ca/en/product/violence-against-women -in-canada.

10 Lucie Ogrodnik, "Child and Youth Victims of Police-Reported Violent Crime," Canadian Centre For Justice Statistics, Statistics Canada, March, 2010, 12, accessed February 29, 2016, http://www.nccdglobal.org/sites/default/files/publication_pdf /focus-dating-violence.pdf.

11 Antoinette Davis, "Interpersonal and Physical Dating Violence among Teens: Views from the National Council on Crime and Delinquency Focus," National Council on Crime and Delinquency, 2008, accessed February 29, 2016, http://www .nccdglobal.org/sites/default/files/publication_pdf/focus-dating-violence.pdf.

12 Girls Action Foundation et al., *Beyond Appearances*, 10.

13 Alicia W. Stewart, "#IamJada: When Abuse Becomes a Teen Meme," CNN, Friday, July 14, 2014, accessed February 28, 2016, http://www.cnn.com/2014/07/18 /living/jada-iamjada-teen-social-media/. See also Kate Dailey, "#BBCtrending: Is #Jadapose a Social Media Low?," BBC, July 14, 2014, accessed February 28, 2016, http://www.bbc.com/news/blogs-trending-28239914.

14 American Civil Liberties Union, "Know Your Rights: Title IX and Sexual Assault," accessed February, 28, 2016, https://www.aclu.org/know-your-rights/title-ix -and-sexual-assault?redirect=womens-rights/fact-sheet-title-ix-and-sexual-assault -%E2%80%94-know-your-rights-and-your-colleges-responsibilities.

15 Vanessa Grigoriadis, "Meet the College Women Who Are Starting a Revolution Against Campus Sexual Assault," *The Cut*, September 21, 2014, accessed

February 28, 2016, http://nymag.com/thecut/2014/09/emma-sulkowicz-campus
-sexual-assault-activism.html.

16 Ibid.

17 Angela Mulholand, "#BeenRapedNeverReported Hashtag Trending, as Women
Share Stories of Assault," CTV News, October 31, 2014, accessed February 29,
2016, http://www.ctvnews.ca/canada/beenrapedneverreported-hashtag-trending
-as-women-share-stories-of-assault-1.2080744.

18 Sara Ashtaryeh, "Meet the 13-Year-Old Girls Changing the Sexual Consent
Conversation," *ELLE*, February 2, 2015, accessed February 29, 2016, http://www
.elle.com/culture/news/a26488/tessa-hill-lia-valente-peitition-consent-sex-education/.

19 Girls Action Foundation, *From the Ground Up: Community-Based Tools To Address
Violence And Seek Justice: A Facilitation Guide*," Montréal: Girls Action Foundation,
2015, accessed February 26, 2016, http://girlsactionfoundation.ca/files/from_the
_ground-up_final.small_.pdf.

20 Ibid., 92.

21 United Way Toronto, "Yes Means Yes: Sexual Consent," The Teen Health Resource,
accessed March 10, 2016, http://teenhealthsource.com/sex/sexual-consent/.

22 The Good Men Project, "The Healthy Sex Talk: Teaching Kids Consent, Ages 1–21,"
March 20, 2013, accessed February 28, 2016, http://goodmenproject.com/families
/the-healthy-sex-talk-teaching-kids-consent-ages-1-21/#sthash.7lj3dP2n.dpuf.

Chapter 8: Cutting is Normal

1 Tristan Simpson, "More Canadian Girls Inflicting Self-Harm, Hospital Admissions
Double," *The Globe and Mail*, November 18, 2014, last updated November 18,
2014, accessed February 28, 2016, http://www.theglobeandmail.com/life/health
-and-fitness/health/more-canadian-girls-inflicting-self-harm-hospital-admissions
-double/article21645697/. See also: http://www.theguardian.com/society/2014
/feb/19/concern-girls-admitted-hospital-stress

2 John Freeman and King Luu, "The Health of Canada's Young People: a Mental
Health Focus," Public Health Agency of Canada, last modified March 16, 2012,
accessed February 28, 2016, http://www.phac-aspc.gc.ca/hp-ps/dca-dea/publications
/hbsc-mental-mentale/health-sante-eng.php.

3 The Missrepresentation Project, *Keep It Real ToolKit*, June 26, 2012, accessed
February 28, 2016, https://issuu.com/missrepresentation/docs/keepitrealtoolkit.

4   The Girls Scout Research Institute, *The State of Girls*, 2.

5   Girls Action Foundation et al., *Beyond Appearances*, 16.

6   Ibid., 16.

7   Ibid., 17.

8   Girls Action Foundation and British Columbia Centre for Excellence in Women's Health, "Girls, Alcohol and Depression," Montréal: Girls Action Foundation, 2012, accessed February 29, 2016, http://girlsactionfoundation.ca/files/alcohol_depression _1.pdf.

9   Jen Wieczner, "Drug Companies Look to Profit from DSM-5," Market Watch, June 5, 2013, accessed February 29, 2016, http://www.marketwatch.com/story /new-psych-manual-could-create-drug-windfalls-2013-06-05.

10 Girls Action Foundation et al., "Girls, Alcohol and Depression," 2.

11 Ken Flegel, "Big Alcohol Catches up with Young Girls," CMAJ, June 10, 2013, accessed February 29, 2016, http://www.cmaj.ca/content/early/2013/06/10 /cmaj.130766.

12 Susan Krashinsky, "Alcohol Ads Push Underage Girls to Drink More, Research Finds," *The Globe and Mail*, June 13, 2013, accessed February 29, 2016, http: //www.theglobeandmail.com/report-on-business/industry-news/marketing/alcohol -ads-push-underage-girls-to-drink-more-research-finds/article12536741/.

13 John Hopkins Bloomberg School of Public Health, Center on Alcohol Marketing and Youth, "Women, Girls and Alcohol" (facts sheet), July, 2011, updated 2012, accessed February 29, 2016, http://www.camy.org/factsheets/sheets/Women_Girls _and_Alcohol.html.

14 Canadian Women's Foundation, "A Girl's Journey to Resilience" (fact sheet), accessed February 29, 2016, http://www.canadianwomen.org/sites/canadianwomen .org/files/blog-tipsforparents.pdf.

Chapter 9: Power Playing

1   Marion Brown, "Discourses of Choice and Experiences of Constraint Analyses of Girls' Use of Violence," *Girlhood Studies*, 5 no. 2 (2012): 65–83, doi:10.3167 /ghs.2012.050205.

2   Originating in the 1930s, roller derby is an international full-contact sport dominated by all-female teams. It is played by two teams, with fourteen players per team and five players on the track at a time during short, two-minute match ups referred to as jams.

3   *Wikipedia*, s.v. "Bullying," last modified April 14, 2016, https://en.wikipedia.org
    /wiki/Bullying.

4   Shelley Hymel, "Preventing Bullying In Schools Through Social Emotional
    Learning" (keynote presentation for the Peace Grantmakers Conference: "Creating
    Caring School Communities Symposium," Montreal, QC, February 7, 2014),
    http://www.peacegrantmakers.ca/symposium/documents/ShelleyHymel_part1.pdf.
    See Dr. Hymel's presentation here: http://www.peacegrantmakers.ca/symposium/en/.

5   The Girls Scouts Research Institute, "The Resilience Factor: A Key to Leadership
    in African American and Hispanic Girls," New York: The Girls Scouts Research
    Institute, 2011, 2.

6   Ibid., 5.

7   Sarah Hampson, "Their story: 'I want to be somewhere between two fixed points of
    gender,'" *The Globe and Mail*, last modified February, 1, 2016, accessed February 29,
    2016, http://www.theglobeandmail.com/news/national/their-story-i-want-to-be
    -somewhere-between-two-fixed-points-ofgender/article28456135/?click=sf_globefb.

8   Angie Wolf, Callie Long, and Stephanie S. Covington, "Girls at Risk: A Trauma-
    Informed Approach," webinar hosted by the National Girls' Institute, June 26, 2013,
    accessed March 1. 2016, https://www.nttac.org/index.cfm?event=trainingCenter
    .traininginfo&eventID=100.

9   Amber Richelle Dean, *Locking Them up to Keep Them Safe: Criminalized Girls
    in British Columbia, A Systemic Advocacy Project Conducted for Justice for Girls*,
    Vancouver: Justice for Girls, 2005, 2, http://homeless.samhsa.gov/ResourceFiles
    /JFG_report_final.pdf.

10 Angie Wolf et al., ibid.

11 Dean, ibid.

12 Ibid., 3.

13 "Those Who Take Us Away: Abusive Policing and Failures of Protection of Indigenous
    Northern Girls in Northern British Columbia," Human Rights Watch, 2013, 46,
    https://www.hrw.org/sites/default/files/reports/canada0213webwcover_0.pdf.

14 Ibid., 51–52.

Chapter 10: What About the Boys?

1   Tressie McMillan Cottom, "Brown Body, White Wonderland," *Slate*, August 29,
    2013, accessed February 29, 2016, http://www.slate.com/articles/double_x/doublex

/2013/08/miley_cyrus_vma_performance_white_appropriation_of_black_bodies
.2.html. To read more about Miley Cyrus's cultural appropriation at MTV Video
Music Awards ceremonies, see Madelyn Chung, "Miley Cyrus Accused Of Cultural
Appropriation For Wearing Dreadlocks To The 2015 MTV VMAs," *The Huffington
Post*, January 9, 2015, accessed February 29, 2016, http://www.huffingtonpost
.ca/2015/08/31/miley-cyrus-dreadlocks_n_8067106.html.

2   *Wikipedia*, s.v. "Women and Video Games," last modified April 18, 2016, https:
//en.wikipedia.org/wiki/Women_and_video_games.

3   Jay Hathaway, "What Is Gamergate, and Why? An Explainer for Non-Geeks,"
Gawker, October 10, 2014, accessed February 29, 2016, http://gawker.com
/what-is-gamergate-and-why-an-explainer-for-non-geeks-1642909080.

4   Thank you to The Next Level Conference and the NRW KULTURsekretariat's
International Visitor's Program, who invited Caia Hagel to attend the two-day
workshops on evolution, activism and art in video games held in Dortmund,
Germany in December, 2014, http://www.nextlevel-conference.org/konferenz
/start/#/.

Chapter 11: Cracks Through The Cracks

1   The Truth and Reconciliation Commission of Canada, "Honouring the
Truth, Reconciling for the Future: Summary of the Final Report of the Truth
and Reconciliation Commission Canada," 2015, http://www.trc.ca/websites/
trcinstitution/index.php?p=890. See also *Wikipedia*, s.v. "Canadian Indian
Residential School System," last modified April 24, 2016, accessed March 1, 2016,
https://en.wikipedia.org/wiki/Canadian_Indian_residential_school_system.

Chapter 12: Girls As Changemakers

1   Caia Hagel, "UNGEI #YouthTalks Meets Zeitun Tifow," United Nations Girls
Education Initiative (blog), June 17, 2015, accessed February 29, 2016, http:
//blog.ungei.org/ungei-youthtalks-meets-zeitun-tifow/.

IMAGE AND TEXT CREDITS

Thank you to all the girls, girl groups and affiliated organizations who created posters and artwork for their grassroots initiatives and campaigns, and allowed us to reprint them here.

Artwork

p. 10: Rock Camp for Girls, Montreal, logo, image courtesy of Rock Camp for Girls, Montreal.

p. 20: The Mission Girls poster art, image courtesy of The Mission Girls, San Francisco.

p. 58: Project Slut poster art, image courtesy of Project Slut.

p. 94: Project Slut poster art, image courtesy of Project Slut.

p. 122: "Start Something Fierce" Zine art by Indigenous artist and graphic designer Cherri Low-Horn, image courtesy of Girls Action Foundation.

p. 150: Volley for Violence, Detroit girls volleyball fund and awareness raising poster art, image courtesy of Michele Lewis Watts and Detroit Sports Factory, page 150.

p. 170: Poster art, image courtesy of Project Slut.

p. 186: Leaping Feats group dance shot, image courtesy of Borealis Soul.

p. 212: Montreal Roller Derby poster art, image courtesy of the Montreal Roller Derby.

p. 236: Image courtesy of White Ribbon, "It Starts With You" campaign, www.itstartswithyou.ca.

p. 262: Land as Body, 2015, Acrylic on canvas, art courtesy of Megan Kanerahtenha:wi Whyte.

p. 282: Image courtesy of Left Hand Gang.

Text Permissions

Grateful acknowledgement is made to reprint from the following:

p. 66: Quotation from "Feminist Ideals for a Healthy Female Adolescent Sexuality: A Critique," by Sharon Lamb, in *Sex Roles*: March 2010, Volume 62, pp 294-306. Used by permission.

ACKNOWLEDGEMENTS

Thank you Jean-Michel, Morganne and Zachary and Tim, Nova and Blue, you are our rocks.

Thank you to our agent Carolyn Forde, our editor Deirdre Molina and our phenomenal team at Random House Canada, and also freelance editors Linda Pruessen and Chandra Wohleber for helping us bring this work to life.

Thank you to our mothers, Eleanor and Carol, and our grandmothers, Rose, Oma, Grundles and Dorothea, and to all the warrior women who've come before us, for passing their spirit on.

Thank you to all the incredible girls and young women who shared their stories, their visions and their hearts with us for this book.

Thank you to the young leaders who appear by name, Khadra Ali, Muna Ali, Anjali Katta, Andy Villanueva, Megan Kanerahtenhawi Whyte, Enoruwa Osagie, Schanelle Campbell, Zoe Craig and Rebecca Cohen Palacios, you are so inspiring!

Thank you to all the mentors who welcomed us into their communities, introduced us to the girls they work with, gave us context and impassioned us in every place we visited: Andrea Simpson-Fowler, Susana Rojas, Michele Lewis Watts, Natasha Burford, Michaela Brooks, Mickey Decarlo, Chelby Daigle, Jessica Van Tuyl, Ann Brillante, Emanuela Sheena, Emily Jones.

Thank you to the smart thought leaders and academics who helped us with expert additional information: Dr. Nisha Sajnani, Dr. Carolyn Carron, Dr. Lara Karaian, SooJin Pate, Dr. Sarah Banet-Weiser, Dr. Amy Hasinoff, Glen Canning, Dr. Michael Kaufman, Denisse Temin,

Christine Grumm, Annabel Webb, Asia Czapska, Dr. Nancy Poole, Dr. Nancy Heathe, Dayna Chatman, Dr. Shauna Pomerantz, Dr. Lena Palacios, Dr. Dawn Currie, Dr. Sandra Weber, Dr. Brenda Morrison, Dr. Shanly Dixon, Dr. Candis Steenbergen, Sarah DeCarlo, Farrah Mohammed, Dr. Bronwen Low, Dr. Shareen Shariff, Dr. Claudia Mitchell.

Special thanks to Joshua Gibson-Fraser for your work in chapter 10, *What About the Boys?* and for helping us at critical moments in chapter developments. Special thanks to Dr. Robyn Diner for being a sounding board to think through the political nuances in pop culture and gender violence. Thank you to Jenny Berman, SooJin Pate, Stephanie Austin, Juniper Glass, Amanda Sheedy and Jordan Gibson-Fraser for your careful proofreading, editorial suggestions and reflective feedback.

Thanks to our awesomely awesome interns Taylor Lecky and Anjali Katta.

Thanks to all the vibrant and open young women who filled out our survey.

Thank you to Girls Action Foundation, Montreal Roller Derby, Oasis for Girls, WORC It, Rock Camp for Girls Montreal, Mission Girls, Head & Hands, Justice for Girls, Gashanti Unity, Leaping Feats Creative Danceworks, Detroit Public Schools Volleyball, Detroit Sports Factory, White Ribbon and Pixelles.

Thanks to the amazing boys and men who are taking on the work of next wave equality.

Gratitude to all our cherished family members, friends and colleagues who've stood by us being energizing, patient and supportive in the years it's taken us to write this book. Thank you to our mutual friend, Alisha Piercy, for introducing us to each other.

May this work stir all of us to be activists for and with girls.

INDEX

abuse. *See also* sexual harassment
    sexual, 134, 268, 269
    verbal, 29, 238
activism, 287–93, 300, 302, 303–4
    anti-poverty, 287, 289
    environmental, 273–78, 296–98
    for gender equity, 286–87
    Indigenous, 277–78, 279
    international, 278, 287
    online, 40, 46–50, 129–30, 176, 275
    political, 49–50, 240, 273–78
    against sexualization, 48–49
    against sexual violence, 17–18,
       176–82, 185
    on social media, 17–18, 156, 176–79,
       181–82, 245
Actua, 56
Adichie, Chimamanda Ngozi, 157
advertising, 101, 109–10. *See also* media
    literacy
African-Americans. *See* girls, black
aggression, 6, 159–60, 213–14. *See also*
    anger; bullying
    expressing, 195, 213, 225–26
    racist, 129–30
    sexual, 66, 151, 162–63, 175–77
alcohol use, 15, 194, 202–4, 210, 266
    impacts, 203–4, 268–69
Ali, Khadra, 288, 291–92, 294

Ali, Muna, 288, 291–92, 293–94
alienation, 127, 172–73, 188
ALIVE, 138–39, 140
Allahyari, Morehshin, 49–50
Allen, Zariya, 147
American Association of University
    Women (AAUW), 168–69, 185
American Psychological Association,
    100–101, 103, 108
anger, 160, 214, 222–28, 231, 235. *See*
    also aggression
Anonymous (online group), 173
anxiety, 192, 204
Art Hoe Collective, 49, 55
Ask.fm, 29, 117
Assassin's Creed (video game), 51
assertiveness, 40–41, 61–62, 235
Auder, Lauren, 256

Banet-Weiser, Sarah, 21, 22, 26–31, 59,
    110, 112
Barbie dolls, 22, 126
The Beauty Myth (Wolf), 22
beauty standards, 28, 44, 109. *See also*
    stereotypes
    challenges to, 48–49, 63–64, 113,
      286
    as pressure, 29–30, 34, 35
    redefining, 37–39, 40, 234

+++

TATIANA FRASER is a writer, speaker, activist and social entrepreneur. She has twenty years of experience leading social innovation to advance girls' and women's empowerment and leadership. Fraser is co-founder and past executive director of Girls Action Foundation, a national organization that believes in the power of girls as agents of social change. Fraser is recognized as a Global Ashoka Fellow and was named one of Canada's Top 100 Powerful Women in 2010 by The Women's Executive Network. She has served on numerous boards and advisory committees including The Carold Institute, Food Secure Canada, Exeko, and Actua, among others.

CAIA HAGEL is a writer, creative director and entrepreneur. Her written work on culture and innovation has appeared in many publications from *Art Papers* to *Vogue*. Hagel is co-founding director of GuerrillaPop+MediaLab, a boutique media co-op that invented "moral offsetting" to create avant-garde media. She is also co-founding director of HungryForFortune, an all-female entrepreneurial collective whose projects pioneer new movements in technology and culture. She has been a speaker on art, design, pop and youth media at several events, including X Contemporary at Art Basel Miami and Forum D'Avignon@Paris, where her presentation on selfies contributed to a new Bill of Digital Human Rights.